the monstrous debt

the monstrous debt

Modalities of Romantic Influence in Twentieth-Century Literature

Edited by
Damian Walford Davies
Richard Marggraf Turley

With a Foreword by Lucy Newlyn

W
WAYNE STATE UNIVERSITY PRESS
DETROIT

10 09 08 07 06 5 4 3 2 1

Library of Congress Cataloging-in-Publication Data

The monstrous debt : modalities of romantic influence in twentieth-century literature /
edited by Damian Walford Davies and Richard Marggraf Turley ;
with a foreword by Lucy Newlyn.
p. cm.
Includes bibliographical references and index.
ISBN 0-8143-3058-4 (alk. paper)
1. English poetry—20th century—History and criticism. 2. American poetry—20th century—History and criticism. 3. Romanticism—Great Britain—History—20th century. 4. Romanticism—United States—History—20th century. 5. English poetry—19th century—History and criticism. 6. English poetry—18th century—History and criticism. 7. Romanticism—Influence. 8. Influence (Literary, artistic, etc.)
I. Davies, Damian Walford. II. Turley, Richard Marggraf, 1970–
PR605.R64M66 2006
821'.9109—dc22
2006012986

∞ The paper used in this publication meets the minimum requirements
of the American National Standard for Information Sciences—
Permanence of Paper for Printed Library Materials, ANSI Z39.48-1984.

Designed by Elizabeth Pilon
Typeset by Maya Rhodes
Composed in Berkeley and Century Gothic

Contents

Foreword
Lucy Newlyn

> To try to find the "sources," the "influences" of a work, is to fall in with the myth of filiation; the citations which go to make up a text are anonymous, untraceable, and yet *already read:* they are quotations without inverted commas.
>
> Roland Barthes, *Image-Music-Text,* 160

Do poems refer to the world, to each other, or to their authors? To all three, readers would now say. But was the answer always so self-evident? Whether we trace the question back to the preface to *Lyrical Ballads* in 1800, or to Eliot's "Tradition and the Individual Talent" in 1919, or locate it in the heady pages of *Tel Quel* during the 1960s, we find that it has perennially been at the center of literary debate. Nowhere is this more evident than in the field of Romanticism, where critics have examined its implications using a range of methodologies. This timely collection of essays on Romantic influence explores the debate from several angles. In particular, though, the editors acknowledge their "monstrous debt" (a Keatsian borrowing) to two major father figures who have cast their long transverse shadows across the field of Romantic studies.

The first of these is Harold Bloom. Thirty years ago, in *The Anxiety of Influence,* Bloom argued that "poetic history . . . is indistinguishable from poetic influence, since strong poets make that history by misreading one another."[1] In emphasizing the role of *interpretation* in intrapoetic relationships, Bloom did away with the idea of influence as the straightforward transmission of ideas. It used to be thought that poetic traditions could be "charted," like rivers flowing back to sources, across the pages of books. Bloom replaced this passive model of influence with the idea of an active engagement between reader-writers. His idea took hold because it appealed to the excited reader in all of us, to our sense that poets speak directly, across the centuries, in a personal voice that awakens an answering voice in ourselves. Bloom's focus on *misreading*—the struggle of reader-writers to find their voice by grappling with poetic tradition—became hugely influential, not least because it joined the broader movement of hermeneutics, reader-response, and reception studies that followed Barthes' announcement of the "death of the author" in 1968.

Criticism, for Bloom, is "the art of knowing the hidden roads that go from poem to poem" (*Anxiety of Influence,* 96). This model of intertextuality has some affinities with post-structuralism, viewing literature as heavily mediated by other literature but finding no use for old-fashioned source hunting. "The profundities of poetic influence cannot be reduced to source-study, to the history of ideas, to the patterning of images," Bloom claims (*Anxiety of Influence,* 7). For him—as for Barthes or Kristeva—the intertextual is a condition of all poems, whether or not they consciously allude to other poems. However, to claim that "the meaning of a poem can only be another poem" (*Anxiety of Influence,* 94) is not quite the same as claiming that everything written is in quotations without inverted commas. In Barthes' terms, Bloom is guilty of subscribing to an outdated "myth of filiation" derived from a Romantic model of authorship.

Bloom is nothing if not Romantic. Poems, he believes, are written by authors, not by anonymous scribes; and authors have psychic compulsions. Romantic authors were preoccupied above all else with *identity,* which they saw as more or less synonymous with originality: "a poet's stance, his Word, his imaginative identity, his whole being, must be unique to him, and remain unique, or he will perish as a poet" (*Anxiety of Influence,* 71). Laboring under the burden of the past, poets had to "clear imaginative space for themselves" by overcoming the "baleful" influence of their precursors. Since Romantic poems offer an intricate system of "swerves" away from powerful origins, reading between their lines involves treating them as if they were psychiatric subjects. To undo the defenses of Romantic poets would be to lead them back to health. However, since their identity consists precisely in the strength of their defenses, this would also strip them of their poetic voice. Defensiveness, in the Bloomian system, is both damaging and crucial to creative expression: "Poetic influence need not make poets less original; as often it makes them more original, though not therefore necessarily better" (*Anxiety of Influence,* 7).

The second critic identified by the editors as a formative influence on this volume is Jerome J. McGann, whose approach to Romanticism (and "poetic history") is the exact opposite of Bloom's. A pioneering figure in the school of new historicism, McGann's aim was to locate texts in their material circumstances. In this endeavor, he had to negotiate not just the specialists in Romanticism who were his immediate predecessors (Bloom, Hartman, McFarland) but the central tenets of Romanticism itself, which he saw as complicit in an evasion of the real. Literary allusion is just one of the ways in which poetry avoids dealing with reality. "Romantic Ideology," as McGann defined it, involves a displacement from the political or sociocultural plane (events, times, circumstances, and places) onto the imaginative plane (subjective impressions, personal illusions, psychic defenses, transcendental aspirations).

The challenge facing new historicism was to gain critical purchase on Romanticism by laying bare its acts of displacement. This meant restoring the occluded or repressed references to the real that lay hidden in the poetic imaginings of Romantic writers and their acolytes. Just as, in its initial phase, new historicism accused Romantic writers of "eliding" the materiality of history, so it repudiated the post-structural theories of Barthes, Kristeva, Derrida, and Bloom, all of whom saw writing as a system of secondary codes and lateral references. Either there was a real world or there wasn't. Poems could not be the utterances of a historically situated individual while being a tissue of always-already written signs.

But once McGann and his generation had set to work, and succeeded in putting a wide range of Romantic texts back in their proper times and places, later scholars began to turn their attention to the more subtle ways in which history makes itself known through literary language. More recent developments in new historicism have taken onboard a post-structuralist historiography, which sees events, times, circumstances, and places as themselves textually mediated. In other words, intertextuality has come to be recognized as a function of historical consciousness. This has repercussions for the study of Romantic and post-Romantic literature. The worlds "behind" poems can be observed in a more complex, layered fashion by investigating the connections they make (consciously and unconsciously) with each other.

Does this mean that there is now a meeting point between the historicists, who claim that our knowledge of the past is inevitably textual, and the theorists of intertextuality, who claim that all writing is a system of "quotations without inverted commas"? And if so, where does this leave the scholars and literary critics who, all along, have been tracking allusions back to their sources? How have advances in literary theory affected the habit of source hunting, as it was practiced before Bloom and McGann came along? And what place is there, in Romantic studies now, for the belief that echoes are acoustic patterns to be heard, or that verbal resemblances between poems are empirically discernible?

One critic upholding this belief is Christopher Ricks, a third éminence grise whose spirit suffuses this book. Over a period of thirty years, Ricks has been exploring the allusiveness of literary language, working on a range of writers from Milton, Keats, and Tennyson through to Bob Dylan. As an experienced editor, Ricks brings to his literary criticism a forensic precision in noticing verbal, rhythmic, and formal echoes. In his scholarly essays, he is mainly content with tracking likely allusions from poet to poet across the English canon. But in his work on Bob Dylan, he hears and sees the most unlikely things.[2] Dylan's work becomes a kind of "thoroughfare"[3] (Keatsian echo intended) for the themes, words, and images that make up Western literary tradition. Whether or not they are conscious on the writer's part, echoes and allusions are always welcomed by Ricks as openings for interpretive ingenuity. The "citations which go to make up a text" are not, for him "anonymous, untraceable" as they are for Barthes. Nonetheless, he has strikingly adopted an almost post-structuralist conception of poetry as an unending bricolage of recycled materials.

"Atheoretical" though they are, Ricks's books are deeply informed by intertextual theory across the centuries. Specifically, they have engaged in a continuing dialogue with Harold Bloom, whose presence is "not to be put by," even outside Romantic studies. Ricks contends that influence is a benign process for writers after Milton. In place of Bloom's angst-ridden evocations of filial competition, burden, debt, and atrophy, he presents their positive counterparts: inheritance, gratitude, brotherhood, geniality, amplitude. In his book *Allusion to the Poets,* the working-through of this argument in relation to individual writers is attentively achieved, with each writer evincing a slightly different version of benign influence. Thus, allusion in Dryden is seen as a way of dealing with "the predicaments and responsibilities of the poet as heir," while for Burns it is an expression of companionable fraternity.[4] Wordsworth, for his part, never uses the word "influence" without suggesting benignity, and his poems are "exquisitely and calmly alive to the nature of influence and of allusion" (90). And so it goes on. Bloom's argument is laid to rest, not so much by the resoluteness and consistency of Ricks's overarching claims as by the cumulative detail of his inflected close readings.

So, turning to *The Monstrous Debt,* how do we place it in the field of intertextual and Romantic studies? What, in particular, has the unlikely trinity of Bloom, McGann, and Ricks contributed to its methodology? As the volume's title indicates, current thinking about influence is still beholden to Bloom's "myth of filiation." Playing with the Keatsian quotation in their introduction, the editors take us back to Mary Shelley's *Frankenstein* (not Milton's *Paradise Lost*) as the paradigmatic Romantic text for theorizing influence. Negative associations in the word "monstrous" call up Bloom's idea of the damage visited by fathers on sons, even as they evoke the piteous quandary of the creature in Shelley's text. The "monstrous debt" thus provides a metaphor for the double-bind of responsibility paid by the creator to his creature, and vice versa.

"Debt" is a fiscal word, and one might expect it to connote a materialist analysis of the circulation of texts that enabled the twentieth century's "inheritance" of Romanticism. But this volume does not concern reception in the economic sense. The interlocking of Frankenstein and his creature (like God and Satan, or Laius and Oedipus at the crossroads) provides an organizing figure for the ambivalent interdependence of reader-writers. This reminds us of the extent to which Bloom's reconfiguration of influence as personal agon exerts a continuing hold on critics. All the essays here observe elective affinities between twentieth-century writers and their Romantic forebears. They treat elective affinity not simply as a meeting of minds but as a temporal occurrence and an interpretive opportunity. Bloomian theory has helped the contributors to notice the intense psychic investments involved in the identification between writers, and to develop a hermeneutics of suspicion toward their subjects. Michael O'Neill approaches Wallace Stevens's declaration, "while I come down from the past, the past is my own and not something marked Coleridge, Wordsworth, etc.," with a wariness, an openness to the possibility of the poet's self-deception, which would not have been possible without Bloom.

Bloom's influence is also evident in the volume's emphasis on canonical authors; in its almost exclusive focus on poetry; and in its belief that there might still be such a thing as "Romanticism," despite the extraordinary variety of modes and ideologies now acknowledged to proliferate in that period. Where the approaches in these essays break away from a Bloomian framework is in their variety, their eclecticism, and their readiness to test hypotheses against the evidence of biographical circumstance and textual complexity. The contributors do not claim to offer an overall picture of the influence of Romanticism on twentieth-century writers, and they resist a single umbrella theory for their approach to influence. Instead, with a double allegiance to Ricksian formalism and new historicist sleuthing, they concentrate on painstaking detail.

The findings of new historicism have been helpful in leading to a complex and nuanced understanding of intrapoetic relationships. Historical circumstances are filled out, and writers are here carefully situated in their respective times. Several of the contributors alert us to the persistence of "Romantic Ideology" in twentieth-century writing, focusing on moments of elision similar to those practiced by Romantic poets. Lisa M. Steinman, for instance, writing of Stevens's "The Idea of Order at Key West," argues that the lights seen in the harbor "were not on fishing boats but on twenty-nine U.S. battleships sent by President Roosevelt to Cuban waters" (110); and Hugh Haughton suggests that Seamus Heaney's return to childhood has its roots in the same adult recoil from violence that we see in *The Prelude*'s retreat from the French Revolution (72). The spirit of these arguments is not accusatory, as it was in the early investigations of Jerome J. McGann and Marjorie Levinson. So practiced are critics at noticing the ways in which history is silently elided that the elisions themselves have come to be regarded as poetic tropes or, as Bloom might put it, "revisionary ratios."

Bloom's theory of the anxiety of influence has never helped in the close reading of poetry. It is not in the nature of generalizing theories to illuminate minute particulars. One might argue, however, that Bloom has been indirectly responsible for the emergence of an antithetical school of influence studies, headed by Ricks, to which this volume's contributors subscribe. Several are careful to align themselves with Ricks when determining whether influence is damaging. Damian Walford Davies treats Dylan Thomas's triumphant claim, "I am in the path of Blake," as registering not simply Thomas's sense of "belatedness" (that, pace Bloom, is a given), but also his "sense of the precursor as an enabling presence delivering the latecomer into his own promising future" (13). Similarly, Hugh Haughton examines "the forces of envy and identification" in Heaney's relationship with his precursors, only to conclude that "he is never happier than when he is acknowledging debts and influences" (61). To argue that the benign model of influence offered in this volume simply *reverses* Bloom's malign one would be to subscribe to a "myth of filiation" as single-minded as Bloom's own. It would, perhaps, be more accurate to say that the Ricksian art of resisting generalizations through close reading is here practiced as an antidote to the reductive dogmatism of Bloomian theory.

Among the current generation of scholar-critics on both sides of the Atlantic, a healthy respect is being reawakened for the hearing of echoes, the noticing of allusions. *The Monstrous Debt* pays careful attention to them. It is becoming clear that this Ricksian turn in recent criticism need not lead us away from the findings of hermeneutics and new historicism. Even as literary theory appears to be undergoing a decline, alternative avenues for intertextual studies are opening. As this collection of essays shows, we are now ready for an integrative model of influence that brings together the various preoccupations of the past thirty years.

Notes

1. Harold Bloom, *The Anxiety of Influence: A Theory of Poetry*, 2nd ed. (Oxford: Oxford University Press, 1997), 5.

2. See Christopher Ricks, *Dylan's Visions of Sin* (Harmondsworth: Penguin, 2004).

3. "The only means of strengthening one's intellect is to make up ones mind about nothing—to let the mind be a thoroughfare for all thoughts." John Keats to George and Georgiana Keats, *The Letters of John Keats, 1814–1821*, ed. Hyder Edward Rollins (Cambridge, MA: Harvard University Press, 1958), 2:213.

4. Christopher Ricks, *Allusion to the Poets* (Oxford: Clarendon Press, 2002), 9.

Acknowledgments

We wish to thank Kathryn Wildfong, Jane Hoehner, Kristin Harpster Lawrence, and former director Arthur B. Evans at Wayne State University Press. Thanks also to copyeditor Jennifer Backer.

We are very grateful to the University of Wales, Aberystwyth, for two research grants in support of the project.

Our greatest debts—in a book about debts—are to Francesca Rhydderch and Brychan and Cristyn Rhydderch Davies; and to Anne, Leah, and Nils Marggraf-Turley.

Introduction

Damian Walford Davies
Richard Marggraf Turley

Never on such a night have lovers met,
Since Merlin paid his Demon all the monstrous debt.

Keats, *The Eve of St Agnes*

This book joins an animated debate on the persistence of Romanticism. Our sense of the influence of Romantic writers on twentieth-century literature and culture is surely less settled than our understanding of the Victorian legacy. One reason for this may be that dominant twentieth-century cultural movements responded equivocally to their Romantic inheritance, clearly recognizing the significance of Romanticism, while believing that an open-eyed (post)modernity depended on rejecting Romantic "myths" of redemptive Nature, individualism, perfectibility, the transcendence of art, the holiness of the heart's affections. One might also suggest that the contested nature of the Romantic survival is bound up with the fact that literary movements (and, for that matter, critical schools) have engaged in the "creation of a Romanticism which is fit to act as a precursor," as Edward Larrissy puts it in a stimulating collection of essays exploring the complex Romantic genealogy of postmodernism.[1] In other words—Wordsworth's, almost—the twentieth century created the Romanticisms by which it was to be enjoyed. This, then, is a book about the *modalities* of Romantic influence in the work of writers of the last century; it is also a book about how these writers have chosen to construct Romanticism.

We are all of us—poets and critics—burdened latecomers. As a title for a collection of essays on literary indebtedness, one might reasonably expect "The Monstrous Debt" to elicit Harold Bloom's approbation. Keats's puzzling phrase in *The Eve of St Agnes* certainly seems to suggest a Bloomian paradigm of anxious negotiation between the precursor-father and the unsettled ephebe, conscious of his (emphatically not *her* in Bloom's patrifilial model) belatedness, and suffering the *influenza* of influence.[2] In addition, coming from a Keats who, for Bloom, is forced, for his own poetic survival, creatively to "misread" both Milton and Wordsworth, the phrase would seem to be freighted with a further legitimization of the Freudian family romance, deployed in *The Anxiety of Influence* as a model for elucidating the agonistic relations between poets.

There is, however, an implied question mark after Keats's phrase as we offer it, for while Keats famously said of Milton that "Life to him would be death to me," he could also envisage influence in terms of convivial fraternity—this is the grateful, "unmisgiving" Keats recently reclaimed by Christopher Ricks in *Allusion to the Poets.*[3] Bloom's tendentious, and anxiety-inducing, essay was published some thirty years ago, during which time critics have questioned the adequacy of its superb (in both senses) monolithic schema.[4] While all of Bloom's "revisionary ratios" are imbued with anxiety, the modalities of influence identified by writers in the present volume are on the whole less fraught, more enabling, and redemptive. In other words, we reject a wholly joyless, wholly demonic view of intrapoetic relationships that can describe "the living labyrinth of literature" as being "built upon the ruin of every impulse most generous in us."[5] While anxiety should certainly be acknowledged as powerfully operative in the modern writer's response to what he or she has been bequeathed, this book on the whole explores influence not as victimization and disease but as assistance and health. The essays in this volume reveal that the anxiety *for* influence is just as strong as the anxiety *of* influence.[6]

Our title may also seem to invoke the monstrous family drama of Mary Shelley's *Frankenstein.* Ambiguously "inscribed" to a Grand Father, the novel is closely attuned to issues of influence, indebtedness, and responsibility, and offers itself, we suggest, as a compelling allegory of intrapoetic relationships that affirms the agonistic energies of Bloom's myth while also reversing their polarity. This is a tale of an anxious, then violently vengeful, relationship with the father. But in *Frankenstein,* the burden of debt falls not on the son, as in the Bloomian model, but on the father, who is urged to pay his "filthy daemon"[7]—his monster-son—the debt of paternal responsibility. Victor Frankenstein fantasizes about the gratitude of children: "A new species would bless me as its creator and source" ("source" resonating suggestively here); "many happy and excellent natures would owe their being to me. No father could claim the gratitude of his child so completely as I should deserve theirs" (52–53). Here, Victor sounds like the baleful literary precursor, as imagined by the anxious latecomer/ephebe. But just as the father can reasonably lay claim to the gratitude of his son, so, the monster insists, the son is entitled to the love and attention of his father. The cause of the struggle that ensues (its language, if not its dynamics, is in places strikingly Bloomian: "[I am] thy creature, to whom thou art bound by *ties only dissoluble by the annihilation of one of us*"; "Come on, my enemy; *we have yet to wrestle for our lives*" (96, 198), is the son's desperate need, not for individuation or autonomy, but for recognition from and union with the precursor-father. The monster's lament is that "No father had watched my infant days" (117), and his rejection by Victor leads to his campaign of terror. The father's victimization of the son (in Bloom's schema) is reversed: it is the monster-son who now victimizes Victor: "You are my creator, but I am your master—obey!" (162). This son—as both devoted *fils* and avenging fury—is in pursuit of, not in flight from, the father; Victor's tracking of his creation at the end of the novel is in fact invited and enabled by the monster, who engages him in a game of allusion by leaving haunting textual "inscriptions" of himself (compare Mary Shelley's "inscription" of her book to her father, Godwin): "marks in writing on the barks of trees, or cut in stone . . . 'Follow me; I seek the everlasting ices of the north'" (198). One can take further this reading of *Frankenstein* as an allegory of poetic relationships. Why does Victor turn with loathing from that which he has labored to create? Why does he disavow paternity? We would suggest that he recognizes the creature at the moment of its "birth" as a living misprision, a work that is literally—literarily—stitched together from other works, bodies of writing, *disjecta membra*. Victor recognizes that the monstrous text can never be original; it is always the result of filchings from the dead bodies of literature's dissecting rooms, slaughterhouses, and charnel houses. The Great Original realizes with horror that he himself is nothing but an anxious ephebe. *Frankenstein,* then, demonstrates the inadequacy of a rigidly Bloomian reading of influence.

In place of Bloom's grand narrative of anxious revisionism,

therefore, we do not offer another totalizing system. Any attempt to frame a single theory to account for the manifold and complex relations between poems and poets runs the risk of being viewed as an act of anxious revisionism. Blake's pronouncement "I must create a system or be enslaved by another man's" could be seen as the motto of Bloom's enterprise as critic; but what was liberating in 1973 now seems enslaving. Though trumpeted as an emancipating model "for practical criticism" that would "free us from [the] more absurd myths (or gossip grown old) of literary pseudo-history," and though influential, the severe Freudian mythopoeia of *The Anxiety of Influence* never actually established itself as an enduring critical orthodoxy in Romantic Studies, or as an authorized view of literary history.[8]

The last thirty years have seen the rise (and, in some cases, the fall) of a number of pretenders to orthodoxy: psychoanalytic criticism; formalism; Yale School deconstruction; feminism; theories of gender and sexuality; postcolonial theory; historicism and new historicism; ecocriticism; theories of canon formation. Most of these approaches seem alive and well, often invigorating Romantic Studies in hybrid forms. There is, then, a healthy plurality of critical viewpoints within the academy, enabling the issue of literary influence to be interpreted from a variety of perspectives.

If there is a prevailing critical orthodoxy in the field, it can reasonably be claimed to be new historicism. Its materialist approach has broadened our sense of what "influence" is by alerting us to the complex of relations that go into the making of the literary text. Notions of cultural embeddedness and circulating social energy trouble and enlarge our understanding of "originality" and "indebtedness." The only "history" that concerns Bloom, of course, is the chronology of early and late, priority and belatedness; he has no interest in the contingencies of time as lived experience or in a poet's, a text's, cultural "debts." As Lucy Newlyn states, "If Bloom's analysis is insufficient, this is partly because it examines anxiety at the purely psychic level, ignoring the social and cultural constraints which might also shed light on influence."[9] Recent critical approaches such as life writing, which brings the personal present into an "ennobling interchange" (*The Prelude* [1805], 12:376) with the literary past, open another critical window on influence; and cultural studies have shown how the Romantics are packaged, rewritten, and overwritten in a variety of new media such as films and popular music.

The Romantic canon has expanded radically in the last decade, bringing into focus marginalized authors and thereby giving us a more precise understanding of the debts canonical writers often owe noncanonical contemporaries. We have made a conscious decision in *The Monstrous Debt,* however, to focus primarily on the influence of canonical Romantic writers on established twentieth-century authors. A factor in this decision is the obvious reality that hitherto elided Romantic figures have not yet been able to achieve the cultural currency—the "monstrous" debt in the sense of the extensive debt—on which significant, mappable influence depends.

Damian Walford Davies's essay begins by profiling the scope of William Blake's influential "coming on earth" (in Michael Horovitz's phrase) during the twentieth century. It then moves to focus on the complex negotiations with a number of Blake's poetic and graphic works discernible in a notoriously obscure sonnet by Dylan Thomas—a poet for whom the Romantic precursor was an "incomparable and inimitable master," not a baleful Nobodaddy. Walford Davies argues that recourse to Blake "crucially contests, clarifies, and extends" the interpretations of the sonnet hitherto offered by other critics; Blake's work helps unlock Thomas's obscurity. Thomas's sonnet, which articulates a momentous cosmic drama within a Christian frame, represents "an impressively close, astute, and creative" reading of Blake. Blake is viewed as inspiring "complex transformative maneuvers" in Thomas's work—"redemptive translations" that amount to "interpretative insights into the great precursor's mythology."

This focused reading of a single text is followed by a broader survey of influence. Harriet Devine Jump considers the ways in which Mary Wollstonecraft became a vital and relevant presence—intellectually, politically, and emotionally—for Virginia Woolf during the course of her research for an essay on Wollstonecraft, published in the *New York Herald Tribune.* Having suffered the vicissitudes of a particularly dramatic posthumous life, Wollstonecraft is reclaimed by Woolf who, Jump contends, "makes [Wollstonecraft's] work and her thought rest firmly on the basis of her experiences of life." Woolf's rehabilitation is thus a return to the very grounds on which Wollstonecraft had been stigmatized during so much of the Victorian period. Jump goes on to trace strong resemblances between the arguments of Wollstonecraft's *Vindication of the Rights of Woman* (1792) and Woolf's discussion in *Three Guineas* (1938) of female education, the legal status of women, and the links between domestic and political tyranny, gender, and social inequality.

In Hugh Haughton's essay on Wordsworth and Seamus Heaney, we find a Heaney who "forged a poetic image of himself out of Wordsworth." For Haughton, Wordsworth laid down the "ground rules of Heaney's poetic enterprise" ("ground" being a resonant term in Heaney's poetics). Wordsworth has clearly helped form Heaney's poetic taste: the Irish poet's view of other writers (Plath, Larkin, and Kavanagh, as well as his contemporaries from Northern Ireland) is conditioned by how "Wordsworthian" they are. Haughton sees Heaney invoking Wordsworth's "poetry of redemption" as a "template with which to understand the work of the writers of his own generation from Northern Ireland"—who, like Wordsworth, were writing out of historical crisis. Haughton charts Heaney's strategic invocations of Wordsworth within a political and autobiographical frame, tracing the shifting ground of the allegiance. Haughton suggests, interestingly, that the excavatory Wordsworthian Heaney, in digging back into childhood, into hiding places of power, may well be escaping not only violence but modernity and "the power of the contemporary world."

Lisa M. Steinman's challenging essay looks at three "creative rereadings" of Wordsworth's "The Solitary Reaper" in Wallace Stevens's "The Idea of Order at Key West," John Ashbery's "Le Livre Est Sur La Table," and Adrienne Rich's "Blood-Sister." Steinman outlines how the three American poets offer consecutive rereadings of the famous Romantic poem, giving us a new—perhaps a distinctly transatlantic—Wordsworth. The essay is interested in the way in which (in Wai Chee Dimock's formulation) "a weak signal is boosted by background noise and becomes newly and complexly audible"—how "words in a text yield different meanings or signals across time." Steinman is stimulating on the idea of the self-consciously anachronistic reading of Romantic texts: "it is more difficult, after 1934, to read 'The Solitary Reaper' without Stevens . . . putting in an appearance." According to this seductive take on influence, part of the meaning of a Romantic poem resides in its twentieth-century rereading. Steinman contends that even the American poets' arguments with Wordsworth reinscribe "aural, representational, and narrative qualities of the lyric" inherited from their Romantic precursor.

At a time when dipping into the myth-kitty was unfashionable, Ted Hughes began to cultivate a profound interest in the mythological underpinning of poetry. John Beer reveals that Hughes's fascination with Coleridge's great visionary works of the late 1790s—"Kubla Khan," "The Ancient Mariner," and part 1 of "Christabel"—was ignited by a recognition of the poems' mythic force. Hughes homed in on Coleridge's pregnant symbolic images of animals and natural organisms. Beer acknowledges that Hughes's detailed readings are creative compositions that represent "a poetic canvas of his own"; he also emphasizes that Hughes's personal exegesis often verges on the eccentric. However, for Beer, Hughes's "critical" writings insightfully posit a double identity (a "Christian Self" and an "Unleavened Self") in Coleridge's life and art—elements of his personality that were in creative but often debilitating tension. A suggestive parallel is posited between the dynamics of the Ted Hughes-Sylvia Plath relationship and the symbiosis of the Wordsworth-Coleridge pairing. Beer is interested in identity here: Wordsworth's and Hughes's "monolithic self-confirming" sense of self; Coleridge's "mercurial," snake-identified character; and the "intricate interweaving of sinuosities" that characterizes Plath's poetic identity.

Swerving from a Bloomian model of influence, Michael O'Neill's essay explores how the word "air"—with which the Romantics were imaginatively preoccupied—serves to position twentieth-century poets in relation to their Romantic precursors. Moving from Hart Crane and W. B. Yeats to Wallace Stevens, Elizabeth Bishop, and Adrienne Rich, O'Neill sees the Romantics offering "a supply of imaginative oxygen to later poems," inspiring "new imaginative breathing[s]." The essay goes on to offer a sparkling discussion of the ways in which Stevens and Bishop negotiate Romantic metaphor, and of how twentieth-century poetry articulates a "double response to Romanticism's visionary quest" by adopting an ironic stance vis-à-vis Romantic ideals—one in which "sustaining air" can support sardonic heirs as well as grateful latecomers.

How can a "conversation" with a Romantic precursor help focus a modern writer's sense of the historical moment of his or her art? John Whale reads Tony Harrison's verse-epistle, "A Kumquat for John Keats," as a meditation on the post-holocaustal burden of history for the late twentieth-century poet. The gift of the exotic fruit is initially a site of identification between the poets, who are joined in a fraternal bond on the grounds of shared sensual relish. However, the grim reality of Harrison's world—one in which "a thing no bigger than an urn explodes / and ravishes all silence, and all odes," and in which "Flora [is] asphyxiated by foul air / unknown to either Keats or Lemprière"—gives rise first to a "measured ambivalence" in Harrison's response to Keats, then to a rupture between the poets. As Whale contends, in Harrison's historically self-conscious poem, "Keats's historical innocence is posed against the terrible difference of twentieth-century experience," and Keats's classical and pastoral imagination is revealed as inadequate "for [Harrison's] own contemporaneity."

Turning aside from debates on the respective *quality* of John Keats's and Bob Dylan's work, Richard Marggraf Turley's essay examines, as an alternative basis for comparison, the two iconic writers' "poise in the presence of the precursor." Where Keats can often appear to be tremulous in the terms Harold Bloom describes in *The Anxiety of Influence*, for Marggraf Turley, Dylan emerges as a new kind of writer, one who "effectively steps out of Bloomian paradigms." Indeed, Dylan is seen as enacting a return to the days "Before the Flood"—the title of Dylan's 1974 live album, and the phrase Bloom uses to designate writers who lived before the age of influence anxiety. Identifying a series of hitherto unnoticed instances where Dylan's work carries verbal traces of Keats—"repeated quotations," as Dylan would put it—the essay finds the latecomer's lyrics "largely untroubled by any original Romantic disquietude."

Emma Mason's essay seeks to recover and rehabilitate the value of a particular mode of Romantic feeling: that exemplified by the poetry of Felicia Hemans. How, asks Mason, did one of the most popular authors of her day become reconfigured by twentieth-century readers as a poet of "gushy and saccharine individualism"? Mason's focus is on three key twentieth-century critical and creative readings of Hemans—by T. S. Eliot, Alan Liu, and Elizabeth Bishop. Eliot's conflicted "indictments" of Romantic feeling are problematized and redressed by the responses of Liu and Bishop, both of whom find ways of reconstituting Hemansian feeling as "restorative." Engaging Hemans's "Casabianca," Mason's essay allows us to become inward with the complex emotional freight of a poem that has for so long been relegated to the status of the sound bite of its opening line.

In the final essay in the volume, an eminent Keatsian returns to Keats to examine the "later modalities of the Romantic Vision."

Hinging on an aperçu regarding the Cockney colloquialism of a line in "Ode to a Nightingale," John Bayley's incisive contribution, delivered from a high vantage point, considers how twentieth-century poetry (that of Dylan Thomas and John Betjeman) seeks to "overcome the shadow of kitsch" by self-consciously "shocking the whole concept out of itself." Bayley suggests, for instance, that Betjeman's transformations of fatigued reality into something newly and ecstatically seen would have been recognized by Keats as something akin to his own linguistic and visionary scheme.

Taken as a whole, then, the essays in *The Monstrous Debt* trace the many and diverse inscriptions of Romanticism's afterlife. They show twentieth-century authors seeking out—and constructing—their Romantic precursors, recognizing in them energizing and necessary models to appropriate and react against in the articulation of their own contemporaneity.

Notes

1. Edward Larrissy, ed., *Romanticism and Postmodernism* (Cambridge: Cambridge University Press, 1999), 3.

2. Harold Bloom, *The Anxiety of Influence: A Theory of Poetry,* 2nd ed. (Oxford: Oxford University Press, 1997), 38, 95.

3. See Christopher Ricks, *Allusion to the Poets* (Oxford: Clarendon Press, 2002), 157–78.

4. For a recent critique, see Robert Douglas-Fairhurst, *Victorian Afterlives: The Shaping of Influence in Nineteenth-Century Literature* (Oxford: Oxford University Press, 2002), 28–43. See also Sharon Ruston and Lidia Garbin, eds., *The Influence and Anxiety of the British Romantics: Spectres of Romanticism* (Lewiston: Edwin Mellen, 1999), and John Beer, *Romantic Influences: Contemporary—Victorian—Romantic* (Houndmills: Macmillan, 1993). For the *ur*-discussion of influence, see W. Jackson Bate, *The Burden of the Past and the English Poet* (London: Chatto and Windus, 1971).

5. Bloom, *The Anxiety of Influence,* 85.

6. See Douglas-Fairhurst, *Victorian Afterlives,* 34.

7. *Frankenstein,* ed. Maurice Hindle (Harmondsworth: Penguin, 1992), 73.

8. Some of Bloom's most resonant terms have certainly entered the critical vocabulary of Romantic Studies and often seem to be deployed in a casual—one might say unconscious—manner. See, e.g., the introduction to Larrissy, *Romanticism and Postmodernism* (Cambridge: Cambridge University Press, 1999), 2, where Larrissy uses "misprisions" and "belatedness" in the context of Jerome J. McGann's new historicism.

9. Lucy Newlyn, *Paradise Lost and the Romantic Reader* (Oxford: Clarendon Press, 1993), 17. Newlyn's study offers a wide-ranging and nuanced negotiation with Bloom.

"In the Path of Blake": Dylan Thomas's "Altarwise by Owl-Light"

Damian Walford Davies

> Blake is not a poet of the Romantic period.
>
> Edward Larrissy, *Romanticism and Postmodernism*

> Blake is a fire-source but enjoins those who catch flame from him to shine according to their own genius. While imitation of this master is a contradiction, dawn-wrestling with him like Jacob with the angel transfers prophetic intensity. Blake does not usurp a writer's voice but rather delivers the individual into his own songs.
>
> James Bogan and Fred Goss, *Sparks of Fire: Blake in a New Age*

"1957—the second hundredth coming of Blake on earth turned my displaced and under-graduating scholar gipsy's head—to listen—taste—& witness—first fruits of the subsequent decade's farther fields & subterranean zones—now borne aloft to Penguins [*sic*] shore."[1] So begins Michael Horovitz's "Blakean cornucopia" of "Afterwords" to the seminal anthology, *Children of Albion: Poetry of the "Underground" in Britain*, published by Penguin in 1969 and featuring Blake's *Glad Day* on the cover. Horovitz's startling performance amounts to a major poetical and political manifesto. As a student at Oxford in the late 1950s, he had seen "budding talents buried alive, most elegantly—taught—to lie," poets on whom fell "the baleful Shadow—of [T. S. Eliot's] influence," which was buttressed by the "professional hollow men—brandishing standards of 'The New Criticism'" (*Children of Albion*, 316). Horovitz was delivered from a similar conformist fate by a Blake-inspired epiphany ("a Glad Day") that led him to "kick the entire mental block" he had "felt [his] body and spirit prisoned in." In the summer of 1948 in East Harlem, Allen Ginsberg (whose own "Blakean way" Horovitz charts in *Children of Albion*) had also experienced a life-changing "Blake Moment." Horovitz's "Afterwords" celebrate Blake as a central influence on the forms and ideology of performance and jazz poetry in the 1960s and as the presiding spirit of the momentous International Poetry Incarnation at the Albert Hall, London, in June 1965. The *New Departures* enterprise and the proliferation of new poetry presses such as Ferry, Fulcrum, and Goliard were part of this politicized Romantic renaissance. For these Blakeans, the "true voice" of their "master" cut across the "closeted 'game-reserve' influences"[2] of Auden (who, Horovitz notes, "has tried to dismiss Blake as 'dotty'") and the "trivial ingenuity," ironic urbanity, and anti-Romantic program of the Movement's poetics. Blake revealed to the poets of the Underground an Albion sick and in need of political and imaginative redemption, just as, with Whitman, Blake had showed Ginsberg, the Beats, and the counterculture movement an America unregenerate, materialistic, and Urizenic. "Yet if the prophet of Jerusalem were on his ancient feet," Horovitz concludes, "I don't doubt but he'd be sending more men to higher mountains by singing his songs and blowing his ever present mind of prophecy to the many who rejoice to hear today." Horovitz's pun ("blowing his . . . mind of prophecy") neatly captures the prophetic, psychedelic Blake of the 1960s—Adrian Mitchell's "Blakehead, babyhead," "shaking tyger-lamb," "Inventor of . . . / The human form, jazz, Jerusalem," who "sucked the sun like a gobstopper,"[3] and whose birthday was to signal the emancipation of canonical worthies imprisoned in Westminster Abbey's Poets' Corner:

> You stony bunch of pockskinned whiteys,
> Why kip in here? Who sentenced you?
> . . . .
> On William Blake's birthday we're going to free you,
> Blast off your platforms with a blowtorch full of brandy . . .[4]

The 1960s marked the most dramatic "coming of Blake on earth" during the twentieth century. But Blake's influence on twentieth-century culture generally was profound and multifarious, as the lively exploration of the "propagation of Blake" recently offered in

Dent and Wittaker's *Radical Blake: Influence and Afterlife from 1827* (2002) has emphasized. Blake's transmission transcends and contests cultural boundaries: as well as the Blake of the Beats and the Underground, there is the Blakean presence in the neglected Romantic (or, as the Movement saw it, the "Id-Romantic"[5]) legacy within British Modernism; the influence of Blake's cosmology on the critical discourse of Bloom's *The Anxiety of Influence* ("The original sin of art . . . is that a False Tongue vegetates beneath nature, *or to use less Blakean language* . . ."[6]); the Blake-saturated lyrics of Jim Morrison and The Doors; Adrian Mitchell's musical, *Tyger* (1971); the countless, diverse musical settings of Blake poems; the homage to Blake performed by Patti Smith, Tori Amos, and other artists at the 2005 Meltdown festival; Blake's Japanese incarnation in Kenzaburo Oe's novel *Rouse Up O Young Men of the New Age!* (2002); "self-help" books such as *The Healing Power of Blake;* and films such as *Dead Man* (1993) and *Red Dragon* (2002), the former taking Johnny Depp's William Blake into the territory of the spiritual Western and the latter presenting a Blake inscribed on the body and literally consumed by a devotee.

In this essay, I have chosen to focus on a specific, circumscribed manifestation of Blake's persistent currency in twentieth-century literature. I offer a detailed exploration of the complex negotiation with Blake's poetry and graphic work traceable in a notoriously (or, as one commentator has it, "nefariously"[7]) obscure sonnet published in 1934 by a poet who is regarded in Horovitz's *Children of Albion* as a neo-Romantic precursor of the 1960s "renaissance of 'the voice of the bard'"[8] and by Blake Morrison as a writer who induced a measure of Bloomian anxiety in the poets of the Movement:[9] Dylan Thomas.

"I am in the path of Blake," Dylan Thomas told Pamela Hansford Johnson on 15 October 1933, "but so far behind him that only the wings on his heels are in sight"[10] (a remark that is in the path of other Romantics, too, since it echoes Coleridge's assessment of Wordsworth, as reported by Hazlitt in "My First Acquaintance with Poets": "He strides on so far before you, that he dwindles in the distance!"[11]). The comment figures Thomas's belatedness in terms that suggest not Bloomian anxiety regarding the priority of the poetic father but a sense of the precursor as an enabling presence delivering the latecomer into his own promising future. Two years before his death, Thomas referred to Blake as one of his "incomparable and inimitable masters."[12] On learning in 1934 that a "Professor Somebody" had fulsomely praised his work in an article, Thomas asserted ironically in a letter to Johnson, "The excerpts I send you show that I'm a greater poet than Blake" (*Collected Letters,* 106)—which, of course, is another way of saying that Blake is incomparable and inimitable. Thomas's was no naïve, unthinking devotion to the master, however. With the moralistic *Proverbial Philosophy* of Martin F. Tupper (1810–89) in mind, he could also state in a 1935 review that "Much of [Blake's] Prophetic Books reads like Tupper after absinthe." He went on to explain:

> The importance of Blake lies in the importance of his poetry and his monstrous mythology, not in his borrowed Judaisms. He lives because he could put words together well. He lives because he had a glorious vocabulary, a divine enquiry, the key to the files of a mystic Rogues' Gallery, and possibly epileptic vision. He does not live because he was a wise man, a man with a message, a constructive philosopher. . . . Possibly he was. But if he had been that and nothing much else, the Marriage of Heaven and Hell would be as little read to-day as the Divine Love and Wisdom of Swedenborg. (*Early Prose Writings,* 177)

Thomas was also conscious of the dangers of merely faddish debt. In 1938, responding to John Goodland's invitation to contribute to a symposium of Apocalyptic writing—another neo-Romantic strain in twentieth-century literature—he recognized that many young poets, "hitherto content with imitations of the queenly social verse," would be "whipping [themselves] into a false delirium, snatching—in case the apocalyptic game flourishes—at the chance of a frenetic reputation, downing Auden on a pylon for Blake on a bough" (*Collected Letters,* 394).

My discussion of the Blake-Thomas poetic relationship rejects a Bloomian reading that sees Blake as an anxiety-inducing poetic father and "Great Inhibitor," in reaction to whom Thomas struggles to free up "imaginative space" for himself through creative misprision. Thomas recognized Blake as a great facilitator, not as his Nobodaddy or, in Bloom's words, as "the Other whose baleful greatness is enhanced by the ephebe's seeing him as a burning brightness against a framing darkness, rather as Blake's Bard of Experience sees the Tyger"

(*Anxiety of Influence*, 35). As we shall see, Thomas certainly recasts and reconfigures Blake, but to see him performing certain of Bloom's dark revisionary ratios on his precursor's work according to the "joyless wisdom of the family romance" (*Anxiety of Influence*, 78) would be—to borrow Christopher Ricks's recent description of Bloom's paradigm—melodramatic.[13] Thomas, in the words of Blake's "Proverbs of Hell," is a "thankful receiver."

Thomas's familiarity with Blake's poetic and graphic work is well documented. In 1951, he claimed that along with Scottish ballads, hymns, the Bible, and Shakespeare, it was Blake's *Songs of Innocence* that had first made him "love language" as a child, inspiring him to "work *in* it and *for* it" (*Early Prose Writings*, 157). On Christmas Day 1933, the nineteen-year-old Thomas wrote to Pamela Hansford Johnson informing her that along with many cigarettes, a "startlingly yellow tie," a "peculiar pair of string gloves," and "a knitted thing," he had received "the complete Blake" from one of his uncles (*Collected Letters*, 91). The years 1925–32 had seen a spate of Blake editions, and Thomas's present was either Max Plowman's 1927 single-volume selection for Everyman or, more probably, one of Geoffrey Keynes's "complete" Nonesuch volumes (1925, 1927, and 1932). In the same Christmas letter, Thomas also told Johnson that he was "reading Blake's letters for the first time." The Blakean credentials of Thomas's poetry from the 1930s to the 1950s are inescapable and have been acknowledged by commentators.[14] The debt manifests itself in early imitations,[15] direct allusions, broader analogies, and—Thomas's apparent misgivings about Blake as "a man with a message" notwithstanding—in the general philosophy of such poems as "I see the boys of summer in their ruin" (1934), which attacks conventional social codes that lead to the suppression of one's sexual urges, and "There was a saviour" (written 1940, published 1946), which contests the comforting simplifications and distortions of institutionalized religion. Thomas's conception of the relationship between body and soul; his distrust of the "ratio" and his "attempt to establish imaginative truth as an element necessary to temper the arrogance of intellect"; his "cultivation of myth"; his "efforts to transcend the categories of good and evil"; his "dualistic view of the world"; his preoccupation with the theme of generation and creation; his "bardic" voice; and his linking of "compassion and physical love" have all been read as either specific endorsements or close analogues of Blake's heterodox vision.[16] Less obvious are Thomas's debts to Blake in the first of his "Altarwise by Owl-Light" sonnets.

> Altarwise by owl-light in the halfway-house
> The gentleman lay graveward with his furies;
> Abaddon in the hang-nail cracked from Adam,
> And, from his fork, a dog among the fairies,
> The atlas-eater with a jaw for news,
> Bit out the mandrake with tomorrow's scream.
> Then, penny-eyed, that gentleman of wounds,
> Old cock from nowheres and the heaven's egg,
> With bones unbuttoned to the halfway winds,
> Hatched from the windy salvage on one leg,
> Scraped at my cradle in a walking word
> That night of time under the Christward shelter,
> I am the long world's gentleman, he said,
> And share my bed with Capricorn and Cancer.
> (*Collected Poems*, 58)

The ten "Altarwise" sonnets, probably written between Christmas 1934 and Christmas 1935,[17] and first published as a group in the poet's second collection, *Twenty-five Poems* (1936), are among the most cryptic of Thomas's poems, characterized by a metaphorical life so dense that some critics have seen them as self-parody[18]—a view supported by Thomas's comment to Glyn Jones, who had just reviewed *Twenty-five Poems:*

> You're the only reviewer, I think, who *has* commented on my attempts to get away from those rhythmic and thematic dead-ends . . . those wombs, and full-stop worms. . . . But I'm not sorry that [in the "Altarwise" sonnets] I did carry "certain features to their logical conclusion." It had, I think, to be done; the result had to be, in many of the lines & verses anyway, mad parody; and I'm glad that *I* parodied those features so soon after making them, & that I didn't leave it to anyone else. (*Collected Letters*, 272)

The sonnets—which William Empson considered mannered but also in places "ragingly good"[19]—have inspired a host of editorial glosses, elaborate explanatory zodiac charts,[20] and celebrated paraphrase contests in *The Explicator.*[21] Thomas's later reaction to them appears somewhat apologetic. Replying to questions at the University of Utah on 18 April 1952, he described them as "only the writings of a boily boy in love with shapes and shadows on his pillow."[22] The impressively off-the-cuff reference is surely to Oothoon's lament in Blake's *Visions of the Daughters of Albion:*

> The moment of desire! The moment of desire! The virgin
> That pines for man shall awaken her womb to enormous joys
> In the secret shadows of her chamber. The youth, shut up from
> The lustful joy, shall forget to generate and create an amorous image
> In the shadows of his curtains and in the folds of his silent pillow.
> Are not these the places of religion, the rewards of continence,
> The self-enjoyings of self-denial?[23]

Representing the sonnet-sequence as the product of adolescent mawkishness, Thomas brilliantly reverses Oothoon's Blakean "moral": the creation of the fantastic "images" of the sonnets in the shadows and folds of a "boily" boy's pillow represents the monstrous "self-enjoyings," not of "self-denial" but of imaginative self-indulgence and excess—a state of "self-enchantment when lip-smacking imps of mawk and hooey / write with us what they will," as Auden put it in "The Cave of Making." Auden's poem—an elegy for Louis MacNiece—announces the need for "the companionship of our good dead," who "break the spell" of such egocentric imaginings; one might say that Blake, summoned through allusion by Thomas in his comment at Utah, is one of those "good dead," performing a similar function by giving Thomas the words publicly to break the spell of an earlier infatuation. Another source for Thomas's "boily boy" comment is to be found in Blake's psychological epic, *Vala, or the Four Zoas.* Here again, Blake provides an illuminating context for Thomas's cryptic assessment of the dense and difficult poetry of an earlier self. At the beginning of Night the Second, Luvah and the perniciously seductive fallen Vala—the passionate "Zoa" or elemental spirit and his emanation—usurp the place of Urizen, the rational, controlling Zoa, in the brain of the Eternal Man while Urizen "sleeps in the porch." Vala plants dreams there while Luvah steals Urizen's horses of light. Toward the beginning of Night the Third, Vala walks with the Eternal

Man "in dreams of soft deluding slumber." With Reason asleep, the Eternal Man begins—fatally—to worship a shadow of himself in his delusive sleep:

> Above him rose a shadow from his wearied intellect . . .
> A sweet entrancing self-delusion . . .
> . . . .
> I heard the voice of the slumberous Man, and thus he spoke,
> Idolatrous to his own shadow. . . .
> (ll. 47, 49, 55–56; *Complete Poems,* 334)

Seduced by Vala, the Eternal Man cannot see that the shadow is in fact Luvah in disguise. When the latter reveals himself, the Eternal Man realizes he has idolatrously worshiped an unredeemed part of himself, and a struggle ensues between them. Luvah is cast out, and the Eternal Man is left, significantly, "Covered with boils from head to foot." Thomas's "boily boy" comment at Utah suggests that this episode of *The Four Zoas* was also in his mind when he appeared to dismiss the "Altarwise" sonnets as the productions of tumescent youth. I suggest that the remark shows the later Thomas identifying (ironically?) in Blake's drama of the seduction and dangerous self-absorption of the Eternal Man a suggestive allegory of his own poetic fall as a "boily" adolescent into an "entrancing," self-involved, and private poetry.

In the following exploration (which implicitly challenges any assessment of the "Altarwise" sequence as merely "entrancing" or mawkish), I will concentrate on the first sonnet, crediting the following comments by Thomas: "though [the sonnets] are linked together by a certain obscure narrative, they're entirely self-contained"; "although the [sequence] as a whole is to be a poem in, and by, itself, the separate parts can be regarded as individual poems"; "each [sonnet] is a more-or-less self-contained short poem"; "[the first sonnet is] a particular incident in a particular adventure" (*Collected Letters,* 264, 229, 231, 348). I do not propose to offer a wholly new reading of the first sonnet based on a reading of Blake; nor am I claiming that Blake provides the definitive "solution" to Thomas's poem as a whole. I do contend, however, that the sonnet owes a significant debt to Blake's poetry and graphic work, and that recourse to Blake crucially contests, clarifies, and extends the interpretations critics have hitherto ventured. Blake's work offers a key that helps unlock Thomas's obscurity. Seamus Heaney has written that the "enigmas" of the sonnet "seem to be contrived rather than discovered"[24]—forced into artificial existence, that is, rather than emerging from authentic experience. One might suggest that the apparent "oddness" of Thomas's images may in part be due to their being "discovered" in Blake.

In my view, the most convincing explication of the sonnet so far offered is still Ralph Maud's, which appeared in *The Explicator* in 1955. Maud rehearsed this reading again in *Entrances to Dylan Thomas's Poetry* (1963) and in greater detail and with some modifications in *Where Have the Old Words Got Me?: Explications of Dylan Thomas's Collected Poems* (2003).[25] Maud's analysis, which does not cite Blake, sensibly negotiates the colorful gloss that Thomas himself supplied in a letter to Henry Treece.[26] In the following preliminary explication of the sonnet, I cite Thomas's paraphrase and supplement some of Maud's interpretations with my own. Maud views the first sonnet as "a one-man drama, which Thomas splits into multiple roles."[27] The "gentleman" is Christ, lying in the "halfway-house" of the grave, contending with his earthly, human passions ("furies") after the Crucifixion; "Abaddon," the Angel of the Bottomless Pit of Revelation 9:11 (also, of course, "a bad 'n'"), is the devil in the flesh who "cracks" away from Adam/Man at the moment of Christ's sacrifice on the cross. As Spirit, Christ is also the "dog among the fairies," the "atlas-eater with a jaw for news"—"the rip and cur among the myths, the snapper at demons, the scarer of ghosts, the wizard's heel-chaser" (Thomas's gloss)—who can "taste already the horror that has not yet come . . . can thrust his nose into news that has not been made, can savour the enormity of the progeny before the seed stirs, can realise the crumbling of dead flesh before the opening of the womb that delivers that flesh to tomorrow" (Thomas's gloss). As a dog uproots a mandrake,[28] Christ the Spirit, a sin-eater, bites out the "mandrake"—the "horror of tomorrow" (Thomas's gloss)—from the sexual existence, the reproductive life ("fork"), of Adam/physical Christ as Second Adam/humanity in an act of redemptive castration. The octave portrays an annunciation, a Nativity scene.[29] Christ is here the "gentleman of wounds," born by Virginal Conception ("Old cock from nowheres"; "old cock" also being a form of address to a man in British slang) and "hatched" again after his death on the cross (the "windy salvage on one leg") and his resurrection. He reveals himself, skeleton-like, to young Thomas the nascent poet (Christ is a walking "word" as well as the Word), on "that night of time."

Describing Christ as the "dog ["God" reversed?] among the fairies," "the rip and cur among the myths, the snapper at demons, the scarer of ghosts," Thomas has in mind Milton's ode "On the Morning of Christ's Nativity" (his favorite English poem, according to the eminent Blakean Kathleen Raine)[30] in which the birth of Christ sets the *genii loci* and the pagan gods to flight:

> Peor, and Baalim,
> Forsake their temples dim,
> With that twice battered god of Palestine,
> And mooned Ashtaroth . . .
>
> And sullen Moloch fled,
> Hath left in shadows dread,
> His burning idol all of blackest hue . . .
>
> Nor all the gods beside,
> Longer dare abide . . .
> (ll. 197–200, 205–7, 224–25)

Thomas's "fairies," among whom he lets loose his dog-Christ (compare Eliot's "In the juvescence of the year / Came Christ the tiger" ["Gerontion," ll. 19–20]), may seem somewhat out of place among the more formidable "myths," "demons," and "ghosts" (though Milton's Christ does set "nymphs" as well as the more monstrous Baalim and Moloch to flight). Blake's line "Fairies of Albion, afterwards gods of the heathen," from *The Four Zoas* (Night the First, l. 14), however, helps explain the fairies' presence and function in Thomas's sonnet. Blake's point here is one he had already made in *The Marriage of Heaven and Hell:*[31] as perceived by the "enlarged and numerous senses" of "ancient poets," the fairies of old "poetic tales" embodied imaginative truth, but those visions were subsequently corrupted and institutionalized into "forms of worship," into "systems of gods and goddesses." For Blake (who was to illustrate Milton's Nativity Ode in 1809[32]), those "Fairies of Albion" had become pagan deities—deities whose rout Milton depicts in the Nativity Ode. There is also a resemblance between the terror of the pagan gods in Milton's poem and the choir of demons (compare Thomas's "snapper at demons") who "[howl] around the new-born king" Orc—always Christ-like in Blake—in *The Four Zoas* (*Complete Poems*, 353), which Thomas in his gloss might also be recalling.

No doubt taking his cue from Thomas's autobiographical collection of short stories, *Portrait of the Artist as a Young Dog* (1940), and from Henry Treece's *Dylan Thomas, "Dog among the Fairies"* (1949), W. Y. Tindall sees in the "dog among the fairies" not a canine Christ among the demons but the young Dylan himself among his 1930s contemporaries. John Bayley is more precise, suggesting that the "dog among the fairies" is the heterosexual Thomas "in the homosexual world of London pubs and artists."[33] Although these readings do not sit comfortably in the context of any larger narrative the sonnet offers, the line in apposition to "dog among the fairies"—"the atlas-eater with a jaw for news"—does seem to gesture toward the autobiographical. "Atlas" (Thomas puns on "small atlas," a specific size of paper sheet[34]) and "a jaw for news" (by analogy with "a nose for news," as Thomas's gloss explains) evoke the world of the journalist; significantly, the young Thomas was employed as a reporter on the *South Wales Evening Post* from 1931 to 1932. A dog-Christ, then, or a dog-Dylan? What kind of cat among the pigeons is the "dog among the fairies"?

Milton's Nativity Ode certainly goes to the making of the image, but I suggest that Thomas's phrase is directly indebted to the seventh emblem (plate 9) in Blake's enigmatic poetic and graphic work, *For the Sexes: The Gates of Paradise*[35] (on which Thomas clearly draws in other poems[36]). Further, I argue that while the young Thomas likely saw in this engraving an image of himself as a whippersnapper, the precise significance of the design within Blake's larger mythology ultimately validates the interpretation of the "dog among the fairies" as a reference to a momentous cosmic event or drama involving Christ, as already outlined. The design shows a young boy knocking down fairy creatures with his hat; one lies on the ground while another tries to escape.[37]

The 1793 heading to the engraving reads "Alas!" expanded in Blake's later version to "What are these? Alas! the Female Martyr! Is She also the Divine Image?" The corresponding couplet of the accompanying work, "The Keys of the Gates," runs, "One dies! Alas, the living and dead; / One is slain and one is fled" (ll. 37–38). David

William Blake, *For the Sexes: The Gates of Paradise,* emblem 7, plate 9, copy D, PML 63936. Copyright © the Pierpont Morgan Library.

Erdman describes the design thus: "A boy who combines the forward movement of the hatching cupid [emblem 6, plate 8] and the open body and weapon wielding of the youth in Fire [emblem 5, plate 7] tries to use his hat as the Eve mother [emblem 1, plate 3] used her apron, to trap female spirits within the veil wherein the dead in spirit dwell."[38] In Blake's system, the entrapping boy among the female fairies signifies the binding of the imagination in the incarcerating veil of Vala, as well as the potentially destructive consequences of male desire. Thomas's understanding of this seventh emblem may not have accorded precisely with Erdman's, of course, but deeply read in Blake, he would have recognized it as an emblem of the imagination violated and suppressed. Thomas appropriates the image, boldly recasting it in the context of the drama of the "Altarwise" sonnet to signify the rout of pernicious demons, ghosts, and wizards by an emancipating, redeeming Christ.[39]

In doing so, Thomas, I suggest, shows himself to be an acute reader of Blake's visual language by responding to the dialectical play

William Blake, *For the Sexes: The Gates of Paradise,* emblem 1, plate 3, copy D, PML 63936. Copyright © the Pierpont Morgan Library.

of Blake's designs for *The Gates of Paradise.* Images of confinement are subtly counterbalanced by details that hint at what Erdman calls "imagination's way," "potential journeying," "the reversibility of a moment of incarceration."[40] In the seventh emblem, for example, such hints are embodied in the "upward flight" (Erdman) of the female creature and the chasing youth's arrested stride. In other words, I argue that Thomas's transformation of Blake's iconography of restriction is an imaginative act urged upon the viewer/reader of *The Gates of Paradise* by the complex dynamics of Blake's designs.

There are further examples in Thomas's poem of such redemptive translations. Blake's first emblem (plate 3) in *The Gates of Paradise* shows a woman under a weeping willow uprooting a mandrake—compare Thomas's "Bit out the mandrake with tomorrow's scream"—which looks like a human baby; she already holds two mandrake-children, their long hair now cropped, in her apron. Blake's heading proclaims: "I found him beneath a Tree." The corresponding couplets from "The Keys of the Gates" run: "My eternal man set in repose; /

The female from his darkness rose, / And she found me beneath a tree / A mandrake, and in her veil hid me" (ll. 13–16). Blake's mandrake is a symbol of the child born, with a scream, in the world of generation, an exile from Eternity. The Christ of Thomas's sonnet, offering Eternal Life, bites out the horror of being born to death or damnation—figured by Thomas as the mandrake[41]—from the sexual life of man in the act of redemption. The female in Blake's design I take to be an Eve figure (the next couplet-key corresponding to this design is suggestive: "Serpent reasonings us entice / Of good and evil: virtue and vice"), who plucks (gives birth to) the mandrake-child, confirming the fall into a universe of generation and confinement outside Eden/Eternity. By contrast, Thomas's sonnet has the devil in the flesh "crack" away from Adam, repairing the curse of that fall. The female in Blake's design is also a Vala figure. She plucks man and places him in an apron that represents the veil of Vala ("and in her veil hid me")—in Blake's mythology, our enclosing vegetative bodies, a code of moral law "composed of the spectres of the dead" (*Jerusalem*, plate 47, l. 11; *Complete Poems*, 728) and also the Mundane Shell, formed first in the Blakean system when renegade Urizen built around him a casing of rocks as protection against the flames of outraged Eternity (*The First Book of Urizen*, ll. 110–30; *Complete Poems*, 254). The casing became the vegetative universe that Blake calls the Mundane Egg, bounded by the Mundane Shell that restricts man's vision and separates him from Eternity. The shell is referred to in "The Keys of the Gates" from *The Gates of Paradise:* "Round her snowy whirlwinds roared / Freezing her veil, the mundane shell" (ll. 28–29). Thomas's image of the "Old cock from nowheres and the heaven's egg" has a source, as Kleinman suggests, in ovigenic myths,[42] but Blake's Mundane Egg is more likely to have inspired the line. One might suggest that Thomas once again transforms Blake's iconography of incarceration, as the Mundane Egg becomes "the heaven's egg";[43] equally, the phrase may serve to remind us of the very different Mundane universe of veiled perception and restricted vision into which Christ was incarnated.

After the doubts, "earthbound vision," and "mortal perspective" symbolized by the first five emblems of *The Gates of Paradise*, Blake's sixth (plate 8) is clearly an image of joyful emancipation. The line accompanying the design—"I rent the veil where the dead dwell"—suggests man's rending of the restrictive veil that separates him from

William Blake, *For the Sexes: The Gates of Paradise,* emblem 6, plate 8, copy D, PML 63936. Copyright © the Pierpont Morgan Library.

Eternity. The design itself shows a winged baby breaking out of an egg with one leg already outside the shell; the heading runs, "At length for hatching ripe he breaks the shell."[44] For Erdman, the cherub's hatching "prefigures the universal jail delivery . . . and the consummation of the five senses by the imagination."[45] Occurring toward the middle of a series of designs that appear to depict the passage of human life from birth to death, the sixth engraving figures not birth into the immortality of an "afterlife" as traditionally conceived[46] but the accessing of a Blakean Eternity in *this* life through the liberation of the divine imagination and the rejection of mere "finite organical perception" (*The Marriage of Heaven and Hell,* plate 12, l. 23; *Complete Poems,* 112). For Blake, "our own imaginations" are "those worlds of eternity in which we shall live for ever—in Jesus our Lord" (*Milton,* plate 1, ll. 19–20; *Complete Poems,* 491), and his "great task" was "To open the eternal worlds, to open the immortal eyes / Of man inwards into the worlds of thought—into eternity / Ever expanding in the bosom of God, the human imagination" (*Jerusalem,* plate 5, ll. 18–20; *Complete Poems,* 636). Commissioned to prepare illustrations for a handsome edition of Edward Young's *Night Thoughts,* Blake produced 537 watercolor sketches between 1796 and 1797.[47] His thirteenth illustration, accompanying the lines "An Heir of Glory! a frail Child

(8)

A Beam etherial ſully'd, and abſort!
Tho' ſully'd, and diſhhonour'd, ſtill Divine!
Dim Miniature of Greatneſs abſolute!
An Heir of Glory! a frail Child of Duſt!
Helpleſs Immortal! Inſect *infinite!*
A Worm! a God! I tremble at myſelf,
And in myſelf am loſt! At home a Stranger,
Thought wanders up and down, ſurpriz'd, aghaſt,
And wond'ring at her *own:* How Reaſon reels?
O what a Miracle to man is man,
Triumphantly diſtreſt? what Joy, what Dread?
Alternately tranſported, and alarm'd!
What can preſerve my Life? or what deſtroy?
An Angel's arm can't ſnatch me from the Grave;
Legions of Angels can't confine me There.
'Tis paſt Conjecture; all things riſe in Proof:
While o'er my limbs *Sleep*'s ſoft dominion ſpread,
What, tho' my ſoul phantaſtic Meaſures trod,

O'er

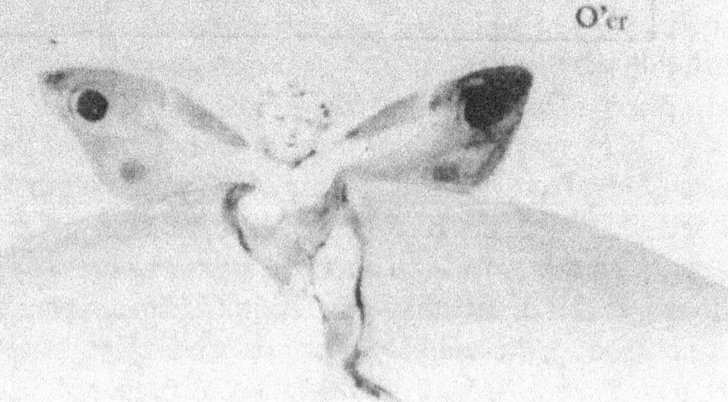

William Blake, Illustration 13 to Edward Young's *Night Thoughts*. Copyright © the British Museum.

of Dust! / *Helpless* Immortal! Insect *infinite*! / A Worm! a God!" (Night the First, ll. 78–80), shows a butterfly-winged infant emerging from an egg-shell.

His sixteenth illustration, accompanying lines 131–33 of Young's first book "On Life, Death, and Immortality"—"Embryos we must be, till we burst the Shell, / Yon ambient, azure shell, and spring to Life, / The life of Gods: O Transport! and of Man"—displays a naked human figure flying upward, with arms outstretched, from a broken eggshell out of which it has emerged. Blake had these lines of Young's in mind when he conceived the cherub emerging from the shell in *The Gates of Paradise.*[48] I suggest that Thomas's Christ, "hatched" from "the windy salvage on one leg" (the cross, with "salvage" suggesting both weather-wracked detritus and redemption, and "windy . . . on one leg" also suggesting a weathervane), is indebted to Blake's sixth emblem of the hatched baby emerging on one leg from the shell, as well as to the link between Christ and the emancipation of the imaginative faculty that the design implies. Thomas's resurrected Christ is "hatched" here, not into a world of time and limitation (as in "Old cock from nowheres and the heaven's egg") but into an Eternity that is now made available to humankind though the salvific sacrifice on the cross. As Blake states in *Jerusalem,* "Jesus, breaking through the central zones of death & hell / Opens Eternity in time & space" (plate 75, ll. 21–22; *Complete Poems,* 798).

With these debts to Blake in mind, the hatching of Thomas's Christ is also to be seen in terms of the enabling of the poetic imagination, which I regard as central to the significance of the annunciation at the end of Thomas's sonnet. The first act of the newly hatched "long world's gentleman," it seems, is to come "scraping" at the infant poet's cradle "in a walking word." Language is central to this meeting between nascent poet and a Savior who in Blake's mythology is the incarnation of that "One Power alone [that] makes a Poet: Imagination, The Divine Vision."[49] Blake equated indwelling divinity with the "Poetic Genius";[50] in *Jerusalem,* plate 70, Imagination is seen specifically as the Divine Humanity (*Complete Poems,* 786) and in *The Laocoön* as "God himself," "The Divine Body," "Jesus."[51] In the annunciation of Thomas's sonnet, imaginative vision and divine revelation are one.

The image of the "graveward"-lying "gentleman" at the beginning of Thomas's poem can also be traced to sources in Blake that further legitimize the readings I have offered thus far. First, there is the obscure reference in "The Keys of the Gates" from *The Gates of Paradise:*

> When weary man enters his cave
> He meets his Saviour in the grave.
> Some find a female garment there,
> And some a male, woven with care
> Lest the sexual garments sweet
> Should grow a devouring winding sheet.
> (ll. 31–36)

It is not clear here whether the Saviour is lying in the grave or merely met there by "weary man." S. Foster Damon sees the "cave" and "grave" as man's body in which the sexes are fashioned and desires fulfilled: "Here, too, in the grave of the flesh, the Saviour descends; and by his power—the Imagination—we can rend the veil, or break this Mundane Shell."[52] Whatever the significance of Blake's lines may be, the "garments" and "winding sheet" certainly recall the account in John 20 of the empty tomb in which Christ lay graveward: "[Peter] stooping down, and looking in, saw the linen clothes lying. . . . Then cometh Simon Peter following him, and went into the sepulchre, and seeth the linen clothes lie, and the napkin, that was about his head, not lying with the linen clothes, but wrapped together in a place by itself."[53] The thirteenth emblem (plate 15) of *The Gates of Paradise,* corresponding to the couplet "But when once I did descry / The Immortal Man that cannot die," depicts the dead body of an aged man stretched "graveward" in a winding sheet, with the spirit rising from it. Indeed, Christ in the tomb, and figures stretched out in death and covered by shrouds, are prominent in Blake's artistic vision. *Christ in the Sepulchre, Guarded by Angels* and *The Entombment* (both c. 1803–5, and part of a series of watercolors depicting the Passion and Resurrection) are particularly fine examples. In the former, Christ, wrapped in a shroud, lies in the half-light (compare Thomas's "owl-light") of the tomb; two angels, reminiscent of the cherubim on the Ark of the Covenant, are placed symmetrically over the body, the tips of their wings touching.[54]

The Eternal Man of *The Four Zoas,* Night the Eighth (with whom Thomas identified himself in his comments on the "Altarwise" son-

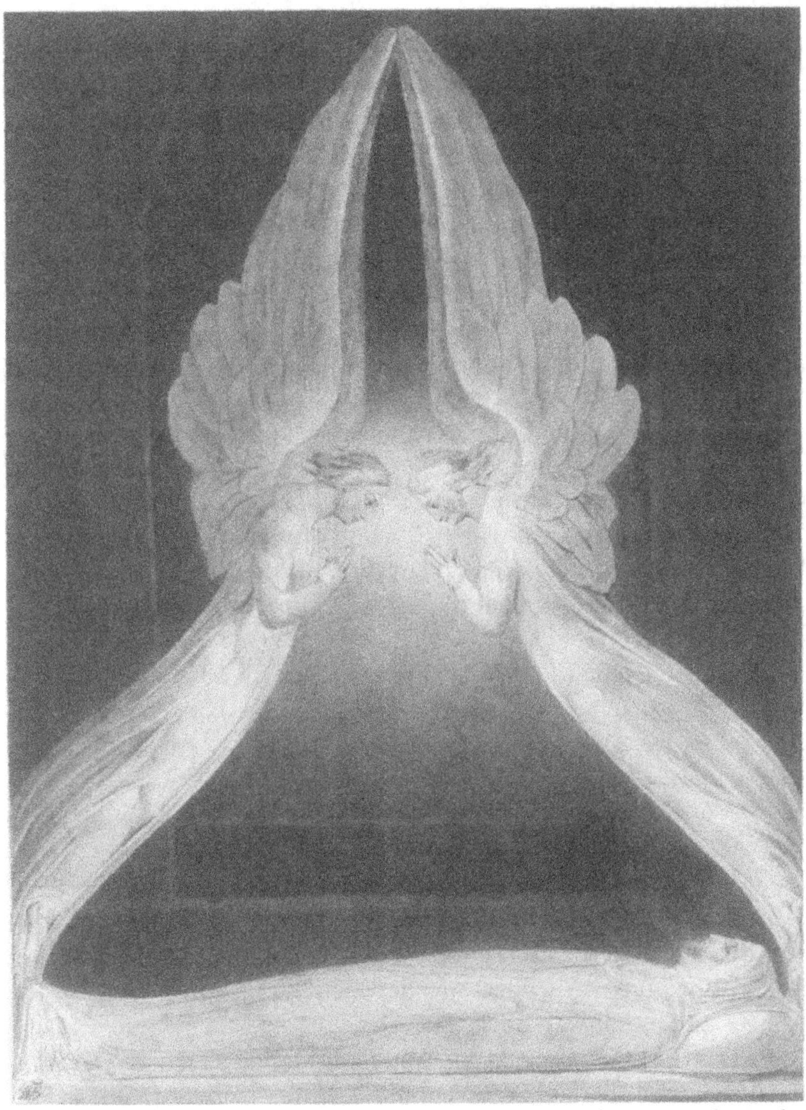

William Blake, *Christ in the Sepulchre, Guarded by Angels.*

nets at Utah), is similarly laid out "graveward" like a sacrificial victim on the Rock of Ages, guarded by angels:

> The fallen Man stretched like a corse upon the oozy rock . . .
> . . . .
> Hovering high over his head
> Two winged immortal shapes, one standing at his feet
> Toward the east, one standing at his head toward the west,
> Their wings joined in the zenith overhead.
> . . . again he reposed
> In the Saviour's arms, in the arms of tender mercy & loving kindness.
> (ll. 4, 6–9, 13–14; *Complete Poems*, 405–6)

Throughout *The Four Zoas*, the Eternal Man, contending with his Zoas on the rock, is guarded by the Divine Vision (compare "the Christward shelter" at the end of Thomas's poem, which suggests "a shelter oriented towards Christ" and "the shelter of the ward of Christ"). In Night the Seventh, Luvah, identified at this stage of the poem with Christ, is "nailed to the tree" and placed in the tomb.

> They pierced him with a spear, & laid him in a sepulchre,
> To die a death of six thousand years, bound round with desolation.
> (ll. 492–93; *Complete Poems*, 392)

Night the Ninth opens with Jesus' body in the tomb: "And Los & Enitharmon builded Jerusalem, weeping / Over the sepulchre & over the crucified body. . . . / But Jesus stood beside them in the spirit" (*Complete Poems*, 432). In Blake's work, then, both Christ (Thomas's "gentleman") and the Eternal Man (with whose fate Thomas was later to identify himself as poet) are depicted lying "graveward" in the half-light of a "halfway-house."

The *Christ in the Sepulchre* watercolor lends weight to the argument that the "gentleman" of Thomas's sonnet is indeed Christ. Further, it can be suggested that Thomas's sonnet about Christ, Adam, and the poet himself is indebted to a number of Blake productions in which links are made between Christ, the Eternal Man, and Blake as creator inspired by "The Divine Vision." Thomas's disturbing "furies," however, are very different from the benign angels who guard both Christ and the Eternal Man in Blake. But Thomas is still in the path of Blake here. The beginning of *The Four Zoas* announces the poem's theme as the fall of the Eternal or Universal Man "into division & his resurrection to unity" (*Complete Poems,* 293). As a result of a conspiracy between Urizen and Luvah,[55] the Eternal Man sickens and is laid to rest by "the Eternal Saviour" "upon the Rock of Ages." Just as Thomas's Christ contends with his earthly passions—figured as furies—in the tomb, so the Zoas contend for supremacy within the Eternal Man in Blake's psychological drama: "O weakness & O weariness! O war within my members!" (*Complete Poems,* 435). Though watched over "with love & care" (*Complete Poems,* 315) by the Saviour himself, he lies from Night the Second to Night the Eighth in painful sleep on the Rock of Ages in a "dark world" which, tellingly, he calls "a narrow house" (*Complete Poems,* 436; compare Thomas's "owl-light" and "halfway-house"[56]). Christ's struggle in Thomas's sonnet is therefore analogous to that of Blake's Eternal Man on the Rock of Ages. But the predicament of Blake's Eternal Man is also transcended—redeemed—by Thomas's Christ. In *The Four Zoas,* the Eternal Man falls from Unity; the result, as always in Blake, is the division of the spirit, a "cracking off" from essential oneness, which heralds further division into Male and Female (Emanation), Shadow and Spectre. As I have argued, however, the moment of "division," of "cracking," in Thomas's sonnet is salvific: it is the cracking away of the devil in the flesh from Adam at the moment of Christ's sacrifice on the cross. Whereas division in Blake's work usually precipitates or marks crisis, in Thomas's sonnet it heralds redemption. And yet, the transformation Thomas effects may also have been suggested by Blake. A link between division and redemption is made only once in Blake's mythology, in plate 42 of *Jerusalem:*

> But when man sleeps in Beulah, the Saviour in mercy takes
> Contraction's limit [Adam], & of the limit he forms woman—that
> Himself may in process of time be born, man to redeem.
> (ll. 32–34; *Complete Poems,* 715)

The design for plate 31 [35] of *Jerusalem* shows the division of Eve from Adam superintended by a Jehovah *who is also Jesus,* the nail wounds clearly visible on his hands and feet.[57] Blake's illustration depicting the creation of Eve in *Paradise Lost,* book 8, shows Eve hovering above Adam underneath the "forming hands" not of the

Almighty, but of Christ.[58] The division of the sexes in Blake is usually the tragic result of the Creation and Fall, and Blake tends to stress this darker aspect of division; here, however, division is seen in terms of a redemptive teleology—as a providential act performed by the Saviour himself. It is a significant moment in the Blakean mythology to which, I suggest, Thomas's image of Abaddon's division from Adam at the moment of Christ's sacrifice is related. In addition, the redemptive division of the "Altarwise" sonnet may well be indebted to Blake as mediated through W. B. Yeats's and Edwin Ellis's *Works of William Blake* (1893), in which a fascinating link is construed between division from Adam (compare Thomas's "cracked from Adam") and Christ's redemption:

> . . . when Los smites Enitharmon; when the horns of the eternal bow separate, and one is called male, one female . . . when . . . God separates into the Incarnate, and the Father . . . the Wound is always the symbol of division. . . . Water, divided from God, reveals its inward dust, which, divided after becoming Adam, reveals its inward Eve, who, divided first from Adam, and then from her own passivity, becomes the Virgin Mary. The wound is healed . . . to reappear on the cross.[59]

The Eternal Man of *The Four Zoas* serves once more as a model for Thomas's Christ at the end of the "Altarwise" sonnet where the resurrected Saviour appears to the infant Dylan "With bones unbuttoned to the halfway winds." Before his redemption, the Eternal Man, lying on the Rock of Ages, is

> . . . enwrapped with the weeds of death.
> His eyes sink hollow in his head, his flesh covered with slime
> And shrunk up to the bones. Alas! that Man should come to this:
> His strong bones beat with snows & hid within the caves of night
> Marrowless, bloodless, falling into dust, driven by the winds.
> (ll. 501–5; *Complete Poems,* 427)

Knowing that the Eternal Man will ultimately be redeemed, Thomas here transfers the attributes of the suffering Man to the resurrected Christ who has just conquered death on the "windy salvage" of the cross. Thomas's skeleton-gentleman, therefore, is no gothic spook.

It is on "that night of time" that the dramatic annunciation occurs at the end of Thomas's sonnet. The phrase is taken from *The Four Zoas,* Night the Ninth, l. 821:

> Tharmas sifted the corn,
> Urthona made the bread of ages, & he placed it
> In golden & in silver baskets, in heavens of precious stone,
> And then took his repose in winter, *in the night of time.*
>
> The sun has left his blackness & has found a fresher morning,
> And the mild moon rejoices in the clear & cloudless night,
> And Man walks forth from midst of the fires, the evil is all consumed.
> (ll. 818–24; *Complete Poems,* 461; my emphasis)

Thomas, famous revitalizer of metaphors,[60] was clearly drawn to Blake's reversal of "that time of night." Writing and illustrating *The Four Zoas* mainly on proof sheets of his engravings for Young's *Night Thoughts,* Blake followed Young in dividing his poem into nine "Nights"—each "book" therefore being a "night of time." Commentators have tended to interpret "that night of time" in Thomas's sonnet in a dark and disturbing sense: Tindall sees it as figuring the womb, which is also a "graveward" "halfway-house";[61] Essig surmises that the phrase refers to "that night as a time of spiritual crisis in the poet's life";[62] Knieger argues that "Since man is fallen, alienated from his God, in a sense all time is nighttime";[63] while Maud has recently interpreted the expression as a reference to "a black moment"—that of "Christ's death on the cross."[64] The precise context of the phrase in *The Four Zoas,* however, leads us to contest these readings; "the night of time" referred to in the apocalyptic finale of *The Four Zoas,* quoted above, *post*dates the deliverance of the Eternal Man and the redemption of Urizen, Vala, and Luvah in a great "Harvest and Vintage of Souls." This supports the contention that the "night of time" in Thomas's sonnet signals an inspiring *postredemption* annunciation rather than biological confinement, debilitating spiritual crisis, or psychological trauma.

Troubling the redemptive resonance of the phrase in the "Altarwise" sonnet, however, is the presence of the same expression in *Adonais* (1821), Shelley's elegy for a Keats lying "graveward" in Rome. After alluding to the sublime achievement of the "Blind, old, and lonely" republican Milton, Shelley turns to contemplate lesser, if happier, spirits, and then the dead Keats himself:

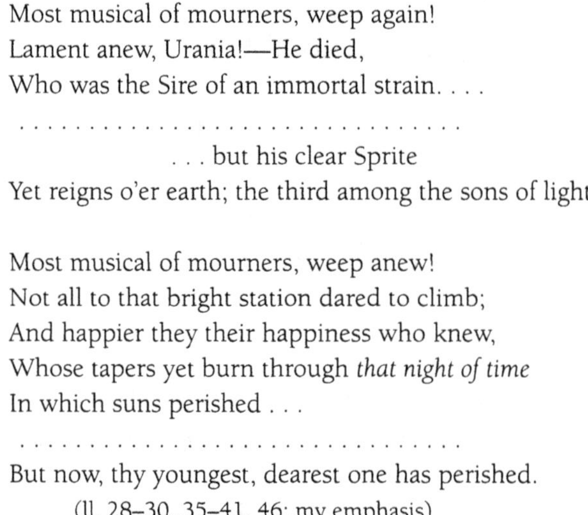
> Most musical of mourners, weep again!
> Lament anew, Urania!—He died,
> Who was the Sire of an immortal strain. . . .
>
> . . . .
>
> . . . but his clear Sprite
> Yet reigns o'er earth; the third among the sons of light.
>
> Most musical of mourners, weep anew!
> Not all to that bright station dared to climb;
> And happier they their happiness who knew,
> Whose tapers yet burn through *that night of time*
> In which suns perished . . .
>
> . . . .
>
> But now, thy youngest, dearest one has perished.
>
> (ll. 28–30, 35–41, 46; my emphasis)

"And happier they their happiness who knew" notwithstanding, Shelley's "night of time" is very much that of a violent, unjust, and slanderous world in which "sons" (Urania is invoked throughout as Adonais's "mighty *Mother*") as well as "suns" die—or are killed off by "savage criticism."[65] The postredemption, Blakean "night of time" of Thomas's sonnet, as I have suggested, is very different, but Shelley's use of the phrase causes the end of the "Altarwise" sonnet to resonate with darker meanings, too—with a recollection of the terrible "Nights" the Eternal Man spent unredeemed in the "dark world" of *The Four Zoas* and of the two nights of time the "long world's gentleman" spent unresurrected in the "owl-light" of the "halfway-house" of the tomb in Thomas's sonnet. Thomas would have welcomed the effect of this ghost presence of past suffering in a sonnet in which time is fundamentally collapsed.

"But why Wordsworth? Why quote that decay? Shelley I can stand, but old Father William was a human nannygoat with a pantheistic obsession," Thomas wrote to Pamela Hansford Johnson on 15 October 1933, having in the same letter proudly proclaimed himself to be "in the path of Blake." On Christmas Day 1933, having recorded the receipt of "the complete Blake" from his uncle and noted his delight in Blake's letters, Thomas informed Johnson of his "theoretical hatred of Byron, Keats, Shelley, and Wordsworth." Blake was the only Romantic poet he read with any enthusiasm. In this essay, I have sought to demonstrate that there is evidence in Thomas's poetry of an impressively close, astute, and creative reading of Blake's poetic and graphic productions. Blake inspired complex transformative maneuvers in Thomas's poetry that amount to interpretive insights into the great precursor's mythology. In addition, Thomas's negotiation with the often obscure symbolism of *The Gates of Paradise*, the Prophetic Books, and the visual work invests the "Altarwise" sonnet with a mythological momentousness while at the same time providing a key to access Thomas's own obscure density. Much work remains to be done on the debt of an unmisgiving latecomer to the master whose winged heels he said he could only just glimpse.

Notes

1. *Children of Albion: Poetry of the "Underground" in Britain*, ed. Michael Horovitz (Harmondsworth: Penguin, 1969), 316.

2. Ibid., 356.

3. Mitchell's poem "Lullaby for William Blake," in ibid., 219.

4. Mitchell's "To the Statues in Poets' Corner, Westminster Abbey," in *Children of Albion*, ed. Horovitz, 225. For another "gathering of Blake's children," see *Sparks of Fire: Blake in a New Age*, ed. James Bogan and Fred Goss (Richmond, CA: North Atlantic Books, 1982), an anthology of creative responses to Blake from writers, composers, artists, and literary critics ("essays high in clarity and low in jive").

5. John Holloway's phrase, quoted in Blake Morrison, *The Movement: English Poetry and Fiction of the 1950s* (Oxford: Oxford University Press, 1980), 155.

6. Harold Bloom, *The Anxiety of Influence: A Theory of Poetry*, 2nd ed. (Oxford: Oxford University Press, 1997), 107, my emphasis.

7. Ralph Maud, *Where Have the Old Words Got Me?: Explications of Dylan Thomas's Collected Poems* (Cardiff: University of Wales Press, 2003), 14.

8. Publisher's summary on the back cover of *Children of Albion*.

9. See the discussion of how the poets of the Movement "revised" paradigmatic Thomas poems in Morrison, *The Movement*, 151–54. Morrison briefly cites Bloom but does not offer a stringently Bloomian reading of these acts of revision.

10. Dylan Thomas, *The Collected Letters*, ed. Paul Ferris, new ed. (London: Dent, 2000), 43.

11. William Hazlitt, *Selected Writings*, ed. Jon Cook (Oxford: Oxford University Press, 1991), 217.

12. "Poetic Manifesto" in *Dylan Thomas: Early Prose Writings*, ed. Walford Davies (London: Dent, 1971), 156.

13. Christopher Ricks, *Allusion to the Poets* (Oxford: Clarendon Press, 2002), 85, 159.

14. For example, the lines "And I am dumb to tell the crooked rose" and "How at my sheet goes the same crooked worm" from "The force that through the green fuse drives the flower" (published 1934) clearly derive from Blake's "The Sick Rose"; the phrase "Man in his maggot" in "I see the boys of summer in their ruin" (1934) indicates Thomas's familiarity with the frontispiece to Blake's *For the Sexes: The Gates of Paradise* (a caterpillar above a chrysalis that looks like a swaddled baby); the lines "brother to Mnetha's daughter / And sister to the fathering worm" in "Before I knocked" (1934) are indebted to the sixteenth emblem (plate 18) of *The Gates of Paradise* (a seated figure in a cloak and cowl, holding a wand, with a worm coiled round), to Blake's underwritten lines "I have said to the Worm: Thou art my mother & my sister" (compare Job 17:14), and to Blake's *Tiriel,* where Mnetha appears as a nurse; and "on a stick of folly / Star-set at Jacob's angle" from "I, in my intricate image" (1936) recalls the famous ninth emblem (plate 11) from *The Gates of Paradise,* titled "I want! I want!" showing a figure with his foot on the lowest rung of a ladder leading up to the moon. Thomas's editors reproduce Blake's designs in *Collected Poems, 1934–1953,* ed. Walford Davies and Ralph Maud (London: Dent, 1988), 179, 181, 197. "The country is holy" from "In Country Sleep" (1952) is unmistakably Blakean. Winifred Nowottny sees in the lines "When hindering man hurt / Man, animal or bird" from "There was a saviour" a debt to Blake's concept of "hindering" another, articulated in his annotations to Lavater's *Aphorisms on Man.* See Nowottny, *The Language Poets Use* (London: Athlone Press, 1962), 204–5.

15. See *Early Prose Writings,* ed. Davies, 156, and "The shepherd blew upon his reed" in *Poet in the Making: The Notebooks of Dylan Thomas,* ed. Ralph Maud (London: Dent, 1965), 62.

16. See Martin Dodsworth, "The Concept of Mind and the Poetry of Dylan Thomas," in *Dylan Thomas: New Critical Essays,* ed. Walford Davies (London: Dent, 1972), 107–35; Nowottny, *The Language Poets Use,* 216–17; *Poet in the Making,* ed. Maud, 28; and Giorgio Melchiori, *The Tightrope Walkers: Studies of Mannerism in Modern English Literature* (London: Routledge and Kegan Paul, 1956), 238–41.

17. The first seven sonnets appeared in the December 1935 issue of *Life and Letters Today* and bore the title "Poems for a Poem." By the time they appeared in *Twenty-five Poems* (London: Dent, 1936), three more sonnets had been added. A prefatory note to the volume declares, "The last poem in the book [the "Altarwise" sequence] contains the first ten sections of a work in progress."

18. See, e.g., David Daiches, "The Poetry of Dylan Thomas," in *Dylan Thomas: Twentieth-Century Views,* ed. C. B. Cox (Englewood Cliffs, NJ: Prentice Hall, 1957), 21.

19. See *A Casebook on Dylan Thomas,* ed. John Malcolm Brinnin (New York: Thomas Y. Crowell, 1960), 114.

20. See Elder Olson, *The Poetry of Dylan Thomas* (Chicago: University of Chicago Press, 1954), 63–89.

21. On the first sonnet, see Ralph Maud, *The Explicator* 14 (December 1955), n.p.; Bernard Knieger, *The Explicator* 15 (December 1956), n.p.; and Erhardt H. Essig, *The Explicator* 16 (June 1958), n.p. For other discussions, see W. Y. Tindall, *A Reader's Guide to Dylan Thomas* (London: Thames and Hudson, 1962), 138–40; and H. H. Kleinman, *The Religious Sonnets of Dylan Thomas* (Berkeley: University of

California Press, 1963), 12–22.

22. Quoted in *Dylan Thomas: The Legend and the Poet,* ed. E. W. Tedlock (London: Heinemann, 1960), 61.

23. Ll. 178–84, in *Blake: The Complete Poems,* ed. W. H. Stevenson, 2nd ed. (London: Longman, 1989), 184. The final piece in Auden's *Poems* (1930) also seems to be indebted to *Visions of the Daughters of Albion:* "Send to us power and light, a sovereign touch / Curing the intolerable neural itch, / The exhaustion of weaning, the liar's quinsy, / *And the distortions of ingrown virginity*" (my emphasis).

24. Seamus Heaney, *The Redress of Poetry* (London: Faber and Faber, 1995), 141.

25. Maud, *The Explicator* 14 (December 1955), n.p.; and Maud, *Where Have the Old Words Got Me?* 14–18.

26. See Thomas, *Collected Letters,* 348 (1 June 1938). Here, Thomas responds to Edith Sitwell's "very vague and Sunday-journalish" analysis of lines 5–6 of his sonnet. In a letter to the *Sunday Times* in 1936, Sitwell had argued that the lines "The atlas-eater with a jaw for news / Bit out the mandrake with tomorrow's scream" referred to "the violent speed and the sensation-loving, horror-loving craze of modern life." Thomas tells Treece: "She doesn't take the literal meaning: that a world-devouring ghost creature bit out the horror of tomorrow from a gentleman's loins. . . . This poem is a particular incident in a particular adventure, not a general, elliptical deprecation of this 'horrible, crazy, speedy life.'" See also Henry Treece, "The Poet Answers a Critic," in *Dylan Thomas, "Dog among the Fairies"* (London: Lindsay Drummond, 1949), 149–50.

27. Ralph Maud, *Entrances to Dylan Thomas's Poetry* (Pittsburgh: University of Pittsburgh Press, 1963), 99.

28. Mandrakes were thought to emit a fatal scream on being uprooted; a dog was therefore tied to the mandrake and lured toward a morsel of food a safe distance away. See the illustration from a thirteenth-century manuscript printed in Kleinman, *The Religious Sonnets of Dylan Thomas,* 17.

29. For an explication of the sonnet as a reworking of Christ's Nativity according to St. Luke, see Kleinman, *The Religious Sonnets of Dylan Thomas,* 13–22.

30. See Thomas, *Collected Poems,* 240. Thomas's poem on the distortions of organized religion, "There was a saviour," makes ironic use of Milton's stanza form.

31. *The Marriage of Heaven and Hell,* plate 11: "The ancient poets animated all sensible objects with gods or geniuses, calling them by the names, and adorning them with the properties, of woods, rivers, mountains, lakes, cities, nations, and whatever their enlarged and numerous senses could perceive. . . . Till a system was formed, which some took advantage of and enslaved the vulgar by attempting to realise or abstract the mental deities from their objects. Thus began priesthood—choosing forms of worship from poetic tales. And at length they pronounced that the gods had ordered such things. Thus men forgot that all deities reside in the human breast" (Blake, *Complete Poems,* 111).

32. See Pamela Dunbar, *William Blake's Illustrations to the Poetry of Milton* (Oxford: Clarendon Press, 1980), 91–114.

33. Tindall, *A Reader's Guide to Dylan Thomas,* 139; *New Critical Essays,* ed. Davies, 59.

34. See note 47 below for an interesting link between Thomas's "atlas," Blake's *The Four Zoas*, and Young's *Night Thoughts*.

35. The work was issued in May 1793 bearing the title *For Children: The Gates of Paradise*. Some time after 1806, Blake enlarged the work to comprise a motto, a prologue, the sixteen design headings (some revised), the sequence of couplets titled "The Keys of the Gates," and an epilogue, "To the Accuser." Some of the designs themselves were also slightly altered. Around 1818, the work was reissued under the title *For the Sexes: The Gates of Paradise*. All the editions of Blake published between 1925 and 1932 mentioned above print the poetry and designs of *For the Sexes: The Gates of Paradise*.

36. See note 14, above.

37. The whole design suggests a child's delight in catching butterflies in a net; compare the prefatory poem to *Europe*, ll. 7–9: "So sang a fairy mocking as he sat on a streaked tulip, / Thinking none saw him; when he ceased I started from the trees / And caught him in my hat as boys knock down a butterfly" (Blake, *Complete Poems*, 225), and "The Fairy" (Blake, *Complete Poems*, 161). See also Blake's illustrations for Young's *Night Thoughts*, Night the Fifth, ll. 369–88, which shows a boy chasing butterflies with his hat, and for Night the Ninth, ll. 437–57, in which a man reaches up toward a small winged human figure: *William Blake's Designs for Edward Young's Night Thoughts: A Complete Edition*, ed. John E. Grant, Edward J. Rose, and Michael J. Tolley (Oxford: Clarendon Press, 1980), vol. 1, design 181, and vol. 2, design 441.

38. *The Illuminated Blake*, ed. D. V. Erdman (London: Oxford University Press, 1975), 272.

39. Interestingly, in the poem "Irish Railway Station" (first published in 1938), the Welsh poet Idris Davies—a friend of Dylan Thomas—sees "Oliver Goldsmith swaggering in green, / Scattering fairies with a walking-stick." *The Complete Poems of Idris Davies*, ed. Dafydd Johnston (Cardiff: University of Wales Press, 1994), 61. Davies, like Thomas, often spoke of Blake as one of his poetic masters.

40. *The Illuminated Blake*, ed. Erdman, 271.

41. See Thomas's comments in his "Poetic Manifesto" in *Early Prose Writings*, ed. Davies, 155: "The words, 'Ride a cock-horse to Banbury Cross,' were as haunting to me, who did not know then what a cock-horse was nor cared a damn where Banbury Cross might be, as, much later, were such lines as John Donne's, 'Go and catch a falling star, Get with child a mandrake root,' which also I could not understand when I first read them."

42. Kleinman, *The Religious Sonnets of Dylan Thomas*, 21 and note. See also John Beer, *Blake's Humanism* (Manchester: Manchester University Press, 1968), 235.

43. Compare the "cloud-formed shell" (with the additional suggestion of a German bomb) in l. 23 of Thomas's poem about the institutionalization of Christ, "There was a saviour."

44. The line is from Dryden's fable, *Palamon and Arcite: or, the Knight's Tale*, book 3, ll. 1069–71: "At length, for hatching ripe, he breaks the shell / And struggles into breath and cries for aid; / Then, helpless, in his mother's lap is laid."

45. *The Illuminated Blake*, ed. Erdman, 271.

46. John Beer finds a "positive" reading of the sixth emblem problematic—"Why should immortality be introduced at the beginning of a series depicting a

human lifetime?"—and therefore offers a very different interpretation of the image as "ambiguous," "satirical," and ultimately satanic: "The breaking egg may release either a winged Eros or a serpent of destruction and the child that Blake depicts has the potential lineaments of both . . . it is fair to suppose that the 'breaking of the shell' reflects Satan's eruption from the bounds of Hell" (see *Blake's Humanism,* 234–36). As I have argued, however, Blake's image does not symbolize "immortality" in the sense of a state entered after death, but rather a Blakean Eternity available through the human imagination (a concept Beer actually mentions on page 232). The position of the sixth emblem, then, is wholly appropriate.

47. Part 1 of Young's poem appeared in the autumn of 1797 carrying forty-three of Blake's engravings. The prospectus describes the engravings as being "in a perfectly new style of decoration, surrounding the text which they are designed to elucidate. The work is printed in atlas-sized quarto." See *William Blake's Designs for Edward Young's Night Thoughts,* vol. 1, 6–7. The reference to the "atlas-sized" quarto is interesting in view of Thomas's reference to "the atlas-eater with a jaw for news" (see my argument above) in which Thomas is punning on a "small atlas," the technical British term for a size of paper sheet (26 ½ × 34 inches).

48. Blake was also familiar at this time with Donne's "Of the Progress of the Soul," in which immortality is figured in terms of hatching: "Thinke thy shell broke, thinke thy Soule hatch'd but now."

49. Annotations to Wordsworth's *Poems* (1815), in *Blake: Complete Writings,* ed. Geoffrey Keynes (Oxford: Oxford University Press, 1992), 782.

50. *All Religions Are One* in Blake, *Complete Writings,* 98.

51. Blake, *Complete Writings,* 776. See also W. B. Yeats, *Essays and Introductions* (London: Macmillan, 1961), 112.

52. S. Foster Damon, *William Blake: His Philosophy and Symbols* (London: Constable, 1924), 85.

53. Compare *The Marriage of Heaven and Hell,* plate 3, ll. 3–4; Blake, *Complete Poems,* 105.

54. The work is inscribed "Exod: C xxv. v. 20." The reference to Exodus 25:20 confirms the resemblance the angels guarding Christ bear to the cherubim of the Ark of the Covenant: "They shall be made with wings outspread and pointing upwards, and shall screen the cover with their wings. They shall be face to face, looking inwards over the cover." The angels' wings are reminiscent of the design of some tombs in Westminster Abbey; Blake served his apprenticeship sketching these.

55. The "usurpation story" in *The Four Zoas* varies as a result of Blake's textual revision; I refer to the "standard"—and first mentioned—version of the story here: Night the First, ll. 201–17; Blake, *Complete Poems,* 302–3.

56. Compare also the "darksome house of mortal clay" of Milton's Nativity Ode, l. 14.

57. *Jerusalem,* ed. Morton D. Paley (Princeton: Princeton University Press/The Blake Trust, 1991), plate 35. See also *The Illuminated Blake,* ed. Erdman, 310.

58. See Martin Butlin, *The Paintings and Drawings of William Blake* (New Haven: Yale University Press, 1981), vol. 1, plates 639, 652, and 658.

59. *The Works of William Blake: Poetic, Symbolic, and Critical,* ed. E. J. Ellis and W. B. Yeats (London: Bernard Quaritch, 1893), 1:396.

60. Obvious examples are: "a jaw for news" from this first "Altarwise" sonnet; "quick of night"; "man in the wind and the west moon" (with an echo of Shelley); "once below a time"; and "I build my bellowing ark / To the best of my love."

61. Tindall, *A Reader's Guide to Dylan Thomas,* 140.

62. Essig, *The Explicator* 16 (June 1958), n.p.

63. Knieger, *The Explicator* 15 (December 1956), n.p.

64. Maud, *Where Have the Old Words Got Me?* 17.

65. Shelley's preface to *Adonais,* in *Shelley's Poetry and Prose,* ed. Donald H. Reiman and Neil Fraistat (New York: Norton, 2002), 410.

"One Cry for Justice": Virginia Woolf Reads Mary Wollstonecraft

Harriet Devine Jump

"I should be tackling Mary Wollstonecraft," Virginia Woolf wrote in her diary on 5 August 1929.[1] Four months earlier, she had agreed to write four articles for Mrs. Irita van Doren, editor of the Book Supplement of the *New York Herald Tribune.* She had been writing commissioned articles for the paper since 1925, but had engaged to do these four only because she needed the money to complete building work—a room of her own—on her house at Rodmell in Sussex. She noted with satisfaction on 13 April 1929 that Mrs. van Doren had "raised her price to £50 an article—so that, whatever the cost, I can have my new room" (*Diary,* 3:221). At what stage, or by what process, she decided on the subjects—Cowper, Brummell, Wollstonecraft, and Dorothy Wordsworth—is not recorded. She seems to have started work on them while she was on holiday in Cassis, noting on 15 June that she had written "a little article on Cowper" (*Diary,* 3:235).

On 30 June, she had hoped, with what seems like wild optimism, that "after tomorrow I shall close down article writing, & give way to fiction for six or seven months" (*Diary,* 3:237), but by 5 August, delayed by having to correct proofs, she was still "in the thick of my four *Herald* articles," now hoping "to be quit of it all by August 14th" (*Diary,* 3:239). On 15 August, however, she was still "[w]riting this compressed article, where every word is like a step cut in the rock—hard work, if ever writing was; & done largely for money" (*Diary,* 3:241). It was not until five days later that she was finally able to record that she had finished "my four little brief hard articles" (*Diary,* 3:245). Her letters of the same period reveal that the pressure of writing them ("four articles, all pressed as tight as hay in a stack"[2]) had contributed to some kind of unspecified collapse, from which, however, she had recovered by 18 August. In her letter of that day to Vita Sackville West, she discusses the subject of her fourth article, adding a little more information to what is a very sparsely documented process:

> The last was Dorothy Wordsworth, and if the written word could cure rheumatism, I think her's [*sic*] might—like a dock leaf laid to a sting; yet rather astringent too. Have you ever read her diaries, the early ones, with the nightingale singing at Alfoxden, and Coleridge coming in swollen eyed—to eat a mutton chop? . . . I like reading them very much; but I cant [*sic*] say I enjoy writing about them, nine pages close pressed. How can one get it all in? (*Letters of Virginia Woolf*, 4:78–79)

As this letter shows, Woolf's problem was chiefly that of compression; so much she would like to say, and so little space in which to say it.

From Woolf's "Reading Notebooks" it is possible to gather a little more about the process by which she composed her essay on Wollstonecraft. Her chief sources of information seem to have been Charles Kegan Paul's *William Godwin, His Friends and Contemporaries* (1876), from which she copied six pages, and Godwin's own *Memoirs of the Author of A Vindication of the Rights of Woman* (1798). The eight pages she took from this volume indicate that she was using W. Clark Durant's edition, which had been published two years earlier in 1927. From Durant's useful "supplement to the Memoirs" she was directed to Wollstonecraft's *Posthumous Works,* to Knowles's life of Henry Fuseli, and to Archibald Hamilton Rowan's autobiography. She also transcribed five pages from Kegan Paul's edition of Wollstonecraft's *Letters to Gilbert Imlay,* and a passage from book 6 of Wordsworth's *Prelude.* From Wollstonecraft's own works she copied very little: one page from what she called in the essay that "eloquent and daring" book, *A Vindication of the Rights of Woman* (she used the edition that had appeared in 1891, edited by Millicent Garrett Fawcett), and one page from the original (1796) edition of *Letters Written during a Short Residence in Sweden, Norway and Denmark.*[3]

Such is the meager total of all references to Wollstonecraft in

Woolf's writings, both private and public. She must certainly have known something of her subject before she began her research for the essay.[4] Her father's largely accurate and not unsympathetic entry in the *Dictionary of National Biography* would have been familiar to her and may indeed have been the starting point for her research. She habitually turned to Leslie Stephen's writings as a way of "filling out [her] ideas . . . to correct; to stiffen [her] vision,"[5] even though, as is clear from her letter to Ethel Smyth of 27 February 1930, she rather quirkily blamed his incessant writing for the weakness of her own nervous system: "I never see those 68 black books without cursing them for all the jaunts they've lost me" (*Letters of Virginia Woolf*, 4:145). Certainly, Stephen refers to three of the same texts that she would later use. He calls Wollstonecraft "an impulsive and enthusiastic woman, with great charms of person and manner," praises the "genuine eloquence" of her writing, and is saddened by the pathos of her letters. The voice of a liberal Victorian gentleman may be heard clearly in his conclusion: "Her faults were such as might be expected from a follower of Rousseau, and were consistent with much unselfishness and nobility of sentiment, though one could wish that her love-affairs had been more delicate."[6] Written at the end of the 1880s, this opinion is representative of the way Wollstonecraft had come to be viewed by the last decade of the nineteenth century. The vicissitudes of her posthumous reputation, both personal and literary, are now well documented. The outcry that had greeted Godwin's well-meaning but scandalously frank *Memoirs of the Author of A Vindication of the Rights of Woman* had ensured that she was scarcely mentioned in any published writing for many years to come. The public perception of her as a sexually voracious virago was confirmed in the early 1830s by two biographies of Henry Fuseli, both of which revealed her unrequited love for the painter and her attempt to initiate a ménage à trois with him and his wife. Her writing was cautiously, but somewhat ambivalently, reappraised by Anne Katherine Elwood in 1843, but after a dutiful struggle to view her subject's life in a sympathetic light, Elwood concluded that her "erroneous theories and false principles" made her a dreadful warning to women endowed with an excess of "enthusiasm and imagination."[7] In 1855, George Eliot included a discussion of her work in an essay published in *The Leader* in which she praised the *Rights of Woman* for its "strong sense and loftiness of moral tone"[8] but described its author as possessing neither erudition nor fancy. Indeed, as one twentieth-century critic has put it, Eliot seemed to be "engaged in the rather unusual task of attempting to revive interest in Wollstonecraft by assuring readers that she [was] intensely dull."[9] It was not until 1876—more than twenty years later—that a full-scale rehabilitation of Wollstonecraft's reputation was undertaken by the somewhat unlikely figure of Charles Kegan Paul, a Church of England clergyman turned biographer. Kegan Paul's impressive two-volume work, *William Godwin, His Friends and Contemporaries,* was commissioned by Sir Percy Shelley, Wollstonecraft's and Godwin's grandson, who wanted to decontaminate the sullied fame of his forebears. Serious and well researched, the book quoted Wollstonecraft's writings, both published and unpublished, to demonstrate her piety and her well-developed moral sense.

The importance of the publication of Kegan Paul's book cannot be underestimated: it proved to be an important turning point in the history of Wollstonecraft studies. Newly respectable, Wollstonecraft could now be recognized as an important precursor in the struggle for women's rights, which had become increasingly urgent throughout the second half of the nineteenth century. A number of sympathetic reassessments of her works appeared in the final decades of the century. A scholarly essay by Mathilde Blind in 1878 was followed by a reappraisal by the veteran essayist, critic, and novelist Margaret Oliphant in 1882. Wary of the more vociferous elements of feminist activism, Oliphant showed evidently pleasurable surprise at the mildness of Wollstonecraft's texts. She declared the *Rights of Woman*—somewhat inaccurately—to be "altogether free from revolutionary principles," and approved of what she called its "warmest religiousness."[10] Three years later, Elizabeth Robins Pennel brought out a book-length study as part of an "Eminent Women" series and, in 1890, celebrated the publication of a new edition of *Rights of Woman* with an article in the *Fortnightly Review.* In 1898 appeared the first book devoted to Wollstonecraft's thought and ideas: Emma Rauschenbusch Clough's *Study of Mary Wollstonecraft and the Rights of Woman,* a work that was adapted from its author's Ph.D. thesis at the University of Bern.

In 1907, Millicent Garrett Fawcett, founder of the National Union of Women's Suffrage, hailed Wollstonecraft as "a pioneer of the movement." Not only was she now said to be "ahead of her own time," but also, according to Fawcett, "her memory has been . . . thoroughly vindicated from the contumely that was at one time heaped upon it."[11] An anthology of extracts from Wollstonecraft's writings, edited by Camilla Jebb, appeared in 1912, and her importance in the history of ideas was acknowledged by two male historians of the French Revolution, W. Lyon Blease (1913) and P. A. Brown (1918).

Whether Woolf was familiar with any of these works is not known. She must, presumably, have been aware of the fact that in 1929, shortly before her own essay on Wollstonecraft was published, an Everyman edition of the *Rights of Woman*—together with John Stuart Mill's *On the Subjection of Women* (1869)—had appeared. The introduction, by the distinguished political historian George Caitlin, began by acknowledging the importance of his edition's historical moment. Both works, he wrote, were "milestones marking the advance of a great social movement . . . to its present day triumph."[12] Contemporary readers would have recognized the reference to the passing, in March 1928, of the Equal Franchise Act, which had given all women, regardless of social or marital status, the right to vote, for which they had been campaigning for over thirty years. To the purists, Caitlin observed, the *Rights of Woman* was "a bad book," but he judged it to be "alive and irritating, as challenging to-day as in the day in which it was written." Although "neither well-planned, well-presented, nor well-written," he considered it to be sincere and honest, and its author, rather against his expectations, perhaps, to be neither hysterical, pessimistic, nor embittered.[13] His analysis of Wollstonecraft's arguments was sensible and fair-minded, and he concluded that her ideas were still relevant: women had a moral right to equal education and economic independence.

Such, then, was the climate in which Woolf's short essay on Wollstonecraft made its first appearance. What is immediately apparent in the essay is the fact that while historians and critics over the previous half century had made obvious efforts to move away from the practice of conflating Wollstonecraft's biography with her texts, Woolf makes her work and her thought rest firmly on the basis of her experiences of life. In fact, she pays very little attention at all to the content of Wollstonecraft's works: the essay cannot by any stretch of the imagination be described as literary criticism. The two *Vindications*, *Rights of Men* (1790) and *Rights of Woman* (1792), are fleetingly characterized as "those two eloquent and daring books . . . which are so true that they seem now to contain nothing new in them—their originality has become our commonplace"[14] (a neat formulation of influence), and though Woolf quotes once from *Letters Written during a Short Residence in Sweden, Norway and Denmark,* she does not mention the text by name. The only other published text cited is the unfinished novel *The Wrongs of Woman, or Maria,* which Godwin had included in his edition of Wollstonecraft's *Posthumous Works* (1798), but this is presented as a book Wollstonecraft was "going to write" (*Common Reader,* 163), and Woolf does not seem to be familiar with it or, for that matter, with her earlier novel *Mary,* her educational texts, or her history of the French Revolution. Wollstonecraft's letters to Imlay and Godwin—which Woolf would have found in Charles Kegan Paul's two volumes—are, on the other hand, frequently quoted from to illustrate what Woolf takes to be the salient aspects of her subject's psychological makeup. As a result, Wollstonecraft's voice echoes through the essay, proclaiming her desire for independence ("Every obligation we receive from our fellow creatures is a new shackle, takes from our native freedom, and debases the mind"; *Common Reader,* 157); being overcome by unexpected sentiment in Paris ("I am going to bed, and, for the first time in my life, I cannot put out the candle"; *Common Reader,* 158); setting out for Imlay the terms she hopes for in their relationship ("I do not want to be loved like a goddess, but I wish to be necessary to you"; *Common Reader,* 159); and crying out, "even in her misery," that "I cannot bear to think of being no more—of losing myself—nay, it appears to me to be impossible that I should cease to exist" (*Common Reader,* 163).

Lively and impressionistic, this essay might best be termed a psychological biography. Woolf does not, of course, use this term. Perhaps she sees herself as what she calls a "picturesque historian," but the context in which she uses the phrase—"it would be easy for a picturesque historian to lay side by side the most glaring contrasts [with other important figures of the Romantic period]" (*Common Reader,* 156)—suggests that she might be using it ironically. "Picturesque" seems right, though, as the essay is composed of a series of vignettes that are often deliberately visual: the young, "ill-dressed" Godwin, "with a head too big for his body and a nose too long for his face" (*Common Reader,* 156); Wollstonecraft's sister (Woolf calls her Everina whereas her name was in fact Eliza) biting her wedding ring to pieces in the coach in which she was escaping from an unhappy marriage; and their father, "that disreputable man with the red face . . . and the dirty hair" (both pure supposition on Woolf's part) (*Common Reader,* 157). Above all there are a number of pictures of Wollstonecraft herself: in tears in her Paris room as the king drives past with the National Guards; gazing with "erotic absorption" at the Baron de Wolzogen rather than at the exquisite sunset; soaking her skirts before throwing herself from Putney Bridge; and putting on her cloak to call on Godwin in Somers Town (*Common Reader,* 175–61). Indeed, Wollstonecraft's face becomes the signifier of her character—conflicted, changing, and contradictory:

> at once so resolute and so dreamy, so sensual and so intelligent, and beautiful into the bargain with its great coils of hair and the large bright eyes that Southey thought the most expressive he had ever seen. (*Common Reader,* 159)

It is the contradictions in Wollstonecraft's thought that seem to be of greatest interest to Woolf. She depicts her subject as, for example, forced to reappraise her revolutionary, republican idealism when she finds herself so profoundly moved by the dignity of the king of France. Above all other tensions, Woolf places the conflict between her desire for independence—"the staple of her doctrine" and "the first necessity for a woman" (*Common Reader,* 157)—and her need for love and security. Far from deprecating her contradictoriness, Woolf seems to value her subject's flexibility:

> Every day . . . for she was no pedant, no cold-blooded theorist—something was born in her that thrust aside her theories and forced her to model them afresh. (*Common Reader,* 159)

Her refusal to marry Imlay was, Woolf argues, called into question by her agonies of loneliness when he left her, and her opinions on the "unnecessary" nature of marriage were overturned by her second pregnancy and the discovery that she was in fact "passionately domestic" (*Common Reader,* 162).

It would be wrong, however, to suggest that Woolf is interested only in Wollstonecraft's personal relationships at the expense of her political convictions. On the contrary, she is shown to be committed above all else to her revolutionary principles:

> The Revolution was . . . not merely an event that had happened outside her; it was an active agent in her own blood. She had been in revolt all her life—against tyranny, against law, against convention. The reformer's love of humanity, which has so much of hatred in it as well as love, fermented within her. (*Common Reader,* 158)

Believing, in Michelle Barrett's words, that "the writer was the product of her or his historical circumstances, and that material conditions were of crucial importance,"[15] Woolf argued that Wollstonecraft's "passion against tyranny" (*Common Reader,* 157) could be traced to the fact that she had witnessed her father physically abusing her mother. Thus Wollstonecraft serves to illustrate one of the cornerstones of *A Room of One's Own,* published just a few months before the Wollstonecraft essay. Here, Woolf had argued that a writer's work "is like a spider's web, attached ever so lightly perhaps, but still attached to life at all four corners," and that

> these webs are not spun in mid-air by incorporeal creatures, but are the work of suffering human beings, and are attached to grossly material things, like health and money and the houses we live in.[16]

For Woolf, then, it is Wollstonecraft's early experiences that account for the fact that all her works can be characterized as "one cry for justice" (*Common Reader,* 157).

Woolf's essay ends with a meditation on the significance of Wollstonecraft's life, which was tragically cut short, Woolf implies, by her last "experiment"—the decision to employ a midwife rather than a doctor at her second confinement.[17] But, says Woolf, "she has had her revenge," and has been vindicated in her posthumous life:

> [A]s we read her letters and listen to her arguments and consider her experiments . . . and realise the high-handed and hot-blooded manner in which she cut her way to the quick of life, one form of immortality is hers undoubtedly: she is alive and active, she argues and experiments, we hear her voice and trace her influence even now among the living. (*Common Reader,* 163)

Among the moderns influenced by Wollstonecraft's arguments and experiments, it should presumably be possible to include Woolf herself. But it would be untenable to suggest that Woolf's research for the Wollstonecraft essay had made her into a feminist. Since 1910 she had been involved, albeit somewhat ambivalently, with the suffrage movement and, from 1912, with the Women's Co-operative Guild. Her first book on women's issues, *A Room of One's Own,* predated the writing of the essay by at least a year. Nor can any special significance be attached to Woolf's interest in her subject's life, since Wollstonecraft was only one of many women about whom she wrote essays and reviews. At various points between 1904 and the early 1930s, she wrote on the duchess of Newcastle, Aphra Behn, Dorothy Osborne, Eliza Haywood, Dorothy Wordsworth, Jane Austen, Emily and Charlotte Brontë, Elizabeth Barrett Browning, Geraldine Jewsbury, Jane Carlyle, George Eliot, Elizabeth Gaskell, Christina Rossetti, Mrs. Humphrey Ward, Ella Wheeler Wilcox, Katherine Mansfield, and Dorothy Richardson, among others. Her reading for these pieces—not only primary texts but also diaries, letters, biographies, and criticism—was sometimes as broad and detailed as it would have been had she been undertaking research for a doctorate, and she evidently enjoyed the process: "To begin reading with a pen in my hand, discovering, pouncing, thinking of theories, when the ground is new, remains one of my great excitements" (8 December 1929, *Diary,* 3:270). Her conclusions, though, were often more whimsical than scholarly. Though clearly interested in a female literary tradition, she was not by any means uncritical of work she considered to be inferior. In her review essay on Haywood, published in the *Times Literary Supplement* on 17 February 1917, she judged her subject to be "a writer of no importance," suggesting that "no one read her for pleasure."[18] She had a great deal of fun at the expense of Ella Wheeler Wilcox's literary and autobiographical pretensions (*The Athenaeum,* 19 September 1919), and of Mrs. Humphrey Ward she wrote that

> the depressing effects of her books must be attributed to the fact that while her imagination always attempts to soar, it always agrees to perch. That is why we never wish to open them again. (*The New Republic,* 9 January 1924)[19]

Admittedly, these are early writings, the latest predating by four years the composition of Woolf's first sustained attempt at a feminist critique of the difficulties faced by women attempting to enter the public world of writing and publishing. It was an invitation to address the students of two Cambridge colleges on the subject of women and literature in October 1928 that led to the appearance of *A Room of One's Own*. The invitation was fortuitous, in that it focused her attention on the causes and effects of female oppression. It is likely, in fact, that the work and thought she put into this pamphlet reminded her of Wollstonecraft's pioneering texts.

If, however, a serious examination is to be made of any influence that rereading and writing on Wollstonecraft may have had on Woolf, then it is necessary to consider her later, less well-known feminist pamphlet, *Three Guineas*. First published in 1938, this text had a long and complicated genesis. Once again, Woolf's starting point was an invitation to deliver a public lecture—this time on professions for women—before the London National Society for Women's Service on 21 January 1931. The day before the lecture was due to be delivered, Woolf wrote excitedly in her diary,

> I have this moment, while having my bath, conceived an entire new book—a sequel to a *Room of One's Own*—about the sexual life of women: to be called Professions for Women perhaps—Lord how exciting![20]

Six days later, the idea had become an "obsession" (*Diary*, 4:7) that was still "forc[ing] itself on [her]" four months later (28 May 1931, *Diary*, 4:28). In September, she was "set off again" by reading Montaigne's remarks on women (3 September 1931, *Diary*, 4:42), and at the end of December, immersed in editing her essays—including the one on Wollstonecraft—for *Common Reader: Second Series*, she was still thinking hard about the project (29 December 1931, *Diary*, 4:57). She began writing what she called *The Pargiters, A Novel-Essay* in the summer of 1932. An ambitious and highly experimental scheme, this was to address the question of women's oppression in a text combining analytical argument with fictional illustration. However, she abandoned the double format in 1932 after writing about 60,000 words, and the "Novel-Essay" ended up as two separate entities, *The Years* (1937) and *Three Guineas* (1938).

> If *The Pargiters, A Novel Essay* had been written to completion as Virginia Woolf originally envisaged it in 1932, it might well have found its place today on that still narrow shelf of books on the equality of women—pressed beside Mary Wollstonecraft's *Vindication of the Rights of Women* [*sic*] (1792).[21]

So writes the editor of *The Pargiters,* Mitchell Leaska. He goes on to argue that the projected text was, for Woolf, "a new and profoundly challenging experiment in form, calling into action both the creative and the analytical faculties almost simultaneously" and that the essay portions (which were adapted to become *Three Guineas*) committed her "to the very difficult task of adopting and sustaining a brand of rhetoric alien to her artistic temperament" (*The Pargiters,* vii). Though the experimental nature of the project cannot be denied (it would in the end, defeat Woolf), Leaska's other claims seem to be questionable. Certainly the combination of fiction with fact and polemic would have been new and exciting, but while regretting what Woolf did not achieve, it is important not to lose sight of what she did. After all, the abandoned project did form the basis of two full-length works, and she continued to think of the two texts as "one book" (3 June 1938).[22] Admittedly, *The Years* has been seen as her least successful novel, and perhaps she herself was not entirely happy with it: certainly, she did not allow Leonard Woolf to read it before she sent it to the printers in March 1936. Of more interest and relevance here is *Three Guineas,* since it seems to bear an important relationship to Wollstonecraft's feminist writings. This text, too, has been much criticized. Q. D. Leavis, in her *Scrutiny* review, called it "silly and ill-informed," and found in it "dangerous assumptions" and "nasty attitudes";[23] more recently, Nigel Nicolson has dismissed it as overstated and muddled, "neither sober nor rational."[24] Readers have had problems with the way in which the essay predicates a pacifist appeal against fascism and war on a sustained argument about the position of women in a patriarchal society. And yet, as Hermione Lee has pointed out, Woolf had an overwhelmingly positive response from a large number of women readers, among them the novelist Naomi Mitchison, who wrote to Woolf, "Your book seemed like part of an eternal argument that is bound to go on in one's mind, on and off, the whole time."[25] As for Leaska's suggestion that Woolf was defeated by "the very difficult task of adopting and sustaining a brand of rhetoric alien to her artistic temperament" (*The Pargiters,* vii), this seems not to be borne out by the facts. Not only do Woolf's diaries show her to have felt obsessively impelled to begin the project in 1931, but over the course of the next year she made notes in her Reading Notebooks from "a score—I might say thousands—of old memoirs."[26] In addition, she cut out newspaper articles illustrating the inequalities and prejudices suffered by women and pasted them into a series of scrapbooks. That these were intended as ammunition in a battle against patriarchy and double standards is clear from the way she described this collection in 1932 as "enough powder to blow up St Pauls" (*Diary,* 4:77).

Three years later, having been diverted by the need to shape the fictional material into *The Years,* her mind was "flooded with the desire" to get back to work on *Three Guineas* (*Diary,* 4:348). As this work neared completion, far from having difficulty in sustaining the rhetoric, she was making a conscious effort to water down the forcefulness of her arguments: "If I say what I mean . . . I must expect considerable hostility. Yet I so slaver and silver my tongue that its sharpness takes some time to be felt" (30 April 1937, *Diary,* 5:84). But the process of writing this text was exhilarating; she often compared the process to a horse race: "once I get into the canter . . . I think I shall see only the flash of the white rails & pound along to the goal" (24 February 1937, *Diary,* 5:62). Looking back on the process of composition she felt she had been whirling "like a top miles upon miles over the downs" (12 March 1938, *Diary,* 5:130).

Written when Britain was on the brink of war with Germany, *Three Guineas* argues forcefully that "the public and the private worlds are inseparably connected; that the tyrannies and servilities of one are the tyrannies and servilities of the other."[27] Patriarchy, according to Woolf, lies at the basis of fascism; she presents a vivid picture of "Man himself, the quintessence of virility":

> His eyes are glazed; his eyes glare. His body, which is braced in an unnatural position, is tightly cased in a uniform. . . . His hand is upon a sword. He is called in German and Italian Führer or Duce; in our own language Tyrant or Dictator. (*Three Guineas,* 257–58)

Woolf's argument here bears a strong resemblance to certain passages in Wollstonecraft's *Rights of Woman.* In this text, Wollstonecraft frequently draws parallels between public and private oppression, between "tyrants of every denomination, from the weak king to the weak father of a family."[28] Writing as she was in the context of the French Revolution—to which she was at this time favorably disposed—Wollstonecraft was not, of course, impelled by quite the same pacifist impulse as Woolf. If one substitutes the rulers of the ancien régime for Hitler and Mussolini, however, the shared basis of their thought becomes apparent: dictators tyrannize over the state, and men tyrannize over women.

Wollstonecraft's equation of the private with the political, of gender inequalities with social inequalities, had also been expressed in her earlier text, *A Vindication of the Rights of Men* (1790). Here she had included a section attacking Edmund Burke for reinforcing gender stereotypes (*Works of Wollstonecraft,* 5:44–46). This theme was to form the basis of her second *Vindication.* Interwoven throughout the *Rights of Woman* are many quotations from male writers who, as she puts it in a memorable chapter title, "Have Rendered Women Objects of Pity Bordering on Contempt." Rousseau is the chief suspect, though Fordyce and Gregory are also found to be culpable. But Wollstonecraft traces the history of misogyny back through Milton's *Paradise Lost* to the Book of Genesis which, if taken literally, she asserts, proves only that "man has, from the remotest antiquity, found it convenient to exert his strength to subjugate his companion" (*Works of Wollstonecraft,* 5:95).

In *Three Guineas,* Woolf uses the same methodology. Scattered throughout the text are quotations that set out to prove that "the creature, Dictator as we call him when he is Italian or German . . . believes that he has the right whether given by God, Nature, sex or race is immaterial, to dictate to other human beings how they shall live; what they shall do" (96). That this is intended to have a specifically gendered frame is clear from the extracts Woolf chooses to quote: "woman has too much liberty" (93); "Homes are the real places of . . . women" (97); "The woman's world is her family, her husband, her children and her home" (97); "It was decided yesterday at a conference of head masters that women were not fit teachers for boys over the age of fourteen" (160). The notes supply more material. One quotes Walter Bagehot writing in answer to Emily Davies's appeal for help in the foundation of Girton:

> I assure you I am not an enemy of women. I am very favourable to their employment as *labourers* or in other *menial* capacity. I have, however, doubts as to the likelihood of their succeeding in business as capitalists. I am sure the nerves of most women would break down under the anxiety, and that most of them are utterly destitute of the disciplined reticence necessary to every sort of cooperation. (276n. 23)

Another supplies an extract from *Under the Fifth Rib* by C. E. M. Joad: "Women, I think, ought not to sit down to table with men; their presence ruins conversation, tending to make it trivial and genteel, or at best merely clever" (*Three Guineas,* 286n. 4). Like Wollstonecraft, Woolf traces much of this misogyny back to the Bible, in this case to St. Paul: "[N]either was the man created for the woman; but the woman for the man . . . if they would learn anything, let them ask their husbands at home" (*Three Guineas,* 297n. 38). Another of Woolf's notes takes up a subject that Wollstonecraft had specifically addressed in *Rights of Woman*—the issue of what Rousseau had called woman's "primary propensity" for the love of dress and of "things to show and ornament; such as mirrors, trinkets, and dolls" (*Works of Wollstonecraft,* 5:151). Woolf quotes a pronouncement by "the late Mr Justice MacCardie [who] remarked . . . 'Dress, after all, is one of the chief methods of women's self expression. . . . In matters of dress women remain children to the end'" (*Three Guineas,* 271n. 16). While Wollstonecraft answers Rousseau by contending that the love of dress is a result of social conditioning rather than a primary propensity ("they were treated like women, almost from their very birth"; *Works of Wollstonecraft,* 5:151), Woolf points out that "the Judge who thus dictated was wearing a scarlet robe, an ermine cape, and a vast wig of artificial curls" (*Three Guineas,* 71). Indeed one of the more entertaining aspects of *Three Guineas* is the photographs that embellish the text: "A General"; "Heralds"; "A University Procession"; "A Judge"; "An Archbishop." "Your clothes," says Woolf, "make us gape with astonishment":

> How many, how splendid, how extremely ornate they are—the clothes worn by the educated man in his public capacity! Now you dress in violet; a jewelled crucifix swings on your breast; now your shoulders are covered with lace; now furred with

> ermine; now slung with many linked chains set with precious stones. Now you wear wigs on your heads; rows of graduated curls descend to your necks. Now your hats are boat-shaped, or cocked; now they are scuttle shaped; now plumes of red, now of blue hair surmount them. . . . After the comparative simplicity of your dress at home, the splendor of your public attire is dazzling. (*Three Guineas,* 35–36)

Some readers have questioned Woolf's argument that these "sartorial splendors" are fundamentally connected with war—"your finest clothes are those you wear as soldiers" (*Three Guineas,* 39)—but Wollstonecraft would have agreed at least in part, since she had asserted that "military men" were as obsessed with their appearance as women were perceived to be (*Works of Wollstonecraft,* 5:93).[29]

Fundamental to both *Rights of Woman* and *Three Guineas* is the question of female education. Wollstonecraft begins her introduction with the assertion that "the neglected education of my fellow creatures is the grand source of the misery I deplore" (*Works of Wollstonecraft,* 5:23), though here she is more concerned, perhaps, with education in its broadest sense. Not only will a proper education help women develop orderly mental activity (5:91), it will also inculcate what she calls virtue and moral sense, dignity and "purity of mind" (5:193). Elsewhere in the text, however, she descends to more practical considerations, deploring the fact that women are unable to get proper instruction to enable them to "earn their own subsistence, independent of men" (5:237). The study of medicine, political theory, and history would be invaluable, she believes, as would training to enable them to go into business, "which might save many from common and legal prostitution" (5:218). Here, her arguments come closer to those of *Three Guineas,* which, at its inception, had been called "Professions for Women." Of course, by the time Woolf was writing, huge advances had been made. For one thing, even in the late 1890s, a university education of sorts would have been open to Woolf if her father had permitted it, and she undoubtedly resented the fact that he had not, attributing it to parsimoniousness: "He spent perhaps £100 on my education."[30] This resentment spills over into her text; even though most of the "daughters of educated men" who are her subject[31] could, by the 1930, acquire a university degree if they so wished, she persists in invoking examples that are, to say the least, anachronistic. Florence Nightingale, the Brontë sisters, Anne Clough, and Mary Kingsley may have been educated by "the four great teachers of the daughters of educated men—poverty, chastity, derision and freedom from unreal loyalties" (*Three Guineas,* 144–45)—but their counterparts in the twentieth century certainly had more, and better, opportunities. "Your class [men] has been educated at public schools and universities for five or six hundred years, ours for sixty" (*Three Guineas,* 33), Woolf declares. This, she argues, will have made for a huge psychological difference between the sexes: "Though we see the same world, we see it through different eyes" (*Three Guineas,* 34). Here again, her arguments resemble the ideas about women's social conditioning that Wollstonecraft had used in the *Rights of Woman:* "Every thing she sees or hears, serves to fix impressions, call forth emotions, and associate ideas, that give a sexual character to the mind" (*Works of Wollstonecraft,* 5:186).

By the 1930s, women had access to professions that had been wholly beyond their reach in Wollstonecraft's time. Nevertheless, as Woolf points out, there were still great inequalities. Women were still unable to join the army or the navy, work on the stock exchange or for the diplomatic corps, or be ordained into the church. Even in the professions that were open to them—the civil service, for example—they were employed only at the lowest of ranks, earning the lowest of wages. While professional men were earning salaries ranging from £3,000 to £15,000 a year, Woolf stresses that as recently as 1934, "To earn £250 a year [was] quite an achievement, even for a highly qualified woman with years of experience" (*Three Guineas,* 81, 287n. 6).

The legal position of women is another issue that concerns both writers. Wollstonecraft had addressed it most forcefully in *The Wrongs of Woman,* in which the heroine, a married woman, realizes that even though she is separated from her husband, she has no legal status as a separate individual: she has become one of the "*out-laws* of the world" (*Works of Wollstonecraft,* 1:146):

> A wife being as much a man's property as his horse or his ass, she has nothing she can call her own. . . . No, he can rob her with impunity, even to waste publicly on a courtesan; and the laws of her own country—if women have a country—afford her no protection or redress from the oppressor. (*Works of Wollstonecraft,* 1:149)

Although many of the laws Wollstonecraft deplored had been changed, it is striking that Woolf offers a remarkably similar argument. Women, she says, constitute a "society of Outsiders" who have had "very little to thank England for in the past." She imagines the outsider giving her reasons for her indifference to patriotism and in doing so echoes Wollstonecraft's words:

> "Our country" . . . throughout the greater part of its history has treated me as a slave; it has denied me education or any share in its possessions. "Our" country still ceases to be mine if I marry a foreigner . . . in fact, as a woman, I have no country. (*Three Guineas,* 197)

The similarities of ideas and terminology here seem too close to be coincidental.

Finally, both *Rights of Woman* and *Three Guineas* have been taken to task for their supposed lack of structure. From late eighteenth-century commentators ("a very unequal performance, and eminently deficient in method and arrangement")[32] to twentieth-century critics ("her lack of education is also shown in her inability to organize material, to follow a consistent train of thought, or to avoid digressions when they are largely irrelevant and in her habit of loose organization. She is incapable either of the coherent organization of ideas or of avoiding repetition"),[33] Wollstonecraft and her texts have been lambasted for deficiencies in logic and structure. Woolf's essay, too, has been described by Hermione Lee as having an "odd structure":

> [A]rgument takes the form of ironical rhetorical questions, and is constantly being interrupted by more examples, or dissolving into suggestive images. . . . There are, disconcertingly, no tidy distinctions between facts and dreams.[34]

It can be argued, however, that Woolf devised, in Lee's words, "a deliberately fluid structure to undermine the rigid insistence of propaganda and polemic" (*Virginia Woolf,* 681). Much the same kind of defense has been mounted for Wollstonecraft: one critic, for example, has argued that to censure her for lack of organization amounts to criticism "by the very standards she is bent on attacking," and that her writing should instead be celebrated for forging "a feminine rhetoric."[35]

There is no doubt, however, that some contemporary feminists have found in *Three Guineas* a "political ambivalence," exemplified, for example, in Woolf's expressed hostility to the word "feminist" ("a vicious and corrupt word that has done much harm in its day and is now obsolete"; *Three Guineas,* 184) and in her apparent inability to decide whether she supports an "equality" or a "difference" view of sexual politics.[36] Significantly, the commentator who made these observations notes that Woolf's essay on Wollstonecraft had celebrated its subject for the very nonrigidity of her views and opinions: "Every day . . . —for she was no pedant, no cold-blooded theorist—something was born in her that thrust aside her theories and forced her to model them afresh" (*Common Reader,* 159).

It seems clear, then, that the views and ideas of these two important writers on women's rights had much in common, despite being separated by one hundred and fifty years of time and change. But this begs the question of indebtedness—"the influence of something on somebody," as Woolf rather scathingly put it in *To the Lighthouse.*[37] And yet, in Woolf's 1929 essay on Wollstonecraft, she herself had written of the persistence, truth, and indeed "influence" of Wollstonecraft's feminist arguments. It would not be going too far to suggest that as Woolf found herself increasingly able to identify and acknowledge the many ways in which her own work could be said to echo that of her important predecessor, she came to see that a continuum existed between them—that together they constituted "one cry for justice."

Notes

1. *The Diary of Virginia Woolf,* vol. 3: 1925–1930, ed. Anne Oliver Bell and Andrew McNeillie (London: Hogarth Press, 1980), 239.

2. *A Reflection of the Other Person: The Letters of Virginia Woolf,* vol. 4: 1929–1931, ed. Nigel Nicolson (London: Hogarth Press, 1978), 78.

3. Brenda R. Silver, *Virginia Woolf's Reading Notebooks* (Princeton: Princeton University Press, 1983), 66–67.

4. It has been suggested that Woolf may have modeled the "experimental" marriage of Katherine and Ralph in *Night and Day* (1919) on what she called in the essay "that most fruitful experiment, [Wollstonecraft's] relation with Godwin." See Herbert Marder, *Feminism and Art: A Study of Virginia Woolf* (Chicago: University of Chicago Press, 1964), 55. The novel also contains a character called Mary, who is a campaigner for women's suffrage.

5. Hermione Lee, *Virginia Woolf* (London: Chatto and Windus, 1996), 71.

6. *Dictionary of National Biography*, ed. Leslie Stephen and Sidney Lee (London: Smith Elder, 1885–1901), 22:61.

7. Anne Elwood, *Memoirs of the Literary Ladies of England* (London: Colburn, 1843), 1:152.

8. George Eliot, "Margaret Fuller and Mary Wollstonecraft," *The Leader*, 13 October 1855, 988–89.

9. Barbara Caine, "Victorian Feminism and the Ghost of Mary Wollstonecraft," *Women's Writing* 4, no. 2 (1997): 261–76, at 267.

10. Margaret Oliphant, *Literary History of England in the End of the Eighteenth and Beginning of the Nineteenth Century* (London: Macmillan, 1882), 2:252.

11. Millicent Fawcett, "A Pioneer of the Movement," in *The Case for Women's Suffrage*, ed. Brougham Villiers (London: Fisher and Unwin, 1907), 188–89.

12. George G. E. Caitlin, introduction to *The Rights of Woman* (London: Dent, 1929), xi.

13. Ibid., xi–xii, xiii.

14. Virginia Woolf, *The Common Reader: Second Series* (London: Hogarth Press, 1965), 158.

15. Michelle Barrett, ed., *Virginia Woolf on Women and Writing* (London: Women's Press, 1979), 5.

16. Virginia Woolf, *A Room of One's Own and Three Guineas*, ed. Michelle Barrett (Harmondsworth: Penguin, 1993), 47.

17. Vivien Jones has recently pointed out that contrary to received opinion, Wollstonecraft's midwife, Mrs. Blenkinsop, was a highly skilled professional woman who was matron at the Westminster New Lying-in Hospital and can in no way be held responsible for Wollstonecraft's death. See Jones, "The Death of Mary Wollstonecraft," *British Journal of Eighteenth-Century Studies* 20, no. 2 (1997): 187–205, at 191–202.

18. Barrett, *Virginia Woolf on Women and Writing*, 93.

19. See ibid., 173–79, 172.

20. *The Diary of Virginia Woolf*, vol. 4: 1931–1935, ed. Anne Oliver Bell and Andrew McNeillie (London: Hogarth Press, 1982), 6.

21. Virginia Woolf, *The Pargiters*, ed. Mitchell A. Leaska (London: Hogarth Press, 1978), vii.

22. *The Diary of Virginia Woolf*, vol. 5: 1936–1941, ed. Anne Oliver Bell and Andrew McNeillie (London: Hogarth Press, 1984), 148.

23. Quoted in *Virginia Woolf: The Critical Heritage*, ed. Robin Majumdar and Allen McLaurin (London: Routledge and Kegan Paul, 1975), 410.

24. *The Sickle Side of the Moon: The Letters of Virginia Woolf*, vol. 5: 1932–1935, ed. Nigel Nicolson (London: Hogarth Press, 1979), xvi–xvii.

25. Lee, *Virginia Woolf*, 693.

26. Silver, *Virginia Woolf's Reading Notebooks*, 67.

27. Virginia Woolf, *Three Guineas*, 2nd ed. (London: Hogarth Press, 1943), 258.

28. *The Works of Mary Wollstonecraft*, ed. Marilyn Butler and Janet Todd (London: Pickering and Chatto, 1989), 5:67.

29. See Barbara Andrew, "The Psychology of Tyranny: Wollstonecraft and Woolf

on the Gendered Dimension of War," *Hypatia* 9, no. 2 (1994): 85–101.

30. Noel Annan, *Leslie Stephen: The Godless Victorian* (London: Weidenfeld and Nicolson, 1984), 121.

31. Compare Wollstonecraft's focus on women "in the middle class" (*Works of Wollstonecraft,* 5:75).

32. William Godwin, *Memoirs of the Author of A Vindication of the Rights of Woman* (Oxford: Woodstock Books, 1990), 83.

33. Eleanor Flexner, *Mary Wollstonecraft: A Biography* (New York: Coward, McCann and Geoghegan, 1972), 164.

34. Lee, *Virginia Woolf,* 681.

35. Laurie A. Finke, "A Philosophical Wanton: Language and Authority in Wollstonecraft's *Vindication of the Rights of Woman,*" in *The Philosopher as Writer: The Eighteenth Century,* ed. Robert Ginsberg (London: Associated University Presses, 1987), 155–76, at 157.

36. See *A Room of One's Own and Three Guineas,* ed. Barrett, xliii.

37. Virginia Woolf, *To the Lighthouse* (St. Albans: Granada, 1977), 16.

Power and Hiding Places:
Wordsworth and Seamus Heaney

Hugh Haughton

In "Envies and Identifications: Dante and the Modern Poet," Seamus Heaney notes that "T. S. Eliot's work is haunted by the shade of Dante." He says that in his influential essay on the Italian poet of 1929, "Eliot was recreating Dante in his own image." "Envies and Identifications" offers a probing account of the contrasting ways in which the Anglo-American Eliot and the Russian poet Osip Mandelstam re-created Dante in their own very different images in their verse and prose. Eliot's Dante is a "seer and repository of tradition," a "stern and didactic" representative of the mind of European Christendom, reflecting Eliot's own journey from "intellectual mysteryman from Missouri" to "English vestryman." By contrast, Mandelstam's is "essentially lyric"; he brought Dante "back from the pantheon to the palate." "Stripped of the robes of commentary" he is made, Heaney says, "to live as the epitome of a poet's creative excitement."[1]

"The palate" and "the pantheon" recall Heaney's own deepest identifications and preoccupations. Heaney is also a poet haunted by Dante, as he is by many other predecessors and contemporaries in the poetic pantheon. In identifying the forces of envy and identification at work in the ways these poets appropriated their great medieval Christian predecessor, Heaney's essay might also make us ask what forces are at work in his own powerful but also self-empowering commentaries on other poets. With this in mind, I want to look at his sustained conversation with the shade of the English Romantic poet, Wordsworth.

As a poet and critic, Heaney is never happier than when he is acknowledging debts and influences. His Dantesque autobiographical sequence, "Station Island," in the 1984 volume of the same title makes this abundantly clear. There the shades of Dante, Carleton, Kavanagh, and Joyce speak authoritatively in Heaney's dream purgatory, finding their place among the priests, friends, relatives, and teachers whose ghosts flock to admonish and instruct him. Early in "Station Island," Heaney tells the "turn-coat" Irish writer Carleton: "Your *Lough Derg Pilgrim* // haunts me every time I cross this mountain— / as if I am being followed, or following." Wordsworth does not figure in *Station Island,* but, to my mind, the Lake Poet's texts haunt Heaney more radically than those of any other poet. The poem about Lough Derg, like "The Strand at Lough Beg," reminds us that Heaney is something of a Lake Poet himself, and it opens with a childhood memory of the Sabbath-breaker Simon Sweeney, who acts as a kind of exemplary antitype of Wordsworth's "Leech-gatherer" in "Resolution and Independence." In an early poem about his father called "Follower," Heaney characteristically represents himself as "being followed, or following": "All I ever did was follow / In his broad shadow. . . . // . . . But today / It is my father who keeps stumbling / Behind me, and will not go away." His declarations of independence (such as the injunction, relayed to him by Joyce at the end of "Station Island" to "swim out on your own") are born of a sense of irresolution and dependence. It was very much as an Irish follower of Wordsworth that Heaney first presented himself as a poet-critic. In critical discussions such as "Feeling into Words" (1974) and "The Makings of a Music" (1978), he not only re-created Wordsworth in his own image but forged a poetic image of himself out of Wordsworth. In 1974, Heaney wrote and presented a BBC television program about Wordsworth ("William Wordsworth Lived Here") in which he acted as modern guide to Dove Cottage, as well as an advocate of the Romantic poet's project to be "at home / In his own place" (*An Open Letter*). It is a virtuoso exercise in envious identification, and Heaney's sustained encounter with the Romantic poet during the 1970s played a crucial part in the forging of his discursive identity as a major poet, not only in the essays of *Preoccupations* (1980), which did so much to shape public perception of his work, but in the autobiographical poems of *North* (1975), *Stations* (1975), and the "Glanmore Sonnets" of *Field Work* (1979).

John Keats, John Clare, Robert Burns, and Gerard Manley Hopkins are other poets who loom large in the Irish poet's thinking about the growth of his poetic mind, and he has written well about all of them. Nonetheless, it was his instinctive, tactical identification with the major inventor of English Romanticism that played the crucial part in his critical self-creation at this time. In earlier poems like "Digging," "Death of a Naturalist," and "Personal Helicon," Heaney began as a poet of rural childhood, the kind of poet Wordsworth learned to become in the late 1790s when he composed the first books of *The Prelude,* his epic investigation into the origins of his poetic power. Though Heaney's early poems do not directly echo Wordsworth, his criticism of the 1970s hitches them unforgettably to the Wordsworthian star. Above all he invited us to see *The Prelude*—that mesmerically rumbling, rambling conversation poem of homecoming, the longest ode to childhood in the language—as laying down the ground rules of Heaney's poetic enterprise. Its first ground rule, after all, is that our first ground rules the rest of our life, an idea that haunts everything Heaney writes.

"I intend to retrace some paths into what William Wordsworth called in *The Prelude* 'the hiding-places.'" So begins Heaney's "Feeling into Words," his first extended autobiographical essay on his own poetry and poetics. Wordsworth's "hiding-places" are "hiding-places of . . . power" (*The Prelude* [1805], 11:335), and in this essay I want to retrace some of Heaney's retracings of Wordsworth, and to ask what power relations might or might not be hiding in them. Wordsworth's poetry, like Heaney's, is very much about influence. It tells of how a poet, during a period of political, personal, and intellectual crisis, is redeemed by his ability to acknowledge the benignity of early influences upon him, and in doing so to ground himself in home ground. For Heaney, there is no "monstrous debt" to Wordsworthian Romanticism and no obvious "anxiety of influence" in Harold Bloom's sense. In fact, to many people, Heaney's keenness to acknowledge his debt to the patenter of the "Romantic Ideology" and incarnation of Keats's "Egotistical Sublime" might even have something monstrous about it.

The Modernists, by and large, resisted Wordsworth. Eliot and Pound, with their desperate suspicions of the whole Romantic project, patronized him at best or passed by on the other side. Even Yeats, though he edited Blake and Shelley, and celebrated Keats as a schoolboy with his face pressed against the sweetshop window, thought Wordsworth a colossal bore. Postwar critics thought otherwise, and

Wordsworth has come to be recognized as one of the shaping forces in Romantic poetry and ideology. In his ongoing negotiations with the ghost of the Lake Poet, however, Heaney is not noticeably engaged with the post-Freudian or deconstructionist Wordsworth of Bloom, De Man, and Hartman or with the politically fraught Wordsworth of the newer historicists, such as Jerome McGann, Alan Liu, and Nicholas Roe. Though the arrival of the two-part *Prelude* of 1799 clearly impinged on Heaney's reading of the poetry—it is included complete in his *Essential Wordsworth* of 1988—his Wordsworth is, in the main, the figure he read at school at St. Columb's College, Derry, and at Queen's, Belfast, and again on returning to Ireland after Berkeley in the early 1970s. Recent criticism has looked back at Romanticism and the Romantic poets through an acutely politicized lens, and most recent criticism of Wordsworth can be read as a defensive critique against what McGann called the "Romantic Ideology." But if the critics seem to be contesting and resisting Romanticism's self-representations, Heaney is not only an unreconstructed admirer of the English Romantic poet but an avowed heir to the Wordsworthian defense of poetry. In a lecture on Sylvia Plath, he declared himself a dedicated follower of Wordsworth rather than of fashion. He said that Plath's best poems

> demonstrate the truth of Wordsworth's wonderful formulation, in his 1802 Preface to *Lyrical Ballads,* of the way poetic knowledge gets expressed. Wordsworth's account is the finest I know of the problematic relation between artistic excellence and truth, between Ariel and Prospero, between poetry as impulse and poetry as criticism of life. . . . Essentially, Wordsworth declares that what counts is the quality, intensity and breadth of the poet's concerns between the moments of writing, the gravity and purity of the mind's appetites and applications between moments of inspiration. This is what determines the ultimate human value of the act of poetry. That act remains free, self-governing, self-seeking, but the worth of the booty it brings back from its raid on the inarticulate will depend upon the emotional capacity, intellectual resource and general civilization which the articulate poet maintains between raids.[2]

Discreetly smuggling in T. S. Eliot's wartime notion of poetry as a raid on the inarticulate, Matthew Arnold's notion of poetry as "criticism of life," and Auden's meditations on Shakespeare's Ariel and Prospero, Heaney's paraphrase incorporates Wordsworth's preface into a developing modern canon while subduing the whole of that canon into his own Wordsworthian defense of the "ultimate human value of the act of poetry."

Yeats edited Blake and Shelley, as I noted earlier, and Heaney has not only edited a selected Yeats[3] (whom he calls both a "national bard" and a "world poet") but a selected Wordsworth. In his introduction to *The Essential Wordsworth* (1988), he calls the Lake Poet's achievement "the most securely founded in the canon of native English poetry" since Milton's. He declares him "an indispensable figure in the evolution of modern writing, a finder and keeper of the self-as-subject, a theorist and apologist whose Preface to *Lyrical Ballads* (1802) remains definitive."[4] Portraying Wordsworth as "finder and keeper" downplays his role as "loser and weeper," as indeed Wordsworth himself sought to do, and the Wordsworthian defense against elegy is one that Heaney repeats. The Wordsworth canon Heaney himself selects and acts as "apologist" for is predictably that of the "great decade." It includes a scatter of the *Lyrical Ballads* ("the volume of poetry that initiates the modern enterprise"), including its preface; the seminal 1799 *Prelude* and extracts from five books of the 1805 *Prelude;* and a range of the *Poems in Two Volumes* such as "Resolution and Independence," "Ode: Intimations of Immortality," and sixteen of the "magnificent sonnets" of 1802–3. Unsurprisingly, the texts are very much those Heaney quotes from repeatedly in his own prose and verse. What is striking, however, is the degree to which he chooses to underwrite his predecessor's whole project:

> "Cheerfulness," a robust, committed, and justifiably positive attitude in the face of evil and injustice, a comprehension that could acknowledge the ubiquity and affront of pain while yet permitting itself to be visited without anxiety by pleasure—this was the goal of Wordsworth's quest in the 1790s and its meaning for our lives in the 1980s is no less central. Equally instructive, however, is the gradual atrophy we perceive in him as the Romantic quester mutates into the Victorian eminence, and an achieved calm turns into an impregnable placidity.[5]

By emphasizing the "cheerfulness" and "justifiably positive attitude" that shape Wordsworth's quest, Heaney reinforces his ideological alignment with Wordsworth's brand of Romanticism. Where modern critics dwell on the massive personal and political anxieties, the contradictions, and the strains that give *The Prelude* its questing power, Heaney reaffirms its fundamental story of "Imagination, How Impaired and Restored." He insists that the "Victorian eminence" is the "inessential" Wordsworth, while the "essential poet remains the one struggling to become a whole person, to reconcile a sense of incoherence and disappointment forced upon him by the external circumstances of his life with those intimations of harmonious communion promised by his childhood visions, and seemingly ratified by his glimpse of a society trembling at the moment of revolution."[6] Nevertheless, though his primary identification is with "the twenty-eight year old poet listening in to himself in the covert of his poetic being," his account of the later Wordsworth, with his "roll call of offices and associations—friend of the aristocracy, Distributor of Stamps for Westmorland, Poet Laureate"—has a certain admonitory force. Heaney, as the most laureated, lauded, and publicly applauded poet of our time, must be aware of the danger of becoming "more an institution than an individual." The prospect of finding himself in a Rydal Mount of his own must occasionally give him pause. He continues, though, to have no qualms about the underlying benignity of the Wordsworthian project, which is simultaneously to underscore the fundamental benignity of the world and the poetic imagination.

Heaney's commitment to such a view is much in evidence in lectures on two poets who do not share it. Philip Larkin is a poet explicitly committed to an altogether less benign take on things, although the Irish poet believes he was capable of writing his own version of *The Paradiso.* In the course of his discussion of Larkin's "Deceptions," Heaney unexpectedly calls up Wordsworth's Pedlar to rebuke the altogether less upbeat Hull Librarian. "I have no doubt that Larkin would have repudiated any suggestion that the beauty of the lines I have quoted is meant to soften the pain," he says, "as I have no doubt he would also have repudiated the Pedlar's advice to Wordsworth in 'The Ruined Cottage' where, having told of the long sufferings of Margaret, he bids the poet 'be wise and cheerful.'"[7] Nonetheless, Heaney sets the image of "light, unanswerable and tall and wide" from "Deceptions" against that of "Those weeds, and the high spear grass on the wall / By mist and silent raindrop silvered o'er" from "The Ruined Cottage." He comments: "It is the authenticity of this moment of pacification which to some extent guarantees the Pedlar's optimism; in a similar way the blank tenderness at the heart of Larkin's poem takes it beyond irony and bitterness, though all the while keeping it short of facile consolation." It is not clear who is more or less deceived here, but it is a powerful reading if only in reflecting the intensity of Heaney's need for "pacification" and "consolation." This is confirmed later in the essay where he says, wittily, that "the minute light makes its presence felt in Larkin's poetry he cannot resist the romantic poet in himself who must respond with pleasure." It goes without saying that Heaney's resistance to the romantic poet in himself is considerably less developed.[8]

An arresting, not to say bizarre, instance of this occurs in his essay on Sylvia Plath. Here, Heaney takes Wordsworth's "There was a Boy" as a "parable" of a poet's changing relationship to his or her work and audience and uses it as a template to map the stages of Plath's career. He relates the "levels of attainment" of her poems as she develops to Wordsworth's story about a boy blowing "mimic hootings to the silent owls." "When the vale fills with the actual cries of owls responding to the boy's art," Heaney says, "we have an image of the classically empowered poet, the one who has got beyond scale practising, the one who Wordsworth says in his Preface, rejoices in the spirit of life that is in him and is delighted to contemplate similar volitions and passions as manifested in the goings-on of the universe." This, for Heaney, "represents the poetry of relation, or ripple-and-wave effects upon audience," so that the poet's personal subjects can become a "common possession of the reader's."[9]

Plath is not an easy vehicle for the Wordsworthian poetry of redemption, and though Heaney finds nothing "*poetically* flawed" about her work, he is clearly deeply troubled by "its dominant theme of self-discovery and self-definition" in which what he calls "the supra-personal dimensions of knowledge" are "slighted in favour of the intense personal need of the poet." Though he does not want to suggest "that the self is not the proper arena of poetry," he believes that poems like "Daddy" and "Lady Lazarus," for all their "valiantly unremitting campaign against the black hole of depression," do not achieve the level of "self-forgetfulness" attained by the greatest poetry.

Plath, that is, remains caught up in the dejection crisis that Wordsworth, if not Coleridge, managed to transcend. The Irish poet goes on to quote Wordsworth's notion of "the active universe" and to affirm the preface to *Lyrical Ballads* as the "finest" account he knows of the articulation of poetic knowledge. Heaney's identification with his Romantic predecessor here enables him to justify his dis-identification with Plath. You would think the "theme of self-discovery and self-definition" to be central to Wordsworth's *Prelude,* too, but Plath's ferocious theater of envies and identifications represents a threat to Heaney's more benign project. Even though in "Digging" the poet imagines his pen "snug as a gun," he offers none of the parricidal bravado of "Daddy."[10]

Although Heaney encountered Wordsworth's poetry at school and his early poems bear the imprint of his poetic investment in rural childhood, it was not until the mid-1970s that the Lake Poet became an explicit force in his intellectual world. From then on, Wordsworth became a potent sponsor of Heaney's project—what he refers to in *An Open Letter* as his "deep design to be at home / In his own place and dwell within its proper name." "Feeling into Words," the influential first autobiographical essay on his own poetics delivered at the Royal Society for Literature in 1974, opened with words from *The Prelude.* From the outset, the rising star of Irish poetry projected himself in his criticism under Wordsworth's banner. The quotation from *The Prelude* was followed by a credo of his own, drawn out of it:

> The hiding-places of my power
> Seem open; I approach, and they close;
> I see by glimpses now; when age comes on,
> May scarcely feel at all, and I would give
> While yet we may, as far as words can give,
> A substance and a life to what I feel:
> I would enshrine the spirit of the past
> For future restoration.

> Contained in those lines is a view of poetry which I think is implicit in the few poems that I have written that give me any right to speak: poetry as divination, poetry as revelation of the self to the self, as restoration of the culture to itself; poems as el-

ements of continuity, with the aura and authenticity of archaeological finds, where the buried shard has an importance that is not diminished by the importance of the buried city; poetry as a dig, a dig for finds that end up being plants.[11]

Heaney translates Wordsworth's seminal lines into the terms of the recent verse of *Wintering Out* (1972) and *North* (1975). Wordsworth's "hiding-places" are personal, locked into early experiences "disowned by memory." Heaney's, by contrast, are communal and cultural, and their archaism is historical as much as psychological. Revelation of the "self to the self" is intimately bound up, for Heaney, with Irish cultural archaeology. The digging he invokes recalls that of his father, portrayed in "Digging," and that of the expert archaeological fieldwork in which he metaphorically engaged in *Wintering Out* and *North*. The restorative "spirit of the past" is Heaney's and Wordsworth's, but also, beyond both, that of his native culture—a culture partly hidden or masked by the dominant culture of Northern Ireland. This is a different kind of "hiding-place" of power.

"Feeling into Words" speaks of "Digging" as the first poem in which he felt he had got his feeling into words. In other words, he frames a poem about his relationship to his actual father by invoking a figure in his literary version of Freud's Family Romance, the sponsoring poetic predecessor, William Wordsworth.[12] Heaney's essay excavates various submerged allusions in "Digging," to the local saying that "the pen is lighter than the spade," for example, and to a local schoolboy rhyme about "Dirty-faced McGuigan." Arguing that he didn't so much "write" the poem as "dig it up," he remarks, "[D]igging becomes a sexual metaphor, an emblem of initiation, like putting your hand into the bush or robbing the nest, one of the various natural analogies for uncovering and touching the hidden thing." "I now believe," he goes on, "that the 'Digging' poem had for me the force of an initiation."[13]

In this retrospective account of the first retrospective poem in which he found his voice, Heaney uses the Wordsworthian metaphor of "hiding-places" quite systematically—the poem puts him in touch with the "hidden thing," and this has the force of a poetic "initiation." *The Prelude* is, of course, Wordsworth's attempt to vindicate and articulate his own peculiar sense of initiation, of being a "chosen spirit," and the metaphors Heaney uses here reproduce scenes from Wordsworth's childhood, notably the bird's-nest robbing incident where Wordsworth remembers hanging over "the raven's nest" by "knots of grass," and the almost erotic despoliation recorded in "Nutting." The lecture recollects his early poems in tranquility, now translated into an explicitly Wordsworthian currency.

In "Feeling into Words," Heaney first uses the image of the young boy listening to different radio "stations" in the fastness of his home as an archetype of his responsiveness to voices from elsewhere and his growing sense of "words as bearers of history and mystery." As we shall see, he returns to it in his Nobel speech, "Crediting Poetry," twenty years later. In fact, the image of the listening boy occurs immediately after his own account of his earliest literary "influence," Hopkins. Explaining the process whereby a poet first finds a distinctive "poetic voice" that is related to his "natural voice," Heaney states that one starts out by "hearing it from somebody else." Originality, that is, originates in unconscious mimicry—ventriloquism of a kind. One's first steps as a writer will then be to imitate, consciously or unconsciously, "those sounds that flowed in, that in-fluence." Heaney does not disown this moment of "in-fluence," as Larkin notoriously disowned Yeats in his introduction to his first book, *The North Ship.*[14] The essay goes on to enumerate the influence of his mother's reciting Latin lists, listings on the radio dial, "the beautiful sprung rhythms of the old BBC weather forecast," and the "litany of the Blessed Virgin" as "providing the unconscious bedding" of his sense of "verbal music." To this was added his experience at secondary school of the "conscious savouring of words" at work in the poetry of Keats, Tennyson, and Wordsworth ("All shod with steel / We hiss'd along the polished ice"). After this faithful and enamored retracing of his developing sense of verbal "craft," Heaney quotes his poem "The Diviner," offering it as a figure for the poet "in his function of making contact with what lies hidden, and in his ability to make palpable what was sensed or raised":[15]

> The pluck came sharp as a sting.
> The rod jerked with precise convulsions,
> Spring water suddenly broadcasting
> Through a green hazel its secret stations.

Quoting Sir Philip Sidney on the classical poet as "*Vates,* which is as much as a Diviner," he notes that the poet, like the diviner, derives his powers from his ability to tap into those Romantically Wordsworthian "hiding-places" of his power. The "green hazel" gives a subliminal Irish inflection to the diviner, as "secret stations" conflates radio stations (once again important for Heaney's poetic radio world) with the Catholic "secret stations" that evoke Penal days. "Broadcasting" brings together sowing and radio, though it makes natural forces sound less like the official voice of the BBC than an underground Irish radio station. The diviner is one of those reassuring local craftsman figures—thatcher and blacksmith—who loom large in early Heaney, but his ability to tune into those "secret stations" has darker resonances.

Wordsworth is often crossed with Kavanagh in Heaney's prose. Heaney first began to float phrases culled from *The Prelude* when reviewing a reprint of Kavanagh's *The Green Fool* in 1972. He describes Kavanagh's autobiographical fiction in terms reminiscent not only of Wordsworth but of his own early work, calling it "an act of piety towards the terrain of this childhood" ("terrain" giving it the Heaney note). Like Heaney, Kavanagh's father had a "small farm," and the memoir's account of its "way of life" clearly strikes Heaney as "a remembrance." After noting its "quieter, secret moments," he portrays it with happy incongruity as a kind of Monaghan *Prelude,* "a prelude to poetry, an account of the unlikely growth of a poet's mind."[16] Heaney takes note of Kavanagh's subsequent denunciation of his "dreadful stage-Irish, so-called autobiography," and his critique of the Irish Literary Movement, with its "Synge-song" and "peasant quality" as a "thorough-going English-bred lie." Nevertheless, he clearly prefers *The Green Fool* to the later *Tarry Flynn,* and celebrates the later Kavanagh in equally Wordsworthian terms. For him, Kavanagh, the born-again poet of the Grand Canal, found "that generous tremor of consciousness that sometimes opens the hiding-places of a poet's power suddenly, memorably and undeniably." Kavanagh, he says, came to distrust the "pieties and postures" of *The Green Fool,* but even this is given a Wordsworthian twist when Heaney says he "might have felt it trailed some corn among its clouds of glory."[17]

If "Feeling into Words" in 1974 first set up a Wordsworthian template for reading Heaney, "The Makings of a Music" (1978) instituted a comparison between notions of poetic composition in Wordsworth and Yeats. Here, Heaney enlisted Wordsworth as an instrument to resist Yeats's aesthetics of "masterful images" in the battle against Yeatsian influence in which later Irish poets are inevitably involved. In neither essay does he reflect on the political Wordsworth. At Grasmere in 1984, however, he launched his most fully fledged account of Northern Irish poetry under the auspices of a more politically inflected Wordsworth. Though it is not an essay on his own work, his account of the strategy of other Northern Irish poets clearly reflects back on his own. At the outset of that essay, "Place and Displacement: Recent Poetry from the North of Ireland," Heaney puts forward *The Prelude* as a "working model" for what Jung calls the "evolution of higher consciousness in response to an apparently insoluble conflict."[18] Noting that "when England declared war on Revolutionary France, Wordsworth experienced a crisis of unanticipated intensity," he goes on to quote the passage from book 10 of *The Prelude* in which Wordsworth describes the "change and subversion" he and his generation experienced at the moment "the strength of Britain was put forth" against the "regenerated" post-Revolution France of the early 1790s:

> Now had I other business, for I felt
> The ravage of this most unnatural strife
> In my own heart; there lay it like a weight,
> At enmity with all the tenderest springs
> Of my enjoyments. I, who with the breeze
> Had played, a green leaf on the blessed tree
> Of my beloved country—nor had wished
> For happier fortune than to wither there—
> Now from my pleasant station was cut off,
> And tossed about in whirlwinds.
> (*The Prelude* [1805], 10:249–58)

"The good place where Wordsworth has been nurtured and to which his habitual feelings were most naturally attuned," Heaney observes, "has become, for the revolutionary poet, the wrong place." Wordsworth has become "displaced from his own affections by a vision of the good located elsewhere," he says, so that "his instinctive being and his appetitive intelligence are knocked out of alignment." The composition of *The Prelude,* according to this argument, was "part of the symbolic resolution of a lived conflict." Describing the poem as "diagnostic, therapeutic and didactic all at once," Heaney presents it as throwing, in a prefiguration of modernist procedures, "the nerves, as 'twere, in patterns on a screen." Wordsworth's case is "symptomatic of the historical moment" for Heaney, with the poem at the eye of the storm of the age, and "the 'I' of the poem at the eye of the storm within the 'I' of the poet." Having cast *The Prelude* in this modernist light with that quotation from Eliot, he seals it by comparing it as a whole to "the extreme of this kind of writing" a century later, *The Waste Land*—"another work where the expression of an acute personal predicament can be read as an expression of the age, and one which has enforced a new way of reading poetry."[19]

Interweaving quotations from Eliot and Wordsworth, Heaney modernizes the Romantic poet (even as he romanticizes Eliot elsewhere).[20] Having done so, he makes Wordsworth's poem a template with which to understand the work of the writers of his own generation from Northern Ireland. These writers also emerged at a time of public crisis, during which the hopes raised by the civil rights movement suffered a traumatic blow during the ensuing violence, a violence that also involved "the strength of Britain" being "put forth." Heaney's account of the moment is more politically outspoken than he usually gives, underpinned as it is by Wordsworth:

> When Derek Mahon, Michael Longley, James Simmons and myself were having our first books published, Paisley was already in full sectarian cry and, indeed, Northern Ireland's cabinet ministers regularly massaged the atavism and bigotries of Orange men on the Twelfth of July. Nothing needed to be exposed: rather, it seemed that conditions had to be outstripped and it is probably true to say the idea of poetry was itself that higher ideal to which the poets unconsciously had turned in order to survive in the demeaning conditions, demeaned by resentment in the case of Nationalists, by embarrassment at least and guilt in the case of Unionists.[21]

"Like the disaffected Wordsworth," he argues, "the Northern Irish writers . . . take the strain of being in two places at once." They "belong to a place that is patently riven by the notions of belonging to other places"—either a Britain that has its capital in London or an Ireland with its capital in Dublin. The Northern nationalist's principles will seem to his Unionist neighbor "as traitorous as Wordsworth's revolutionary sympathies" to his "patriotic neighbours," while his commitment to the "Nationalist myth" means he lives "in an exile from his ideal place." In this context, Heaney says, "the only reliable release for the poet was the appeasement of the achieved poem," that "liberated moment when the lyric discovers its buoyant completion." It is this, he suggests, that lies behind "the typical concern of Northern Irish poets with style, with formal finish, with linguistic relish and play." Emphasizing the "profound relation here between poetic technique and historical situation," he argues that it is superficial to see their "lyric stances" as "evasions of the actual conditions," saying that "their concern with poetry itself wears well when we place it beside the protest poetry of the sixties."[22]

The bulk of the essay consists of brilliant and sympathetic readings of the work of his contemporaries, showing the ways in which, both intellectually and technically, they are committed to "displacement" of many kinds. A case in point is the "large number of poems in which the Northern Irish writer views the world from a great spatial or temporal distance," Derek Mahon's "A Disused Shed" being the most obvious example. Mahon's poems rarely show that "appeasement of the achieved poem" that Heaney talks about, however, and the essay ends with Michael Longley's much more Wordsworthian "Self-Heal" being cited as an example of the way in which the poets "make their poetry a process of self-healing" that is "neither deliberately provocative nor culpably detached."

"Place and Displacement" offers a powerful reading of the poetry of Heaney's generation, but it is also, like Coleridge's discussion of the poetry of Wordsworth in *Biographia Literaria,* an implicit defense of his own poetic stance. Heaney's defense of poetry involves seeing poetry as a defense against other forms of engagement with political conflict. In this, his appeal to Wordsworth is an instance of the displacement he talks about, but it also offers a powerful contemporary reading of the displacements at the heart of the Wordsworthian project. The notion of "displacement" had already occurred in Wordsworth criticism, in both Geoffrey Hartman's psychological account of the Wordsworthian self in *Wordsworth's Poetry, 1787–1814* (1964), which talks of the "developing and self-displacing vision" of *The Prelude*, and, more destructively, in Jerome McGann's *The*

Romantic Ideology: A Critical Investigation (1983), which speaks of the tendency of Romantic poets to "occlude and disguise their own evasion" of politics.[23] In fact, the year before Heaney's talk, David Simpson had subtitled his study, *Wordsworth's Historical Imagination* (1983), *The Poetry of Displacement.* McGann criticizes Wordsworth for a mystifying displacement of the real historical dimensions of his poetic material, while Simpson reads the poems as displaced but still explicit engagements in the world of public debate. They are not, in his reading, "achieved instances of successful displacement," as McGann would have it, but "transcriptions of conflict" that openly register the forces that threaten their own stability. Heaney's sense of Wordsworthian "displacement" differs from both, but his identification with it draws attention to the ways in which Wordsworth's idea of "the good place," like his own, may be seen as a product of trauma, a strategy for psychic survival, rather than evasion. Reading this as a kind of family romance, we might say that it is the "achieved poem," rather than Wordsworth's Grasmere or his own Mossbawn, which ultimately figures as "the good place" for the Irish poet, who speaks as someone literally "displaced" from the north of Ireland to the south.

With Eliot, Yeats, Jarrell, and Stevens, Heaney is not only a highly influential poet-critic but one of the most eloquent ambassadors for poetry in his time. Wordsworth, in his "Supplementary Essay" of 1815, wrote that "every Author, as far as he is great and at the same time *original,* has had the task of *creating* the taste by which he is to be enjoyed." For Wordsworth, the great poet "has to call forth and to communicate *power*" above all, and in his own preface to *Lyrical Ballads* of 1802, as in the later "Supplementary Essay," he used the power of expository prose as a discursive instrument to help create that taste for his own kind of original power.

Heaney tends to downplay originality and play up indebtedness, but he, too, has used critical prose as a powerful instrument in helping define the terms through which his own work can be understood. In readings, essays, interviews, and lectures, he has proved himself a generous commentator on his contemporaries and predecessors but also an eloquent self-promoter of his own art. *Preoccupations* largely shaped the terms of his own critical reception, and Wordsworth, alongside Yeats, is the presiding spirit of the volume. Though he does not figure center stage in Heaney's Nobel lecture, "Crediting Poetry," his is one of the many voices that lie behind Heaney's crediting of poetry. Heaney's lecture pays more attention to the other voices he read and valued early on—those of Keats, Hopkins, Owen, Lowell, Bishop, and Kavanagh—than to the establishment of his own. "Crediting Poetry" is now placed as epilogue to *Opened Ground: Poems, 1966–1996,* so that it fulfills something like the function of Yeats's "A General Introduction to My Work." It opens with another childhood memory, this time of the Heaney family in their thatched farmhouse, listening to both the local sounds of cattle and trees and the national, British, and international voices on the radio, made possible by the "aerial wire attached to the topmost branch of the chestnut tree." We recognize the image of the radio from "Feeling into Words" and the Wordsworthian "Glanmore Sonnet, VII," with its invocation of the "strong gale-warning voice" of the BBC weather forecast. Such a view of the poet as both rooted (by the Yeatsian "great rooted chestnut-tree") and open to other voices is consciously emblematic. It suggests how deeply at odds Heaney is with Harold Bloom's Oedipal account of the strong poet's resistance to literary indebtedness in *The Anxiety of Influence,* published the year before Heaney's "Feeling into Words." For Bloom, poetic history is "indistinguishable from poetic influence," and he is interested only in "strong poets" who make that history by misreading each other, those "major figures with the persistence to wrestle with their strong precursors." For the Nietzschean Freudian Bloom, "weaker talents idealize; figures of capable imagination appropriate for themselves."[24] Heaney's tactic suggests idealization might be another form of appropriation.

Wordsworth is only one radio "station" among many, but he does figure in "Crediting Poetry." Speaking of "The Stare's Nest at My Window" by his Irish Nobel predecessor, Yeats, Heaney saw it as "proof that poetry can be equal to *and* true at the same time, an example of that completely adequate poetry which the Russian woman sought from Akhmatova and which William Wordsworth produced at a corresponding moment of historical crisis and personal dismay exactly two hundred years ago."[25] For Heaney, Yeats, Akhmatova, and Wordsworth here embody achieved poetic adequacy at a "moment of historical crisis and personal dismay" such as his own, but Wordsworth is not only historically the earliest of these but the first to present his life's work in terms of a "moment of historical crisis" of this kind. *The Prelude* is the self-validating template for self-validating poetic adequacy.

"Crediting Poetry" is an apology for poetry in general, but since its inclusion in *Opened Ground* it has also become an essay supplementary to Heaney's own oeuvre. With *Opened Ground* now supplemented by *Finders, Keepers: Selected Prose, 1971–2001* (2002), we can see the two-pronged nature of his prolific output and consider how poetry and prose supplement each other, just as in Yeats's career—or indeed Wordsworth's. Heaney had called Wordsworth "a finder and keeper of the self-as-subject" and the title of his collected prose suggestively reappropriates this. Heaney found Wordsworth an empowering ally and patron in his early criticism and has kept returning to him, as I hope I have shown, with eloquent obstinacy, aligning the "hiding-places" of his own power with those of Wordsworth's.

When we come to the poetry itself, it is a slightly different story, though again we can trace Heaney being followed by, or following, Wordsworth. As in his prose, it was only in the poetry of the mid-1970s that Heaney first explicitly alludes to Wordsworth, from around the time of his BBC film. In reading such allusions, we might bear in mind his own emphasis in a recent lecture on "the literary echoes and allusions" that are fundamental to "poetic energy." In a poem, he says, "words, phrases, cadences and images are linked in to systems of affect and signification which elude the precis maker. These under-ear activities, as they might be termed, may well constitute the most important business which the poem is up to and are more a matter of the erotics of language than the politics and polemics of the moment."[26]

Heaney loves to cross and compound quotations, and at the head of his autobiographical sequence, "Singing School," in *North,* he sets cunningly balanced autobiographical epigraphs from his two most persistent poetic mentors, Yeats and Wordsworth. "Singing School" opens with one of the most quoted passages from *The Prelude,* "Fair seed-time had my soul, and I grew up / Fostered alike by beauty and by fear, / Much favoured in my birthplace." In its wake comes an extract from Yeats's *Autobiographies* in which Yeats confesses that his first experience of "the pleasure of rhyme" was reading a stable boy's "book of Orange rhymes" in a hayloft. Amid this autobiographical cross fire of seed-times and haylofts in the north of England and the north of Ireland, Heaney launches his reminiscences of his own schooldays in Derry and university days in Belfast, framing a story of the "growth of the poet's mind" in the Northern Ireland of his formative years.

The allusion to the Lake Poet's "fair seed-time," favored "birthplace," and "the beloved Vale" to which he was transplanted might seem ironic, given the chronicle of Heaney's encounters with sectarian and political division in Ulster recorded in the sequence that follows. The poems record armed police swinging "crimson flash-lamps, crowding round the car," an RUC constable evoking a sense of "arithmetic and fear" in the Heaney household at Mossbawn, the "giant tumours" of lambeg drums on an Orange parade in Tyrone," and a Belfast in which "the Constabulary covered the mob / Firing into the Falls." The sequence ends with a self-portrait of the poet as "an inner emigré, grown long-haired and thoughtful," having "Escaped from the massacre" in the North, weighing his responsible *tristia* on a damp Wicklow evening in December. Taken together, it might seem an ironic commentary on Wordsworth's idea of a "fair seed-time." Nothing, however, in the rest of Heaney's oeuvre calls in question—or ironizes—the poet's instinctive Wordsworthian loyalty to his childhood experiences, or his grounded sense that his first place was in some sense blessed. "I wrote about my childhood because I couldn't help it," Heaney wrote in a grainily evocative 1971 essay for *The Listener* titled "A Poet's Childhood." He recalls lying in a barn, "snug in a big soft pile of hay, with hayseeds tickling down the neck of my jersey, smelling the dead summer smells of the hay, listening to the rich purrings as the milk rose steadily in my aunt's pail."[27] What Heaney reaps as an adult poet had been sown in childhood and youth and is rooted in his earliest formative sense of place (the flax-dam of "Death of a Naturalist," the "tawny guttural water" of the river Moyola, Anahorish as "the first hill in the world," the "Toome" and "Toner's bog" of the early poems). It resurfaces in "Mossbawn: Two Poems of Dedication" at the start of *North*.

It is also, of course, rooted in his formative literary experience. The title of the autobiographical suite in *North* is "Singing School," which pays tribute to Yeats's "Sailing to Byzantium," with its defiantly un-Wordsworthian affirmation that the only singing school for the poetic imagination is "studying monuments of its own magnificence." The first poem in the sequence, "The Ministry of Fear," opens with a quotation from Patrick Kavanagh's "Epic" ("Well, as Kavanagh said, we have lived / In important places"), returning to that watershed moment in Irish poetry when Kavanagh announced that Homer "made the *Iliad* from such / A local row. Gods make their own importance." Underwritten by texts from Wordsworth, Yeats, and Kavanagh, Heaney returns to his days as a boarder in St. Columb's College, where he "overlooked the Bogside" and "was so homesick I couldn't even eat / The biscuits left to sweeten my exile." Heaney first encountered Wordsworth at St. Columb's, and no doubt the Lake Poet's homely but uncanny conjuration of rural childhood spoke to his homesickness. Wordsworth did not begin as a poet of childhood, autobiography, or memory, of course. It was in Wales, far from the Lakes and on the point of departure for the Continent, that he wrote "Tintern Abbey," the first poem in which he trod the labyrinth of his childhood memories and committed himself to blank verse. And it was in Goslar, Germany, during a sense of acute political and intellectual crisis, that he began to write *The Prelude,* his unprecedented attempt to articulate the "hiding-places" of his power as a poet. The idea that "The child is father to the man" is an adult insight, of course, a retrospective doctrine of childhood most fully articulated in the "dark invisible workmanship" of his autobiographical epic. In all its versions, from the two-part *Prelude* of 1799 to the 1805 and 1850 incarnations, Wordsworth insists on the relation between the poem on the "growth of [his] own mind" and the process of its composition in the late 1790s during what he calls "these times of fear, / This melancholy waste of hopes o'erthrown." We misread the whole tenor of Wordsworth's poem, with its retrospective doctrine of the genesis of inspiration, if we fail to see its genesis in political crisis, in "times of fear."

Wordsworth claims he was "fostered alike by beauty and by fear," and, having declared, "Fair seed-time had my soul," he goes on to relate anecdotes that explore the troubling interplay between power and fear. He tells of his acting as a "fell destroyer," stealing ravens' eggs and trapping birds in springes, and, in the boat-stealing episode, of an "act of stealth / And troubled pleasure" resulting in a terrifying sense of being pursued by a punitive landscape. Heaney, less stealthily, uses the same phrase "It was an act of stealth," in "The Ministry of Fear," if only to describe his throwing away of biscuits in the fog. However incongruously, this aligns him with the young Wordsworth, just as the title of the poem recalls the "severer interventions, ministry / More palpable" invoked in *The Prelude*—a ministry compounded in Heaney's memories of the "leather strap" in the Big Study at school, and then in the punitive encounter with the armed policemen. "The Ministry of Fear," dedicated to the poet and critic Seamus Deane as his contemporary version of Coleridge, offers a truncated parallel to Wordsworth's account of schooldays and his time at Cambridge. "Ulster was British, but with no rights on / The English lyric," he concludes in this first poem, but the poem itself makes good his right to appropriate the words of one of the greatest English lyric poets, however uneasily.

The later poems in the sequence offer Wordsworthian parallels, if not allusions. In "A Constable Calls," Heaney tells a childhood anecdote about his father's encounter with a visiting RUC man. Though it seems little more than a highly sprung genre piece of Irish rural autobiography, it is charged with a sense of the "hiding-places" of power in many senses. As the poet interrogates his memory, the policeman's interrogation of his father starts to pulse with the forces at work in the larger political culture of the north of Ireland ("Arithmetic and fear"; "I sat staring at the polished holster"; "His boot pushed off / And the bicycle ticked, ticked, ticked"). The young Heaney is only a spectator, but, as a young Catholic boy in Unionist Ulster, he is inevitably a guilty spectator: "I assumed / Small guilts and sat / Imagining the black hole in the barracks." It is the very innocence of the scene that makes it so convincing an embodiment of the ministry of fear, a counterpart of such moments as the boat-stealing episode in *The Prelude* when "with trembling hands" the young Wordsworth stole his way "back to the cavern of the willow-tree." But where Wordsworth talks of his intercourse with "high objects, with enduring things, / With life and Nature," Heaney's experience of "pain and fear" are fraught with a whole political history and iconography.

"Summer 1969" tells in a tightened version of Wordsworthian blank verse of Heaney hearing the news of the police entering the Falls Road in Belfast when on holiday in Madrid. The poem then reads Spain, and the art of Goya in particular, where Saturn is "Jewelled in the blood of his own children" and "Gigantic Chaos" turns his "brute hips / Over the world," as displacements of events back home. I am reminded of Wordsworth's uncanny account of passing through Paris after the September Massacres looking upon the sights "as doth a man / Upon a volume whose contents he knows / Are memorable but from him locked up" (*The Prelude* [1805], 10:49–51), or again his account of turning from the "rubbish" of the Bastille, where he had looked "for something which [he] could not find," and being moved instead by "a single picture," the Magdalene of Le Brun (*The Prelude* [1805], 9:70, 77–78). After this, the last two poems are more precisely literary. "Fosterage" sports a Wordsworthian title but describes the influence of Michael McLaverty, Heaney's headmaster and mentor, who tells him that "Description is revelation" and lends him Hopkins's journals. "He fostered me and sent me out, with words / Imposing on my tongue like obols." If McLaverty imposes words on his tongue "like obols," the notion of fosterage is a Wordsworthian obol. In the poem that follows, "Exposure," the poet dramatizes himself sitting "weighing and weighing" his "responsible *tristia*" and pondering his relationship as a poet to the north, the "massacre" and "the people," modeling his position on that of the exiled Mandelstam. Nevertheless, as he takes "protective colouring / From bole and bark, feeling / every wind that blows"—an allusion to Wordsworth's "The Thorn"—he aligns himself intimately with his English predecessor, who also "escaped from the massacre" and settled in the Lake District to work out a redemptive version of poetics that can measure up to, even while it seems to resist, the political crises of the time.

During the years in which the poems of *North* were germinating, Heaney also composed a series of prose poems he called *Stations* and published in Belfast in 1975. Begun in Berkeley in 1970, they were completed in Glanmore in 1975. They, too, suggest *The Prelude* was much upon his mind. Heaney says composition was halted in 1971 partly due to the appearance of Geoffrey Hill's *Mercian Hymns*, a work of "complete authority" that adopted a comparable ritualized prose to explore analogous ground, and partly due to the adverse political conditions in Belfast on his return home from California. The first pieces, he said, were "attempts to touch what Wordsworth called 'spots of time', moments at the very edge of consciousness which had lain for years in the unconscious as active lodes of nodes, yet on my return a month after the introduction of internment my introspection was not confident enough to pursue its direction." It was only "again at a remove, in the 'hedge-school' of Glanmore, Co. Wicklow, that the sequence was returned to, and then the sectarian dimension of that pre-reflective experience presented itself as something asking to be uttered also."[28]

In his preface, Heaney sets up the analogy with Wordsworth's "spots of time" in *The Prelude.* The less explicit biographical analogy between himself and Wordsworth is equally striking. As Wordsworth had begun to explore childhood memory abroad in Goslar, so did Heaney in his year in Berkeley with the first *Stations* pieces and the essay "A Poet's Childhood" for *The Listener* in 1971. *Stations* was published in Belfast and, though nine of the twenty-one pieces are now included in *Open Ground,* they took some time to be admitted into Heaney's oeuvre. There is something overcooked as well as raw about them, and, in hindsight, they remain too much in thrall to the revamped scholastic idiom of Geoffrey Hill's *Mercian Hymns.* Nevertheless, Heaney's prose sketches cast a different light over the childhood described in the earlier three volumes, bringing up from the dark the sectarian dimension largely hidden beforehand. Starting out with early memories of being lost and found as a young child ("Cauled") and weeping on the sofa at home ("Branded"), picking primroses for the altar ("Hedge-school"), and eyeing sandmartins' nests ("Nesting-ground"), there is also a jeweled account of men coming to "sink the pump." These are all memories that surface in later poems, all part of the repertoire of his mythologized "hedge-school" Catholic rural childhood. Soon, however, shades of sectarian politics begin to close upon the growing boy. "Sweet William" ponders the disturbing relation between the garden flower and the Unionists' King Billy ("that king with crinkling feminine black curls"); "The Discharged Soldier" reflects on the impact of the Wordsworthian veteran of Flanders who "stamp[ed] the parish"; "The Sabbath-breakers" chronicles Nationalist rituals (as footballers "raised a tricolour in the chestnut tree and faced it proudly for the anthem"); and "Kernes" relates the sight of a boy on a Raleigh bicycle as "king of the castle" to "Sir Walter Raleigh in his inflated knickers" and to "King Billy," establishing Heaney's identification with the "wood-kerne" in "Exposure." "July" records a Catholic boy's ear being "winnowed annually" by the sound of "Orange drummers" leading "a chosen people through their dream," while "England's Difficulty" portrays the young Heaney in wartime Ulster moving "like a double agent," listening to Lord Haw Haw, lodging with "the enemies of Ulster," "the scullions outside the walls." The collection ends with a handful of poems that take him beyond primary school and on to St. Columb's in Derry where, following in the wake of Joyce's *Portrait of the Artist,* he describes the light "calloused in the leaded panes of the college chapel" and being "champion of the examination halls." There is an unlyrical prose "Ballad" about a boy victim of sectarian violence; an account of a visit to the Gaeltacht in "The Stations of the West" and of being interrogated by a Protestant "christened in Boyne water" in "Inquisition"; and a brief piece, "Incertus," about an "old pseudonym" he "went disguised in."

Heaney likens his poems to the Protestant "spots of time" of Miltonic Wordsworth and to Catholic "stations," like the "stations" at Lough Derg. What is striking about *Stations*, however, is the degree to which his "fair seed-time" was shaped and scarred by the sectarian politics of Northern Ireland. The story told elsewhere of the idealized rural family in Mossbawn is overwritten here—overwritten in many senses—by tribal politics in Ulster. The unresolved politics of Northern Ireland make Heaney's "spots of time" very different from Wordsworth's, just as the "seed-time" and "ministry of fear" recorded in "Singing School" in *North* are more explicitly political than anything in Wordsworth's repertoire of childhood memories. But if, according to Heaney, *The Prelude* is in part a product of traumatic disappointment and dispossession, we could say the same of Heaney's obstinate programmatic need to take possession of his childhood home and "dwell within its proper name" (as he puts it in *An Open Letter*).

It was in 1974 that Heaney researched, wrote, and presented his television documentary about Dove Cottage, titled "William Wordsworth Lived Here." Beginning with the return of the twenty-nine-year-old poet and his sister to Grasmere in December 1799, it calls Dove Cottage a house "socketed into the hillside like an elemental power point," "an emblem of the poet's instinctive decision to make this new and nourishing connection with his origins."[29] The program suggests the scale of Heaney's possibly envious identification with his English predecessor at this time. The celebration of the Wordsworthian "retreat" to Grasmere (a word that has Catholic as well as military resonances) is clearly shaped by his own move to Glanmore in 1972, and suggests the degree to which Wordsworth in the texts of the period may have helped Heaney justify that. "Exposure," the ultimate destination of "Singing School," is Heaney's first explicit self-portrait of the poet in rural exile. The image of the "wood-kerne // Escaped from the massacre" evokes a parallel between Heaney and Irish refugees feeling the horrors of Tudor policy in Ireland; it may also evoke a parallel between Heaney and Wordsworth who, safely home in Grasmere, remembers the September Massacres in post-Revolutionary Paris. The "Glanmore Sonnets" in his next volume, *Field Work* (1979), openly play out Heaney's sense of parallel with Wordsworth, a poet who retreated from the internecine political battles of the 1790s to found a new poetics of interiority, childhood memory, autobiography, and place.

It was at Grasmere that Wordsworth took up the sonnet, and Heaney's "Glanmore Sonnets" represents his first sonnet sequence. Heaney had composed an early political sonnet on 1798—the year not only of *Lyrical Ballads* but also of the rebellion of the United Irishmen commemorated in "Requiem for the Croppies" from *Door into the Dark* (1969). In *North,* one of the two opening poems, "The Seed Cutters," is a very consciously composed sonnet about a dream of composure ("Under the broom / Yellowing over them, compose the frieze / With all of us there, our anonymities"), while "Strange Fruit" is another sonnet about political violence, and "Act of Union" a double sonnet, equally rooted in history. "Act of Union" returns not only to the same form as "Requiem for the Croppies" but also to the same point in time, the political moment that cemented the imperial "Union of Great Britain and Ireland"—the basis of the "Union" affirmed by Ulster Unionists. In returning to it, however, Heaney turns it into a pregnant figure of his wife's pregnancy, his own marriage, and the violence of contemporary politics, reaping what the historical Act of Union sowed. The formal doubleness of "Act of Union" casts a disturbing double light on both Irish history and the poet's marriage, yoking together the heterogeneous realms of the political and the domestic, parliamentary and gynecological processes, marital intimacy and historical violence. There are shades here of Yeats's "Leda and the Swan," another sonnet about sex and political violence, and Heaney's poem ends with the image of his wife's "stretch-marked body, the big pain / That leaves you raw, like opened ground again." It is not clear whether the birth of a child is matched by a political rebirth of some kind, or just "pain" and "an obstinate fifth column."

The first "Glanmore Sonnets" were published in the immediate aftermath of *North* and show Heaney moving away from the tight, packed, drill-like forms that predominate earlier and easing himself into the fuller space allowed by the iambic pentameter. They also show him moving away from the note of "violence and epiphany" that sounds through almost every line of the earlier volume. The phrase "opened ground" recurs in the first line of the first sonnet, now in the context of agricultural and cultural renewal:

> Vowels ploughed into other: opened ground.
> The mildest February for twenty years
> Is mist bands over furrows, a deep no sound
> Vulnerable to distant gargling tractors.
> Our road is steaming, the turned-up acres breathe.
> Now the good life could be to cross a field
> And art a paradigm of earth new from the lathe
> Of ploughs. My lea is deeply tilled.
> Old ploughsocks gorge the subsoil of each sense
> And I am quickened with a redolence
> Of farmland as a dark unblown rose.
> Wait then . . . Breathing the mist, in sowers' aprons,
> My ghosts come striding into their spring stations.
> The dream grain whirls like freakish Easter snows.

Opened Ground is the title Heaney gives to his collected poems, and there is a sense here of a new beginning, the making of a new music, even if it is one anchored in traditional agricultural practices and the traditional cadences of the English sonnet. From "Iniskeen Road" to "Epic" and "The Hospital," Patrick Kavanagh had also adapted the sonnet for his own insouciant vernacular use, employing it to map a road in his parish or a hospital ward in Dublin, helping the poetic gods "make their own importance." Like the "ploughsocks," the cadences and images Heaney uses are old, but the poem's present tense generates a sense of tensed, eager expectation, with the "ghosts" from his past given new energy as they strike into "their spring stations" (again that word). Though the ghosts are not specified or named, in their sowers' aprons, it is soon clear that Wordsworth is among them. "Fair seed-time had my soul," he had written, and this poem is also about a fair seed-time ghosted by Wordsworth's words.

The second sonnet of the sequence returns to familiar Wordsworthian notions with its immediate invocation of "Sensings, mountings from the hiding-places / Words entering almost the sense of touch, / Ferreting themselves out of their dark hutch." The lines recall the "mountings of the mind" recorded in the "Glad Preamble" of *The*

Prelude and, of course, the "hiding-places" of Wordsworthian power. These are poems about the act of composition itself, the making of a music Heaney discusses in the essay of that title on the different compositional practices of Wordsworth and Yeats. "Vowels ploughed into other"; "art a paradigm of earth"; "Words entering almost the sense of touch"; "It was all crepuscular and iambic"—Heaney's lines from the "Glanmore Sonnets" repeatedly explore the surfacing of phrases in the act of composition. There are many echoes of the opening music of *The Prelude* itself and of the sense of enfranchisement Wordsworth records there:

> The earth is all before me—with a heart
> Joyous, nor scared by its own liberty,
> I look about, and should the guide I chuse
> Be nothing better than a wandering cloud,
> I cannot miss my way. I breathe again—
> Trances of thought and mountings of the mind
> Come fast upon me. . . .
> Whither shall I turn,
> By road or pathway, or through open field,
> Or shall a twig or any floating thing
> Upon the river point me out my course?
> (*The Prelude* [1805], 1:15–21, 29–32)

"I breathe again" echoes behind "The turned-up acres breathe." "Now the good life could be to cross a field" might also echo the opening sequence of *The Prelude* in which Wordsworth states, "to the open fields I told / A prophecy; poetic numbers came / Spontaneously" and punningly speaks of the "honorable field" of "music and of verse." "Words entering almost the sense of touch" certainly recalls Wordsworth's description of himself as "soothed by a sense of touch / From the warm ground, that balanced me, else lost / Entirely" (*The Prelude* [1805], 1:89–91).

The Prelude famously opens with the sense of a breeze that is later described as generating "A corresponding mild creative breeze" in the poet's mind. Heaney's third Glanmore sonnet confirms that Wordsworth is palpably in the air, as it ends with an Irish equivalent of Wordsworth's breeze. Heaney says to his wife, "I won't relapse / From this strange loneliness I've brought us to. / Dorothy and

William —," and notes his wife's interruption: "You're not going to compare us two. . . ." "Outside," Heaney writes, "a rustling and twig-combing breeze / Refreshes and relents. Is cadences." The wind in Wicklow blows from the Lake District, carrying with it Wordsworth's description of the River Derwent's "steady cadence," which gave him a foretaste "of the calm / Which Nature breathes among the hills and groves." The comparison between the Irish poet and his wife at home in Glanmore and Wordsworth and his sister Dorothy at home in Grasmere, while gently mocked, is not dispelled. Though questioned, it is not erased. In fact, it is one of the founding inspirations of the sequence, as an earlier, erased version of the second sonnet makes clear. There, after a quotation from Oisin Kelly, Heaney dwells precisely on the parallel between his and Wordsworth's dwelling places and worries about his need to conjure such figures and voices from the past:

> "These things are not secrets but mysteries,"
> Oisin Kelly said. I wonder. Yes
> And no. Glanmore is not Grasmere.
> That was a different ministry of fear.
> Out of the cave of the mouth I would raise
> The antique strains of slug-horns and blown lurs
> That might continue, hold, dispel, assuage,
> Yet something in this conjuring demurs.
> My age demands a sense of my own age
> Perhaps? Perhaps. An eleven-plus aesthete
> Making the daring leap from quote to quote.[30]

Heaney does indeed love to leap "from quote to quote," as he does here from Oisin Kelly to Pound's "The age demanded" via the "ministry of fear," which he quotes from his own earlier poem in *North* as well as out of Wordsworth and Graham Greene. The later version rightly cuts the weak display of misgivings—the "Yes and no," that "Perhaps? Perhaps"—and the schoolboy embarrassment about his schoolboy embarrassment at being "an eleven-plus aesthete" who loves to quote. That Wordsworth's was a "different ministry of fear" hardly needs saying, so what has Heaney in mind here? The declaration of dis-identification ("Glanmore is not Grasmere") is perhaps an instance of the poet protesting too much about his overbearing need to identify with Wordsworth. It suggests a homegrown touch of the "egotistical sublime." In excising it, however, Heaney glosses over the anxieties he harbors about "this conjuring," which I take to be his conjuring of the spirit of Wordsworth as well as of "antique strains" from the "cave of the mouth." It also plays down the intimate connection between the political and poetic "ministry" evident in Coleridge's "secret ministry of frost." The "Glanmore Sonnets" are an apology for poetry at a time of intense political crisis.

Revising the second Glanmore sonnet, Heaney returned to the time he "landed in the hedge-school of Glanmore," where he hoped to raise "from the backs of ditches" the poetic forces of renewal with which the sonnet sequence as a whole begins:

> Vowels ploughed into other, opened ground,
> Each verse returning like the plough turned round.

This verse returns to the first line of the first sonnet, making that return paradigmatically self-reflexive; the verse line reproduces the *versus*, the "furrow" ploughed by the plough that gave the language the word "verse," anchoring poetic practice in the kind of agricultural practice Heaney knows from his childhood. Heaney used the phrase "opened ground" in "Act of Union" from *North*, but here it reflects on Wordsworth, whose "Home at Grasmere" (1800) was written in the year of the Union of Great Britain and Ireland. The choice of *Opened Ground* as the title of his canonical collected poems suggests how deeply Heaney is committed to this particular view of verse and locale.

Heaney in the "Glanmore Sonnets" comes alive to the "crepuscular and iambic" music of the English sonnet, which Wordsworth had discovered when reading Milton at Grasmere in 1801–2. This is ironized at the opening of the third poem ("This evening the cuckoo and the corncrake / (So much, too much) consorted at twilight") but is played out throughout the sequence in cadences such as "He saw the fuchsia at dusk in the risen moon / And green fields greying on the windswept heights," or "The respite in our dewy dreaming faces." "I used to lie with an ear to the line," the fourth sonnet begins, risking a wonderful pun on the railway line he lay on as a child and the poetic line. This is comparable to the moment in *The Prelude* where Wordsworth speaks of "drinking in / A pure organic pleasure from the lines / Of curling mist" (*The Prelude* [1805], 1:590–91).[31] One first sees and hears him drinking in pure organic pleasure from the poetic line itself. Heaney "listens with an ear to the line," as a poet must, but as he does so, he aligns the local Derry railway line where he waits for "an iron tune / Of flange and piston pitched along the ground" with the blank verse line of English tradition, heard again when it sounds on his own ground, and in his own poem about his own ground.

At this point, one might look back at Heaney's early poems of childhood, written before he openly invoked Wordsworth, and compare them to those he wrote later. "Digging" is about a resurfacing childhood memory of his father; Heaney focuses it through the lens of Wordsworth's notion of "hiding-places" of power. The poet looks out of the window and sees, in an abrupt chronological disjuncture, his father "com[ing] up twenty years away / Stooping in rhythm through potato drills / Where he was digging." The idea of rhythm unites father and son, but in tendentiously describing his pen as resting, "snug as a gun," in his hand—in lieu of his father's spade—Heaney draws attention to the dimension of violence that may be involved in his metaphoric identification with and displacement of his father through the power of his pen. Heaney does not dwell on what might be hidden in the "hiding-place" here, but in the reference to the "curt cuts of an edge / Through living roots" that "awaken in [his] head," he addresses the mutilation that is integral to both writing and digging. One might read the metaphoric gun as Oedipal or political. Whichever way, it suggests that in tapping his "living roots," the writer is inevitably involved in more than a version of pastoral.

Wordsworth described himself and Coleridge as "Prophets of Nature." Though they were not naturalists, it was Nature that was at stake. The title poem of the volume *Death of a Naturalist,* though it does not allude specifically to Wordsworth, reads almost like an episode hewn from *The Prelude.* It offers a repellent as well as fascinated vision of the natural world that jars with Wordsworth's. In fact, Nicholas Roe has suggested that it has an unacknowledged "literary background"—a "hiding-place" of power—in one of the childhood "spots of time" in *The Prelude.* Roe is thinking of Wordsworth's account of having been a "fell destroyer" and of hearing among the solitary hills "Low breathings coming after me" (*The Prelude* [1805], 1:317, 330).

For Roe, however, the "consonantal music" and "vivid externality" of Heaney's account of the child's horror in the face of the "angry frogs" at the flax-dam is "disengaged and external" in comparison to the *Prelude* lines, in which Wordsworth "inhabits the child's feelings." "Death of a Naturalist," for Roe, suggests that "Heaney is drawn to the Wordsworthian spot of time, but unable to admit its redemptive adequacy." He goes on to suggest that *The Prelude,* with its roots in Milton's epic, depends on the "inner light and private intercession of Protestant theology," whereas Heaney's resistance to it is related to his "Catholic unwillingness to admit the efficacy of a Protestant redemption."[32]

Heaney's poem does indeed contest the mode of autobiographical interiority pioneered by Wordsworth, though I doubt this is a question of confessional theology. That said, it may well be that ideas of Protestant and Catholic are subliminally at work in Heaney's reconstruction of his childhood encounter at the flax-dam—a shocking solitary encounter that goes far beyond the domestic terms of Miss Walls's natural history lesson ("The daddy frog was called a bullfrog"). The poem's beginning already suggests something more than nature is at work:

All year the flax-dam festered in the heart
Of the townland; green and heavy headed
Flax had rotted there, weighted down by huge sods.
Daily it sweltered in the punishing sun.

The first line ends with that loaded Wordsworthian word "heart" (as in "sensations sweet / Felt in the blood, and felt along the heart" in "Tintern Abbey"). However, at issue here is the "heart / Of the townland"—a term for a rural locality that is thoroughly Irish; at its heart lies not a pond but a "festering" dam. The flax-dam is a piece of agricultural engineering and it is associated with the linen industry that played such a crucial role in the history of the Protestant North of Ireland (Michael Longley's great poem, "The Linen Industry," redeems linen-making in the wake of Heaney's nightmare account). Its "festering" at the "heart of the townland" may be a piece of sensational nature reporting or an implicit critique of the culture of the townland itself.

The second verse paragraph shows more than a touch of the

author's admiration for the nature poetry of Ted Hughes ("Right down the dam gross-bellied frogs were cocked / On sods; their loose necks pulsed like sails"), but its apocalyptic evocation of "the great slime kings" is shot through with other forces. The "slap and plop" of the frogs are seen as "obscene threats"; the frogs are "Poised like mud grenades," "gathered there for vengeance." This not only gives us a feverishly phobic view of the natural forces explained by Miss Walls, but could be read as a displaced version of a Catholic boy's recoil from the kinds of angry, pent-up political forces feared to be at the "heart" of the Unionist State, "gathered there for vengeance." This seems to be confirmed by "Summer 1969," where Heaney describes himself responding while on holiday in Spain to the outbreak of violence in Belfast: "Each afternoon, in the casserole heat / Of the flat . . . / . . . stinks from the fishmarket / Rose like the reek off a flax-dam. / . . . patent leather of the Guardia Civil / Gleamed like fish-bellies in flax-poisoned waters."

The last poem in *Death of a Naturalist,* "Personal Helicon," is, like "Digging," both autobiographical and concerned, if not with "the growth of a poet's mind," then with the adult poet's attempt to convert childhood experiences into emblems of his own poetics. It opens with one of Heaney's most ingrained Wordsworthian tropes, a genially inviting but also self-validating appeal to his childhood in South Derry: "As a child, they could not keep me from wells / And old pumps with buckets and windlasses." This exactly parallels the opening of the 1971 essay for *The Listener,* "A Poet's Childhood": "As a boy I grew up in the country at a place called Mossbawn in County Derry. I remember one place that I loved: the top of the dresser."[33] Heaney's return to childhood experience as a trope for his creative practice is evident in a large number of his essays as well as in numerous poems; "Personal Helicon" is one of his first return journeys and one of his earliest attempts to look into the "hiding-places" of his poetic power:

> Others had echoes, gave back your own call
> With a clean new music in it. And one
> Was scaresome, for there, out of ferns and tall
> Foxgloves, a rat slapped across my reflection.
>
> Now, to pry into roots, to finger slime,

To stare, big-eyed Narcissus, into some spring
Is beneath all adult dignity. I rhyme
To see myself, to set the darkness echoing.

In many of these early poems, we see the poet "fostered alike by beauty and by fear," as in the "scaresome" experience of the rat here. Transporting Helicon to County Derry has a touch of Kavanagh about it ("Gods make their own importance"), but the poet's claim to abjure infantile Narcissism and sublimate it through rhyme is double-edged. What enables Heaney to "see [him]self" is precisely the sense-laden re-creation of his total immersion in well-gazing in childhood, the prying into his own roots he speaks of in an early essay:

> Certainly the secret of being a poet, Irish or otherwise, lies in the summoning of the energies of words. But my quest for definition, while it may lead backward, is conducted in the living speech of the landscape I was born into. If you like, I began as a poet when my roots were crossed with my reading.[34]

The Prelude is the longest example of poetic root-prying in the language, and Wordsworth did occasionally feel embarrassed about the fact ("it seems a frightful deal to say about one's self," he told his friend Richard Sharp). But Heaney's terser "Personal Helicon" is most alive when there is either "no reflection" (l. 8) or when the rat slaps across Heaney's reflection. Where the Wordsworthian Self should be, there is indeed an echoing vacancy, something almost entirely hidden.

In the poems of *Wintering Out*, written during the period where his explicit engagement with Wordsworth begins in his prose, Heaney's developing analysis of the "hiding-places" of power emerges in a clearer light. The last section of "Gifts of Rain" about the River Moyola might be thought of as a tauter, braced equivalent of the watery opening of the 1799 *Prelude* with its invocation to the River Derwent, the "beauteous stream," whose voice Wordsworth says "flowed along [his] dreams," making "ceaseless music" in his early childhood, and whose "steady cadences" "composed" his thoughts. Listening to "the Moyola harping on // its gravel beds"—that "harping" giving the primal river's repetitive volubility an Irish note—Heaney talks of his need for "antediluvian lore," and then addresses the river as a paradigm for poetry, as does Wordsworth:

The tawny guttural water
spells itself: Moyola
is its own score and consort,

bedding the locale
in the utterance,
reed music, an old chanter

breathing its mists
through vowels and history.

Though he says the river rises to "pleasure" him and names himself "Dives, / hoarder of common ground," the celebration of the river is articulated not in terms of the way it composed Heaney but in terms of the way it composes itself: the Moyola is described as "bedding the locale / in the utterance"—its own utterance, that is—rather than bedding the local river dialect in the poet's imagination (as in Wordsworth). There is common ground between the Derry poet and the Westmorland one, but also a world of difference, as the river speaks of a communal Irish music of "reed" and "chanter" as well as of its own name. But then in *The Essential Wordsworth,* Heaney, having evoked the "fluvial procedures" of Wordsworth's verse, proceeds to describe it in terms of "bagpipe music," explaining that one has to "let the drone of the manner count for as much as the chanters of the meaning." What Heaney hears is the music of a hidden Ireland, a music associated with its own name. Wordsworth wrote a set of poems about the "Naming of Places"; Heaney's "Gifts of Rain," like "Broagh" and "Toome," are about Irish place-names, whose "hiding-places" can be tapped through the poet's sounding of his own language, as his mouth holds round "the soft blastings." These are all poems about his earliest place, but what they offer are epiphanic glimpses of a culture—not of a poet in "nature." In this respect, they are in line with recent readings of Wordsworth in the wake of Geoffrey Hartman, which see him very much as a poet of culture rather than nature, or with readings indebted to David Simpson's *Wordsworth's Historical Imagination.* Heaney's early poems about his childhood terrain are underpinned less by "imagination" as such than by his Dives-like sense of the historical and cultural riches lurking on home ground. Though the naturalist dies, the cultural nationalist does not.

As time goes on, however, Heaney increasingly returns to his home ground and memories of childhood for something more like Wordsworth's sense of ontological rather than cultural renovation. Late Heaney, like middle-period Wordsworth, is a Romantic ontologist, a Heideggerian poet of being and of home. Memories of his first ground continue to ground that sense of being, and poetry.

Heaney continues to mine his childhood with apparently inexhaustible fascination. Take, for example, "The Railway Children" from *Station Island,* which describes youngsters viewing telegraph wires and imagining how "words travelled the wires / In the shiny pouches of raindrops"; or the resurrected school memories of section 5 of "Station Island"; or the evocation of actual "hiding-places" in section 3 with its return in memory to the family kitchen, where the poet forages for a "toy grotto" hidden away in the "big oak sideboard":

> It was like touching birds' eggs, robbing the nest
> of the word *wreath,* as kept and dry and secret
>
> as her name, which they hardly ever spoke
> but was a white bird trapped inside me
> beating scared wings when *Health of the Sick*
> fluttered its *pray for us* in the liturgy.

Heaney thinks of "walking round / and round a space utterly empty, / utterly a source, like the idea of sound; // or like the absence sensed in swamp-fed air." This has the authentic Wordsworthian and Joycean smell, with the sense of robbed nests and the stale aura of Catholic piety, focused around emptiness and death. It evokes something like one of those "uncanny moments" Heaney found in Wordsworth, which for all its emptiness is a "source" (a word that is important for both poets).[35]

Poems about childhood from this time include "Alphabets," "Terminus," and the wonderful sequence of memorial sonnets for his mother, "Clearances," from *The Haw Lantern* (1987), as well as "Markings," "Seeing Things," and "Wheels within Wheels" from *Seeing Things* (1991). Their viewpoint is summed up by "Fosterling," a sonnet with a Wordsworthian title, which announces that it was only when he was nearly fifty that Heaney learned "to credit marvels."

The poems of the "Squarings" section of *Seeing Things* are consciously marvel-crediting, such as the one beginning, "A boat that did not rock or wobble once / Sat in long grass one Sunday afternoon / In nineteen forty-one or two." Despite their luminous sense of design, these poems can seem all too designing, four-square exercises in visionary memory that are more akin to the late Wordsworth of what John Jones called "the baptised imagination"[36] than to the early Wordsworth of "There was a boy." In one of the poems from the "Settings" sequence in the same volume, the poet remembers his father bending over a tea chest packed with salt, a hurricane lamp in his fist, but he frames the memory with a kind of aesthetic religiosity far removed from early Heaney. "And strike this scene in gold too, in relief," it begins, going on to conjure a consciously painterly "Rembrandt-gleam" around the memory, and ending with a self-congratulatory sense of visionary wealth: "That night I owned the piled grain of Egypt. / I watched the sentry's torchlight on the hoard. / I stood in the door, unseen and blazed upon." Exploring "Memory as a building or a city, / Well lighted, well laid out, appointed with / *Tableaux vivants,*" or a "scene from Dante," these poems genuinely mark a new development in Heaney's engagement with the material of his life. Now bent on forging a visionary world comparable to Yeats's, Dante's, Henry Vaughan's, or that of "the sage Han Shen," the poems seem to operate in an altogether more iconographically fixed spiritual universe of would-be "perfected vision." Heaney, though he wants to escape the "doldrums of what happens" and yearns for "lightenings," does not seem as fluent a metaphysical poet as his masters. The uncanny note of angelic heterodoxy sounded in their different dialects by Emily Dickinson, Rainer Maria Rilke, Wallace Stevens, or Fanny Howe eludes him.

Two of the poems in the "Squarings" sequence of *Seeing Things* bring these questions into particularly sharp focus, while raising the ghost of Heaney's earlier commitment to Wordsworthian memory. The first begins with Heaney giving a new jolt to his sense of his childhood contact with an earlier world: "I was four but I turned four hundred maybe / Encountering the ancient dampish feel / Of a clay floor. Maybe four thousand even." It concludes on a different note:

> Ground of being. Body's deep obedience
> To all its shifting tenses. A half-door

Opening directly into starlight.

Out of that earth house I inherited
A stack of singular, cold memory-weights
To load me, hand and foot, in the scale of things.

Like his early "mould-hugger" Antaeus, Heaney is one of the great ground-hugging poets, and "ground" is one of his most resonant terms. A later poem in the sequence talks of spirits who are "still territorial, still sure of their ground," but the move from the "clay floor" to "ground of being" is less sure of its ground. He wants to resist, it seems, the "cold memory-weights" that load him allegorically "in the scale of things," as souls were weighed, but the "rank puddle-place" evoked in the poem resists that resistance. The quantitative "Memory-weights" seem altogether more emblematically calculated than the muddier currency of memory in earlier Heaney.

In the second poem, having evoked his pleasure in words such as "sand-bed" and "gravel-bed" (echt Heaney vocables), he says:

The places I go back to have not failed
But will not last. Waist-deep in cow-parsley,
I re-enter the swim, riding or quelling

The very currents memory is composed of,
Everything accumulated ever
As I took squarings from the tops of bridges

Or the banks of self at evening.
Lick of fear. Sweet transience. Flirt and splash.
Crumpled flow the sky-dipped willows trailed in.

The daring, self-conscious allegorical play of "banks of self" replays the idea of Wordsworth as "finder and keeper of the self-as-subject," but "the places" he goes back to here are more conceptually determined. In portraying himself as reentering the "swim, riding or quelling // The very currents memory is composed of," Heaney gives rein to the sense of mnemonic exploration we find in *The Prelude*, but the "prospect of the mind" here displaces the "places he goes back to." It is one of the best poems of the sequence since it is pulled back and forth between those places and Heaney's new metaphysical project. The project has to do with the limits of "the ground of being," the places that "will not last," but the poet has to work too hard to square the material of memory with allegory.

I want to end by looking at two more recent poems, "Markings" from *Seeing Things* (1991) and the concluding poem "Mycenae Lookout" from *The Spirit Level* (1996). "Markings" re-creates his memories of playing Gaelic football as a child, when the boys "marked the pitch," and recalls his love of "lines pegged out in the garden." His account of "Youngsters shouting their heads off in a field / As the light died" with their "hard / Breathing in the dark and skids on grass" is not unlike Wordsworth's numerous accounts of boyhood pastimes in *The Prelude*. As with Wordsworth, Heaney portrays such activities as paradigms of poetry. The "pitch," the "line," and the "field," marked on "bumpy thistly ground," establish familiar Heaney terms for the grounding of his poetry, so that when he goes on to talk of "lines pegged out in the garden" or "the imaginary line straight down / A field of grazing, to be ploughed open" we know he is contemplating yet again the analogy between the agricultural world of his childhood and his adult devotion to verse, while anchoring the latter in the former. The poem uses a form that is not unlike the "line" of Wordsworthian blank verse, and in the third section, Heaney marks a further literary origin in *The Prelude:*

> All these things entered you
> As if they were both the door and what came through it.
> They marked the spot, marked time and held it open.
> A mower parted the bronze sea of corn.

Surely here, in saying "They marked the spot, marked time," Heaney is alluding, consciously or unconsciously, to the "fructifying virtue" of Wordsworth's "spots of time." The idea of poetic "marking" is founded on childhood marking. His solitary mower calls him back to his childhood as a "visible scene on which the sun is shining" (*The Prelude* [1805], 1:663).

Some of the strongest poems in *The Spirit Level* and *Electric Light* return to home ground, though, for me, the current of memory is beginning to fail. There are too many dutiful occasional poems—elegies or christening poems—and the Eclogues and "Sonnets from Hellas" in *Electric Light* exhibit a stale classicism that has a whiff of the Parnassian tourist poetry of the later Wordsworth. "Mycenae Lookout"—a meditation in time of civil war recast in a classical setting—is the real thing, however, whether we think of it as a re-creation of classical mythology and geography or as an evocation of Heaney's first world. Its concluding section, "His Reverie of Water," is about that most characteristically Heaney space, a "hiding-place" that is also a source. It describes "the well at Athens," but unsurprisingly ends with a return to a well at home in South Derry (one of those wells from which adults could not keep him, according to the closely related "Personal Helicon"):

> And then this ladder of our own that ran
> deep into a well-shaft being sunk
> in broad daylight, men puddling at the source
>
> through tawny mud, then coming back up
> deeper in themselves for having been there,
> like discharged soldiers testing the safe ground,
>
> finders, keepers, seers of fresh water
> in the bountiful round mouths of the iron pumps
> and gushing taps.

Those "discharged soldiers" remember Aeschylus's *Agamemnon* and may also anticipate "discharged soldiers" on both sides in Northern Ireland; but they also remember the discharged soldier Wordsworth recalls meeting in *The Prelude*. In *Stations*, Heaney has a poem about "Sinking the Shaft" that prefigures this and, as mentioned above, a poem titled "The Discharged Soldier" about a world war veteran who is his equivalent of Wordsworth's soldier. Once more, we find the allusion to "finders, keepers" is associated with Wordsworth as in Heaney's prose, as the poet, in response to the affront of war, writes a kind of Ode to Water, a recasting of "Personal Helicon" that brings together the classical and the native place.

Speaking of "safe ground" makes sense only in time of war, as in "Mycenae Lookout." This might prompt one to ask to what extent Heaney's cult of childhood memory, of indebtedness to his own childhood, like Wordsworth's before him, can be read as a defense against an implicit violence. We can understand that violence in terms of Heaney's vein of thwarted cultural nationalism, the dream of belonging discussed in "Place and Displacement." We could also think of it, however, in the context of the violence of modernity. Wordsworth was alive to the political violence of his time, but more than that, I think, to the disorienting modernity represented by the French Revolution and by the modern metropolis mapped in book 7 of *The Prelude*. It may be that Heaney's return to childhood has its roots in the same adult recoil not just from "The Troubles" but from the troubling pressure of accelerating cultural change in Ireland and elsewhere. His work constitutes an extraordinary set of Irish variations on a theme by Wordsworth. In poems such as "A Sofa in the Forties" (from *The Spirit Level*) and "Electric Light" (from *Electric Light*) this engagement continues to generate power out of the Heideggerian "hiding-places" of his Northern Ireland childhood. However, there may be a sense in which these are not only places charged with hidden power and underwritten by a Romantic dream of chthonic homecoming, but places in which to hide from the power of the contemporary world.

Notes

1. Seamus Heaney, "Envies and Identifications: Dante and the Modern Poet," originally published in *Irish University Review* 15, no. 2 (1985) and reprinted in *Finders, Keepers: Selected Prose, 1971–2001* (London: Faber, 2002), 168–79.

2. Seamus Heaney, "The Indefatigable Hoof-taps: Sylvia Plath," in *Finders Keepers*, 230–31.

3. Originally for the *Field Day Anthology of Irish Writing*, now as a Faber book: *W. B. Yeats: Poems Selected by Seamus Heaney* (London: Faber, 2000).

4. Seamus Heaney, ed., *The Essential Wordsworth* (New York: Ecco Press, 1988), 4.

5. Ibid., 12.

6. Ibid.

7. Heaney, *Finders, Keepers*, 148.

8. Elsewhere, in "Joy or Night: Last Things in the Poetry of W. B. Yeats and Philip Larkin," he says "we must imagine Yeats as the reader in eternity who resists Philip Larkin's 'Aubade.'" Heaney, *Finders, Keepers*, 326.

9. Heaney, *Finders, Keepers*, 223–24.

10. Ibid., 229–31.

11. Seamus Heaney, "Feeling into Words," Royal Society of Literature Lecture, October 1974, in *Finders, Keepers*, 14.

12. See "The Family Romance" in Sigmund Freud, *The Uncanny and Other Essays*, ed. Hugh Haughton (London: Penguin, 2003).

13. Heaney, *Finders, Keepers,* 15.

14. Heaney discusses this in "The Main of Light," in *Finders, Keepers,* 145–52.

15. Heaney, *Finders, Keepers,* 20.

16. Seamus Heaney, "After the Synge-song—Seamus Heaney on the Writings of Patrick Kavanagh," *The Listener,* 13 January 1972, 55–56.

17. Ibid.

18. Seamus Heaney, "Place and Displacement: Recent Poetry from Northern Ireland" (1984), in *Finders, Keepers,* 112.

19. Heaney, *Finders, Keepers,* 115.

20. See Seamus Heaney, "Learning from Eliot," in *Finders, Keepers,* 26–38.

21. Heaney, *Finders, Keepers,* 116–17.

22. Ibid., 118.

23. Geoffrey Hartman, *Wordsworth's Poetry, 1787–1814* (New Haven: Yale University Press, 1964), 65. Jerome J. McGann, *The Romantic Ideology: A Critical Investigation* (Chicago: University of Chicago Press, 1983), 81–92.

24. Harold Bloom, *The Anxiety of Influence: A Theory of Poetry,* 2nd ed. (Oxford: Oxford University Press, 1997), 5.

25. Seamus Heaney, "Crediting Poetry," in *Opened Ground: Poems, 1966–1996* (London: Faber and Faber, 1998), 464.

26. Seamus Heaney, "Through-other places, through-other times," in *Finders, Keepers,* 373.

27. See Seamus Heaney, "A Poet's Childhood," *The Listener,* 1 November 1971, 660–61. The incident recalls "The Barn" in *Death of a Naturalist* (1966) and "Servant Boy," published in *Honest Ulsterman,* November/December 1971.

28. Seamus Heaney, *Stations* (Belfast: Ulsterman Publications, 1975), 3.

29. My quotations from the program derive from a transcript by my Ph.D. student at York, Michael Kinsella. I am grateful to him for permission to use these and for the influence of our innumerable conversations about Wordsworth, Heaney, and influence.

30. Seamus Heaney, "Glanmore," *Prospice* 5 (1976): 64.

31. Christopher Ricks has written a brilliant essay on this. See Ricks, *The Force of Poetry* (Oxford: Oxford University Press, 1987), 89–116.

32. See Nicholas Roe, "Wordsworth at the Flax-Dam: An Early Poem of Seamus Heaney," in *Critical Approaches to Anglo-Irish Literature,* ed. Michael Allen and Angela Wilcox (Gerrards Cross: Clin Smythe, 1989), 166–70.

33. Heaney, "A Poet's Childhood," 660.

34. Seamus Heaney, "Belfast," in *Preoccupations: Selected Prose, 1968–1978* (London: Faber, 1980), 36–37.

35. Heaney, ed., *The Essential Wordsworth,* 3.

36. See John Jones, *The Egotistical Sublime: A History of Wordsworth's Imagination* (London: Chatto and Windus, 1964), 154–92.

"Beauty, Resonance, Integrity": Creative Rereadings of Wordsworth in Twentieth-Century American Poetry

Lisa M. Steinman

In this essay, I want to explore poetic "resonance," using the term in a similar fashion to Wai Chee Dimock, although in my title the word is drawn from a line in "Le Livre Est Sur La Table," the final poem in John Ashbery's 1956 volume, *Some Trees*.[1] In her 1997 article, "A Theory of Resonance," Dimock notes that resonance has a precise definition in acoustics, with stochastic resonance in particular being the way in which "a weak signal is boosted by background noise and becomes newly and complexly audible."[2] Using "weak signals" metaphorically, Dimock asks us to consider the way in which words in a text yield different meanings or signals across time. Ashbery's (and, later, Adrienne Rich's) use of the trope is less technical, calling attention to how resonance has become a loose term employed in discussions of lyric poetry to mark an unclearly defined sense of richness or suggestiveness. I here want to reclaim the term to explore a relationship between poems that involves both reciprocity and authorial agency by way of four texts that embody what might be called creative rereading. The poems I have in mind are—along with the Ashbery poem that provides my title—Wordsworth's "The Solitary Reaper" (1805), Wallace Stevens's "The Idea of Order at Key West" (1934), and Rich's "Blood-Sister" (1973).

There are obvious echoes of the earlier poems in the later: the series could be called "women, usually singing, by real or metaphorical seas." That is, most simply, Wordsworth's Scottish reaper who sings in a vale "overflowing" with sound is compared with (and found superior to) a nightingale, whose voice offers respite from the desert, and then with a cuckoo "[b]reaking the silence of the seas / Among the farthest Hebrides" (ll. 15–16). Stevens's singer sings "beyond the genius of the sea," her voice positioned "among / The meaningless plungings of water and the wind" (ll. 1, 29–30);[3] Ashbery's woman walks in a less localized landscape but is associated with the placement of "a bird-house / Against the blue sea," and a "line-drawing / Of a woman, in the shadow of the sea" (ll. 13–14, 18–19). Rich, finally, turns from "[s]horing up the ocean" (l. 1) to the desert, one that in various ways recalls Wordsworth's "Arabian sands" (l. 12), but without Wordsworth's oasis of overheard (or, as Rich would have it, appropriated) sound.

Typically, readers of "The Solitary Reaper" note Wordsworth's investment in his female figure, who allows him to align poetry with work and, in particular, with rural, humble, physical labor. The most straightforward reading of this short, four-stanza, ballad-like poem, which appeared in the second volume of the 1807 *Poems, in Two Volumes* under the heading "Poems Written during a Tour in Scotland," would regard it as a typical Wordsworthian georgic (some would say pastoral) about the power of song (or poetry). Contemporary readers would be more alert to the tacit political investments of the poem. That is, we know that Wordsworth would not have understood his reaper, from whom he was separated by gender, class, and nationality, as well as by a language barrier; his use of her as a figure for his own vocation (and sense of isolation) is thus open to critical comment.

Indeed, critical comment on the status of the reaper is not solely a twentieth-century phenomenon, although the basis on which the figure is criticized has shifted over time. Francis Jeffrey's 1807 review of *Poems, in Two Volumes* scorned Wordsworth's "low, silly, [and] uninteresting" subjects—a judgment on the lowly status of the people and events represented in the poems that was widely echoed at the time.[4] In a letter of 1807 to Walter Scott, for instance, Anna Seward mentions Wordsworth's manufacturing "of metaphysic importance upon trivial themes,"[5] while on the other side of the Atlantic the reviewer for the *Port Folio*'s March 1809 issue pronounced that Wordsworth had "mistaken silliness for simplicity."[6] Wordsworth provided a critical gloss on the poem that suggests a more self-conscious emphasis not on the "simple" reaper but precisely on the narrator's distance from her (and his own distance from both narrator and reaper);

Wordsworth's note points out the source of the poem in Thomas Wilkinson's manuscript version of *Tours to the British Mountains*, where an entry reads: "Passed a female who was reaping alone: she sung in Erse as she bended over her sickle; the sweetest human voice I ever heard: her strains were tenderly melancholy, and felt delicious, long after they were heard no more."[7]

I will return to "The Solitary Reaper," but first I want to offer a sketch of how three American poets—Stevens, Ashbery, and Rich—over roughly half of the twentieth century offer consecutive rereadings of Wordsworth, giving us a new—perhaps a distinctly transatlantic—Wordsworth, and of how these poets (the later two triangulating their relationship with Wordsworth through Stevens) carry forth a Wordsworthian project in their conversations with Romantic modes of representation and narrative.

Wordsworthian gestures and tropes appear in several of Wallace Stevens's poems. The first part of "The Comedian as the Letter C" (1922), for instance, titled "The World without Imagination," puts Stevens's persona, Crispin, to sea and asks: "Could Crispin stem verboseness in the sea, / The old age of a watery realist, / Triton, dissolved . . . / . . . nothing left of him, / Except in faint, memorial gesturings, / That were like arms and shoulders in the waves" (ll. 37–39, 45–47). This exorcism of Triton, the poem hypothesizes, might leave the demystified poet "some starker, barer" self // In a starker, barer world," in which he confronts "the veritable ding an sich" (ll. 61, 69). This is most obviously the obverse of what Wordsworth was writing a year or so before he composed "The Solitary Reaper," in a poem about being "out of tune" with the spirit of the natural world:

It moves us not. Great God! I'd rather be
A Pagan suckled in a creed outworn;
So might I, standing on this pleasant lea,
Have glimpses that would make me less forlorn;
Have sight of Proteus rising from the sea;
Or hear old Triton blow his wreathed horn.
("The world is too much with us," ll. 9–14)

Stevens, it seems, would rather be post-pagan but is unable entirely to imagine a poetry of the material natural world demythologized. Indeed, by the time Crispin is said to face the world in itself, it has become "the veritable ding an sich"—a typical Stevensian piece of rhetorical legerdemain whereby the real ("a vocable thing" [l. 70]) is mediated by Latinate adjectives and philosophical German phrases before it even appears on the page. The effect, again typically, seems not so much an invocation of the world (in what Paul Fry categorizes as an odic "calling," signifying an impossible desire for language to make present what it invokes) as a representation of desire always-already frustrated.[8]

We know that in 1922, and even more by 1934 during the Depression, the pressures of getting and spending in an increasingly corporate American culture were what Stevens hoped poetry might resist. Rather than the sense of "outworn" belatedness (and the more Fry-like embodiment of odic desire) of Wordsworth's "The world is too much with us," however, Stevens seems to propose a new creed, namely that all creeds are and always have been human fictions—embodiments of human making—and that viewed in this light, imaginative power (the power of poetry, in particular) might be reclaimed. The ways in which I have qualified the stance that underwrites poems like "The Comedian"—"seems to propose" and "might be"—echo Stevens's own consistent qualifications, both within individual poems and throughout his work. For example, Triton returns, lightly, at the beginning of "The Idea of Order at Key West," where Stevens says of the relationship between a singing woman and the world she animates that the "water never formed to mind or voice, / Like a body wholly body, fluttering / Its empty sleeves" (ll. 2–4). If, earlier, Triton dissolves, leaving only "faint, memorial gesturings, / That were like arms and shoulders in the waves," here he has slipped out of costume, or rather become all costume. Wordsworth is after a sense of immanence, but it seems the sleeves of Triton are always-already empty, "outworn," and out of fashion. For Stevens, if one is after the physical world (the ding an sich), by the time one has named what one is after ("wholly body"), it has jumped ship, waving good-bye ("fluttering its empty sleeves"). Both poems ultimately represent an absence, but what is absent in each is not quite the same thing. Stevens, in an early (1906) journal entry, suggested he wished there were still sacred groves, something free of doubt "that day unto day still uttered speech,"[9] but by 1934 when he wrote "The Idea of Order," he courted a voice that was no longer free from doubt.

Stevens's "Idea of Order" is also conspicuously framed, which is to say that we, as readers, are positioned as eavesdroppers, overhearing the speaker's questions to someone named Ramon Fernandez about the relationship between the poem's singing woman and that of which she sings (the ocean), which complicates the issue. The question becomes not simply one of the status of representation, or the impossibility of invoking or giving voice to the world in the poem, but also one of the "the maker's rage to order words of the sea" (l. 52). The ambiguous syntax—turning here on the equivocal "of"—is another common Stevensian rhetorical gesture. At the level of the framed scene—composed by the singing woman—the poem's questions are repeated: are these her words about the sea, her order? "She was," the poem suggests, "the single artificer of the world / In which she sang"; "there never was a world for her / Except the one she sang and, singing, made" (ll. 36–37, 41–42). Yet the poem also leaves open the possibility "that in all her phrases stirred / The grinding water and the gasping wind" (ll. 12–13). More interestingly, after listening, the speaker states that the world is put in order; the lights of the fishing boats in the harbor (not any human speech) "[m]astered the night and portioned out the sea." Implicitly, the natural world is back in tune (to use Wordsworth's trope) or in order (Stevens's), and, while for Stevens the order is human (in the song, the poem, the lights, the speaker's perception), what is ordered may, the poem suggests, be "of" (that is, belong to) the world. As Douglas Mao has noted, many of the poems that were published with "Idea of Order" "use music as a figure for an ordering that is also an embodying."[10]

At the same time, in "The Idea of Order at Key West" the questions raised about those represented as makers—the singing woman and the poetic speaker—are deliberately left unanswered: what has the woman to do with the ocean? the speaker to do with the woman, or the reader with the speaker? The poem insists, "Whose spirit is this? we said, because we knew / It was the spirit that we sought and knew / That we should ask this often as she sang" (ll. 18–20). This is in part Stevens reopening and emphasizing the process of imagination and of giving voice (by insisting on the act of questioning—the act of the mind). Still, we too—as readers—find ourselves tracing the frames, and asking, "Whose spirit is this?"

I have already suggested, both explicitly and tacitly, that one answer is: Wordsworth's. Of course, the quest for spirit, however refigured, makes Stevens more generally a late Romantic, and—stylistically—his poetics of process seem more sensibly affiliated with Keats or Shelley (whom he mentions in poems like "Owl's Clover" and clearly alludes to in poems like "Notes Toward a Supreme Fiction") than with Wordsworth (whom he does not seriously mention, unless one grants my suggestion that Wordsworth's poems surface in the tropes—glimpses of Triton, music, and singing women—and in the insistence that some internal or perceptual shift occurs, even after the singing ends). Moreover, one can certainly offer a reading of Stevens's poem resembling the one sketched above without drawing on the specific Wordsworth poems I have cited.

However, it is more difficult, after 1934, to read "The Solitary Reaper" without Stevens—like Stevens's never-quite-dissolved Triton—putting in an appearance. Let me give two quick examples—one relatively small and local, the other broader—of the reciprocal workings of resonance in these two poems. After Stevens's images of how song orders "words of the sea," Wordsworth's image of a cuckoo breaking "the silence of the seas" takes on a new resonance. At first reading, Wordsworth's comparisons between the reaper's voice and bird voices seem designed simply to emphasize the comfort or respite song (and by implication metered verse) offers and, at the same time, to mark how the foreign reaper's song surpasses songs heard in apparently more exotic settings (Arabia, the farthest Hebrides), while making the reaper herself more exotic or "other" than a farm laborer would have seemed to most of Wordsworth's contemporary readers. After reading Stevens, however, the way in which song is set against "the silence of the seas" in Wordsworth's poem figures the difference between organized sound—ordered words—and (to use Stevens's image) "meaningless plungings of water." After all, the seas do not break on the shores of the Hebrides without sound. The silence of Wordsworth's seas is that of sound irrecoverably separate from human meaning, that is, the image is of the seas' sound as mere noise, not of the total absence of acoustic activity. We are told that Stevens's singer is one who "measure[s]" (l. 35). This, coupled with the blank verse of "The Idea of Order," allows us to hear how the way poetic lines order or measure time is part of the effect Wordsworth claims for *his* reaper's overheard song. The association between affective or conceptual orders and rhythmic patterning is in interesting juxtaposition with the speaker's later claim: she "sang / As if her song could have no ending." Given the distinction between measured sound (which is humanly meaningful) and mere noise (like that of the sea, tantamount to silence), we attend to the hypothetical status of the song's eternal quality: it only appears or feels to the speaker "as if" it is unending.

One could argue that these are idiosyncratic associations, of course, which place undue weight on one word ("silence"). Yet the associations make sense of a larger feature of Wordsworth's poem, also brought into focus by its relationship with Stevens's poem—namely the way Wordsworth's apparently simple poem is also framed. For all that it seems first a simple portrait, on closer inspection, "The Solitary Reaper" says very little about the woman cutting and binding grain. In fact, that she is alone, "singing at her work, / And o'er the sickle bending" (ll. 27–28), is all we know about her. Finally, as in Stevens's "Idea of Order," Wordsworth's poem is composed of the speaker's questions, which are deliberately left open: if the speaker knew the theme, not only would the focus of the poem—the uncanny effect of being moved by something "vocable," something all ordered sound but with no discernible theme—shift, but fully a quarter of the poem would simply disappear, in that one full stanza is (again on close reading) composed of questions. When the poem emphasizes that the speaker imagines the song "as if" unending, it similarly focuses our attention on how the scene unleashes the *speaker's* reverie. That is, the poem focuses on the speaker's act of hypothesizing.

Post-Stevens, in other words, "The Solitary Reaper" is no longer a portrait (or still life), framed like the Wordsworth poems that appear on sugar packets in the tea rooms around Grasmere, but rather a poem that enacts how the speaker's imagination is set in motion when confronted by a scene he can neither ignore nor understand. The poem's unfolding structure calls our attention to the scene and to our distance, like the speaker's, from it ("Behold" . . . "Stop here, or gently pass" . . . "listen!"); it moves to negative comparisons ("*No* nightingale" . . . "A voice so thrilling *ne'er* was heard") that exoticize—that is, distance us from—the scene, gesture toward the difference between the world without imagination and the creations of the ordering imagination—song as opposed to the silence of seas—and ultimately underline the importance of imaginative, linguistic activity—making metaphors, for example, or transforming the Wilkinson tour book entry that Wordsworth cited as his source into the poem we are reading. Indeed, Wordsworth's note, published with the poem, claims as inspiration not Wilkinson's eye for the scene but his "beautiful *sentence*" (my emphasis). Such a view of "The Solitary Reaper" organizes Wordsworth's poetic world for us. That is, a simple poem about a reaper might more properly end after the fourth line ("Stop here, or gently pass"), rather than ranging from Arabia to the Hebrides to antique battles and "far-off things" (l. 19) to more quotidian "sorrow, loss, or pain" (l. 23), as the speaker is unleashed to his own speculations. Thus, we might wonder both *whose* music the speaker bears in his heart as he leaves at the end . . . and whose music we hear.

I have been leaving open the possibility that the above resonance with Stevens's poem means that part of the music I have just described is Stevensian, that reading "The Solitary Reaper" as a "poem of the act of the mind" (as Stevens puts it in "Of Modern Poetry") is a self-consciously anachronistic reading, validated by something like Dimock's theory of resonance. Yet, while more modern judgments query whether Wordsworth's choice of the reaper as his subject is a matter of identifying and humanizing or appropriating and making other, Wordsworth himself made clear to his contemporary readers that he is ventriloquizing not the reaper but Wilkinson's response to her. In short, although straightforward modern responses to the lowly status of the singer and to the poet-figure in the poem stress how the singer is "joyously self-sufficient in her own power of song,"[11] the poem may be, and may always have been, more about how the singer, like her song, resists the viewer's—Wilkinson's, as much as Wordsworth's—gaze, and about the speaker's uncertain relationship to his subject. In fact, William Hazlitt, reviewing *The Excursion*, early on noted Wordsworth's preoccupation with "the workings of . . . mind."[12] Stevens may let us hear Wordsworth, but it is not clear that Stevens's Wordsworth is simply like the ocean in "The Idea of Order at Key West": "there never was a world for her / Except the one she sang and, singing, made." These lines suggest that representations or conceptualizations of the world outside the self never give us the world itself. I am suggesting, on the contrary, that Stevens's Wordsworth does give us something of the historical Wordsworth; it is *not* the case that "there never was a [Wordsworth] . . . [e]xcept the one [Stevens] sang and, singing, made."

I began this rereading of Wordsworth's poem by noting that whether or not Stevens consciously engaged his predecessor's poem, his poem resonates with Wordsworth's, and I employed "resonance" in much the way Dimock uses the term: a weak signal in Wordsworth's poem is boosted by the background "noise" of Stevens's poem. However, Dimock's argument with historicism is not interested in textual meanings that (like acoustic signals) are "present," or even weakly present, in the way suggested by Bill Brown's image of the "material unconscious." Brown's "material unconscious" concerns "literature's repository of disparate and fragmentary, unevenly developed, even contradictory images of the material everyday, demonstrat[ing] the pressure that such materiality . . . exerts on literary texts."[13] Dimock's project similarly involves mining unevenly developed images lodged in literary texts, but it is not as clearly concerned with materiality. Moreover, she wants to claim the background noise that makes her metaphorical weak signals audible as noise, not as ordered sound. That is, my understanding of how Stevens allows us to hear Wordsworth's poem involves more intentionality on Stevens's part than Dimock's model would countenance. Nor would her model accommodate my claim that Stevens offers us a historically plausible reading of Wordsworth's poem since, for Dimock, weak signals are not so much made audible as imaginatively or culturally constructed. She is concerned primarily with eschewing synchronic models and embracing the ways in which texts travel and change in time, with (as she says) no set integrity. Like Dimock, I am interested in how texts travel, but I want to suggest that our critical interest in "integrity" and "resonance," like Stevens's (and Ashbery's and Rich's), can be seen as an integral part of Wordsworth's legacy—an inquiry about the aural, representational, and narrative qualities of the lyric.

This is to propose, among other things, that the pairing of Stevens's and Wordsworth's poems makes audible what is both in Wordsworth's poem and in Stevens's. That is, it is not simply that Stevens reopens Wordsworth's poem for us but that Wordsworth's poem also—like a weak signal, newly audible—informs Stevens's in ways that go beyond the flickering quasi-presence of Triton, the unrecoverable pretext of musical women, or the inward shift in the speakers at the end of the poems. Part of the "background noise" that makes Wordsworth's legacy audible in Stevens's poem is the new interest in cultural and historicist criticism. To illustrate, I want draw on James Longenbach's sensitive reading of "The Idea of Order at Key West," which emphasizes the poem's commitment to ambiguity—its opening, odic "endlessly deferred and contingent sense of the relationship between . . . the self, voice, poetry, and the otherness of the real world"—while also investigating what informs and what is at stake in the commitment to ambiguity.[14] The universalizing answer is: "the human imagination" or, perhaps, "poetic ambition." To cite Harold Bloom, the poem affirms "a transcendental poetic spirit yet cannot locate it."[15] As Longenbach explains, however, the *weight* of not being able to locate the spirit the poem wants to affirm is itself historically locatable.

Without doing full justice to Longenbach's intricate presentation of various strands of Stevens's thought and history, I want to cite three of the moments he finds relevant. First, there is the fact that Stevens wrote the poem shortly after a 1934 visit to Key West, where the lights he saw in that harbor ("[m]astering and portioning out") were not on fishing boats but on twenty-nine U.S. battleships sent by President Roosevelt to Cuban waters to make the American presence visible following the army takeover led by Fulgencio Batista. Stevens's imagined, provisional mastery and ordering are tacitly set against more physical and political impositions of order. Second, despite Stevens's well-known insistence that he simply made up the names Ramon and Fernandez (*Letters of Wallace Stevens,* 798), Longenbach reminds us that Fernandez's work was familiar to Stevens from the *Nouvelle Revue Française,* the *Partisan Review,* and the *Criterion,* in whose pages Stevens was following not only Fernandez's conversion from a sympathy with fascism to an affirmation of the struggle of the proletariat, but also the arguments and positions of others prone to "theorising, which tends to make one highly susceptible to original 'solutions.'"[16] Again, these are ideas of order—fascist, Marxist, imperialist—that did not allow their devotees to rest with ambiguity, foils to Stevens's disorderly "idea" of perceptual and imaginative orderings.

But it is a third moment that I find most interesting here. In a 1935 letter to Ronald Lane Latimer about "ideas of order," Stevens identifies his relating of worldly to poetic orders as "perhaps another version of pastoral," by which he seems to mean that he could be taken as proposing a simplified codification or idealistic representation of poetry's "status." In the same letter, Stevens comments on his rising interest in "passionate disorder," which he opposes to his interest in pastoral order, indicating that his attraction to both order and disorder shows how one "moves in many directions at once" (*Letters of Wallace Stevens,* 300). The reference to "passionate disorder," like the reference to versions of pastoral, draws on Stevens's reading. Stevens's "version of pastoral" alludes to William Empson's 1935 *Some Versions of Pastoral,* where Empson suggests that good proletarian art "is usually Covert Pastoral,"[17] containing a dream of a simpler life; this Empson regards as a potentially useful form of "romanticism" since it serves to criticize actual social conditions, inspiring change in the world. As Stevens tells Latimer, his thoughts about "passionate disorder" come also from a somewhat different discussion of Romanticism—namely, a critique of late Romantic poetry in a review by Anne Treneer published in the *Times Literary Supplement* that makes specific reference to the Wordsworthian "egotistical sublime." Stevens copied into his notebook the opposition Treneer draws between presenting the real human world's "passionate disorder" and presenting the more limited "pursuit of an ideal simplicity of experience," a pastoral ideal she associates with the Romantic creation of a wholly subjective world—an ideal Stevens feared might seem to characterize his "rage for order" in "The Idea of Order at Key West."[18]

To make this rather long story shorter: as he was writing "The Idea of Order at Key West," Stevens knew his commitment to imaginative ordering could be read as another form of pastoral, too removed from disorderly reality. He had just encountered three characterizations of what could be called pastoral. The first two are traced in Ramon Fernandez's conversion from fascist to Marxist ideas of order (the former too rigidly ordered and too inhumanly theoretical according to Fernandez's account in *The Partisan Review;* the latter, in Empson's account of proletarian literature, a form of "Covert Pastoral," which is to say another, if potentially more useful, oversimplification). The third analysis of pastoral, from the *TLS,* also criticized idealized worlds when pursued at the expense of disorderly, "troublesome humanity." Stevens's comments to Latimer suggest his quandary. He notes that he is attracted to (and, moving in many directions at once, exhibits) "passionate disorder," but concludes that system "of some sort is inescapable," whether "political," "military," or "something else" (*Letters of Wallace Stevens,* 300). Given that both Empson and Treneer equate pastoral or idealized order with Romanticism (Treneer, specifically with Wordsworth), the suggestion that the spirit of Wordsworth's "The Solitary Reaper" informs "The Idea of Order at Key West" is far from anachronistic. I have already noted that "The Solitary Reaper" may be read not as a pastoral pursuit of an ideal simplicity or as a proletarian portrait (in Empson's sense, "Covert Pastoral") but as a portrait of "the workings of . . . mind" (*Complete Works of William Hazlitt,* 19:10)—that is, of the mind of the questioning speaker trying to understand a recalcitrant world, in the same way that Stevens's speaker in "The Idea of Order at Key West" orders but then also disorders and reorders the world. Both poems feature the problematic nature of the relationship between speakers and that of which they speak or by which they are moved. In the *TLS,* Treneer recognizes that poets as such cannot escape seeing things in their own minds. For Stevens, what is at stake is how to balance the danger of solipsism (in Depression America, a defect indeed) with the danger of seeking overly rigid solutions (which may be why a second viewer, and in particular Ramon Fernandez with his weakness for grand solutions, appears at the end of "The Idea of Order at Key West"). There were, then, local, political pressures that animated and complicated Stevens's ideas about order. However, Stevens also understood that his poetic gestures were Wordsworthian and that his commitment to the ambiguity of the relationship between speakers and subjects, a relationship that enabled poetry, was open to the same criticisms leveled against Wordsworth.

Moreover, if the disorderly order Stevens proposes is at odds with itself in the poem, this is also widely said to be true of Wordsworth by the late 1790s. Stevens, one hastens to add, almost certainly was not a new historicist or a cultural critic before his time, as he read or rethought Wordsworth's gestures. But his creative reading of Wordsworth—resulting in the ways in which "The Solitary Reaper" resonates in "The Idea of Order at Key West," the ways in which a Wordsworthian sublime is skeptically tested against a recalcitrant, sometimes brutal world—takes place on terms set by the earlier poet. To cite Longenbach again:

> With an innate Emersonian diffidence . . . Stevens approached a disordered world and answered it as a poet—more precisely, as a poet who always felt somewhat insecure commenting on political situations he knew less well than he knew poetry. But Stevens also distrusted the poetry he knew, and "The Idea of Order" does not affirm the sublime power of "Tintern Abbey"

> . . . precisely because its author was skeptical of the ideas of order such power may appear to provide. (*Wallace Stevens*, 161)

Longenbach is not arguing that Stevens had "Tintern Abbey" in mind; he is distinguishing his view of historical content in poetry from that of Marjorie Levinson in her reading of "Tintern Abbey." However, "Tintern Abbey" comes to mind precisely because its author, with and without Levinson's new historicist critique, frames the ways in which we—and Stevens—question the efficacy or availability of a "transcendental poetic spirit" (or of the location of that spirit in the figure of human music).[19] That such questions and the blank verse in which they are measured come to Stevens (and to some of us) also through Emerson's readings of Wordsworth[20] does not make them less of a Wordsworthian legacy.

Similarly, I have borrowed from—even as I have argued with—Dimock in using the concepts of "resonance" and "integrity." But the terms, more generally, are part of a late Romantic and specifically post-Wordsworthian framing of approaches to lyric poetry. "Resonance" means "re-sounding" or "reinforcing sound" (and as such is the aural equivalent of Stevens's "mimic motions" in "The Idea of Order"). Resonance is a corollary of music—as a trope and as an awareness of the aural qualities of poetry. John Ashbery's "Le Livre Est Sur La Table" draws on this understanding of lyricism when it opens with the lines: "All beauty, resonance, integrity, / Exist by deprivation or logic / Of strange position." The poem next imagines a woman who knows all "that she does not know," while a second section presents the figure of a young man placing a birdhouse against the sea and then leaving; the poem concludes with a series of questions about whether there are "communications on the shore," or whether all "secrets vanish" with the disappearance of the woman.

The poem itself is resonant (in the general sense of the word) of Wordsworth's solitary reaper, although it also echoes Wallace Stevens's figure of a woman singing by the sea in "The Idea of Order at Key West." Certainly, Ashbery draws on Wordsworth's nightingale and cuckoo breaking "the silence of the seas." As his title suggests, the book Ashbery puts on our table is in part a volume of Wordsworth's poems but translated, with a new grammar—that of mid-twentieth-century American poetry.

Actually, Ashbery's book is not only Wordsworth's. It would

also be a reference to a French grammar for someone born in 1927, schooled in the United States, and living in France by the time *Some Trees* was published. Generations of Americans learned French prepositions by chanting about books on, over, near, and under tables, just as they learned how to form the possessive by asking, "Où est la plume de ma tante?" Ashbery's logic of strange position, then, becomes almost a joke like the one in Woody Allen's story about a man, granted a wish by a genie, who asks to be transported into the world of a foreign book and finds himself not in something like *Madame Bovary* but rather in a French grammar. On one reading, then, "Le Livre Est Sur La Table" is a self-conscious metadiscourse on poetry, a sampler of the tricks of the lyric poet designed not to move us but to unmask how language moves us to construct narratives and to flesh out lyric gestures. The portrait of a late reaper or Stevensian singer on closer inspection is part of an instruction manual on how to see what desire makes of absence (or "deprivation") in a world that, among other things, had become even more deeply skeptical (both philosophically and practically) of what language can invoke:

> . . . This being so,
> We can only imagine a world in which a woman
> Walks and wears her hair and knows
> All that she does not know. Yet we know
>
> What her breasts are. And we give fullness
> To the dream. The table supports the book,
> The plume leaps in the hand. But what
>
> Dismal scene is this? the old man pouting
> At a black cloud, the woman gone
> Into the house, from which the wailing starts?

Ashbery's genius lies in the way in which his demystification nonetheless *does* move readers. The final sketch of melancholy, for example, comes briefly alive: "dismal," "old," "pouting," "black," and "wailing" so set the scene that it is not difficult to read "the woman gone" (with that abrupt enjambment) as elegy, rather than (equally plausibly) as the poem's winking acknowledgment that it is showing us that the uncanny effects—the spirit—of Wordsworth's and even Stevens's poems is done with smoke and mirrors, that is, with rhetorical devices (the second section of "Le Livre Est Sur La Table" describes a—or the—woman as a "line-drawing," made of poet's lines) rendered meaningful by our familiarity with poems like those of Wordsworth and Stevens. Even Ashbery's use of the language of logical or narrative continuity across stanza breaks—"This being so," "Yet," "And," "But"—to stitch together otherwise apparently discontinuous stanzas simultaneously presents a compelling narrative (ending with the elegiac "dismal scene" of "the old man pouting" and "the woman gone") and an unmasking of the literal and conceptual syntaxes that compel us.

Ashbery's late comments on poetics suggest that he is most interested in representing the vagaries and discontinuities of contemporary consciousness, a consciousness that represents itself in languages drawn from multiple discourses—Romantic poets and popular culture (or novels and grammar books), for example. Yet in such a representation, a Romantic construction of poetry reemerges. We find, as Motlu Blasing has suggested in her pairing of Wordsworth and Ashbery, a Wordsworthian representation of the speaker's act of the mind (if with less clarity about what, if anything, is at stake in that act).[21]

As with the resonance between Stevens and Wordsworth, there is a reciprocity between the poems of Ashbery, Wordsworth, and Stevens. Wordsworth insists that some presence with which to interact—like that of Triton—is needed to move us, otherwise nature remains unresonant ("It moves us not"). Yet, after reading Stevens's and Ashbery's poems, we see that Wordsworth's insistence marks desire, not assuredness, and that the last quatrain of "The world is too much with us," like all but the first quatrain of "The Solitary Reaper," is allowed precisely because of a sense of "deprivation." In this vein, too, the concluding section of Ashbery's "Le Livre Est Sur La Table" raises the possibility that this poem about resonance is still in quest of poetic resonance and that Ashbery, skeptical as he may be about Wordsworthian hauntings, is still haunted by them or by *their* absence.

The end of "Some Trees," the title poem of the volume in which "Le Livre" first appeared, begins with a natural scene—trees that "are amazing"—and raises the possibility that "their merely being there / Means something" (ll. 1, 10–11). The poem then retracts such speculation, moves (albeit with Ashbery's typical ambiguity) to a Stevensian praise of mental motion and the doubt that gives rise to such motion, but ends with the following couplet: "Our days put on such reticence / These accents seem their own defense" (ll. 19–20). Whether the "accents" are the poem's inner voices, the trees against the snow, or the metricality with which the couplet brings the poem to a sense of closure, the claim is that given the silence of everyday life, any "accent" is, at least, a good in itself, if not a sign or revelation of anything more. A similar commitment to utterance and inner life seems to reappear at the end of "Le Livre": "Are there / Collisions, communications on the shore / Or did all secrets vanish when / The woman left?" (ll. 20–23). Typically difficult, the lines may simply push further the demystification of Wordsworthian or Stevensian senses of some spirit (natural or natural supernatural). The secret, in short, would be that there never was a secret. Yet, the very density of the passage presents readers with the sense that something is at issue, and that this is a rhetorical question the poem desires to answer by reaffirming communication—poetic speech, meaningful sound—with or prompted by the unknown. "The Idea of Order at Key West" concludes with an image of ordering words "of ourselves . . . / In ghostlier demarcations, keener sounds" (ll. 54–55). In Ashbery, the seductions of sound remain, although the poetic self and the poet's project become more and more attenuated. At the same time, just as the earlier poets' tropes are mimicked by and haunt "Le Livre Est Sur La Table," so too Ashbery's poem reciprocally illuminates Stevens's "ghostlier demarcations, keener sounds," among other things suggesting how robust Stevens's ghost might be.

The resonance set up by Ashbery's and Stevens's repetitions of Wordsworth's haunting lyric is recast yet again in Adrienne Rich's "Blood-Sister" (1973), which reimagines women but has them talking for themselves, announcing that "the ocean has undergone a tracheotomy / and *lost* its resonance" (ll. 17–18; my emphasis). "Blood-Sister," originally published in *13th Moon*, a feminist poetry journal, has an obvious political bone to pick with the ways in which women have served as vehicles for inspiration or objects for contemplation. Although Rich's view of how the waves become silent, and of what it means to move inland, tries to refigure the tropes in all three earlier poems, it is difficult finally not to read her poem as a response to the concluding two questions posed in "Le Livre Est Sur La Table": "Is the bird mentioned / In the waves' minutes [*No, the waves will have nothing more to say to future poets*], or did the land advance? [*It did*]" (ll. 23–24).

Rich's poem opens by staking a claim to autobiography—the title's reference to biological kinship is followed by a dedication, "For Cynthia," who is further identified as "my sister" in the general dedication to Rich's mother and sister that opens the volume of poems in which "Blood-Sister" appeared in 1975. The first two stanzas, though free verse, are syntactically and narratively decorous, with roughly alternating tetrameter and trimeter lines describing childhood visits to the ocean on summer holidays in the 1940s. The speaker and sister are said to have been dressed in identical outfits "not to show the soot. Like dolls / we sat with our dolls" (ll. 11–12). Plain-spoken, anecdotal, the representation of girls by the sea also contains lightly threatening images of industry (trains, sludge) and even more coded images of what Eisenhower called the military-industrial complex (there are "shells" and coin-like "sand dollars" [ll. 6, 8]). The more serious turn of the poem against an elegiac rendering of the childhood scene comes in the thirteenth line, set apart from the rest: "When did we begin to dress ourselves?" The poem thereafter rejects the objectification of female subjects (no dolls, after all, to be posed) and traditional tropes of womanhood, as well as rejecting formal inheritances, with both stanzaic and sentence structure abandoned in the remainder of the poem.

Rich includes only one partial end rhyme, as the speaker-self describes an old sweater she has worn "*since* / the ocean has undergone a tracheotomy / and lost its *resonance*" (ll. 16–18; my emphasis). In one sense, the poem here issues a declaration of independence. Ultimately, the poem discards the seductive aural feature of rhyme, underlining the thematic rejection of a feminine self dressed by others or for others, presumably including (to follow Rich's logic) the objectified singing women of Stevens and Wordsworth or even the ironic, fleshed-out line drawing of Ashbery. The sister comes to wear, in contrast to the tidy dresses of her youth, the colors of "Navaho turquoise and sand" (l. 20); this allows the poem to reclaim untidiness—a lack of conventional domesticity—and a lack of transparency as beauty: "light flashes off unwashed sheetglass / you are more beautiful than you have ever been" (ll. 24–25). This is most obviously a form of passionate disorder, a gendered response to Stevens's idea of order, as the poem further aligns ice with repressive political orders ("a fist of law and order" [l. 28]), the imagination with fire ("your imagination burns" [l. 29]), ending with an imagined future in which "the ocean may be closed for good" and the woman "will turn / to the desert / where survival / takes naked and fiery forms" (ll. 32–36). Rich's ocean is neither vocable nor invocable; it has no voice or sound. By the mid-1970s in America, the silence of the seas has increased with what we might call Rich's resonant image of the ocean as polluted both literally and metaphorically. Indeed, for Rich, who in this period was writing of and against the "failure of patriarchal politics and patriarchal civilisation," the war, the industrial waste, and the objectification of women culturally and literarily, the inherited sounds and tropes and forms of poetry would be all of a piece.[22] Against this conglomerate, Rich's foreword to the volume that contained "Blood-Sister" proposes touching "the living who share [an] animal passion for existence" (*Poems*, xvi).

Most obviously, Rich proclaims that Ashbery's "secrets"—or the music we bear in our hearts (to use Wordsworth's formulation) when we read poems like the "Solitary Reaper"—are not necessarily the communications on the shore Wordsworth might once have imagined. Both modern American writers suggest Wordsworth's poem is asking the wrong questions. For Ashbery, the apparent integrity, beauty, and resonance of Wordsworth's song are like odic absence ("deprivation") or perhaps a trick of grammar (that "logic" of "strange position"); for Rich, the ocean loses its ability to speak entirely, undergoing a tracheotomy and ultimately, as Rich's poem imagines it, being "closed for good" without the woman as the figure or vessel for that which is alluring but unknown.

To quote Stevens (the mediating voice for both Rich and Ashbery): the ocean's "mimic motion // Made constant cry, / caused constantly . . . a cry . . . / Whose spirit is this? we said" (ll. 2, 4–5, 18). For Stevens, mimic motion or repeated gestures evoke yet more repetitions; the voicings of poetry are similarly both cause and effect. In this vein, Rich's final trope—the naked and fiery forms—most obviously serves as a figure for not accepting and, more important, not reinscribing the ways in which women have been clad or represented. While "naked forms" recalls Stevens's "starker, barer self" in a demythologized world, a fiery form is presumably one without a fixed shape, constantly undoing or consuming what is fixed. In this sense, then, Rich's rejection of the trope of women as an occasion for male verse nonetheless mimics both Wordsworth and Stevens in its emphasis on the activity of creating rather than on what is created. In yet another way, too, her mid-1970s critique of representation can be seen as an unwitting repetition of covert pastoral. That is, with the references to Navahos, sand, and desert, Rich has imagined a simpler, superior existence by appeal to the Native American culture of the American Southwest (a pattern reinforced by the title's secondary play on the Native American ritual of becoming blood brothers, widely circulated through popular culture in the United States). Put bluntly: Rich's Navahos are as pastoral, and as objectified, as Wordsworth's highlander or Stevens's singer. The refusal to serve as a pretext for song, the attempt to foreclose resonance at the level of trope and narrative, nonetheless ends in a resonant gesture. Even if one understands the final image (the fiery forms) as an attempt to refuse all form, the voice of the poem remains audible as a poetic voice both through its repetition of Wordsworth's and Stevens's and Ashbery's increasingly guarded gestures toward what is unimageable or ineffable and, more broadly, through its antagonistic negotiations with Wordsworth and his American heirs.

The uneven lineation of Rich's final five lines barely conceals an underlying iambic (and, in "takes naked and fiery forms," trimeter). Presumably, Rich would hear as appropriation and patriarchy the language and tenor of Wordsworth's final lines—"And, as I *mounted* up the hill, / The music in my heart I *bore*, / Long after it was heard no more" (ll. 30–32; my emphasis)—though she probably did not know the even more appropriative 1807 version of the fifth line of the final stanza of "The Solitary Reaper"—"I listen'd till I had my fill" (*Poems, in Two Volumes*, 185; altered in later editions to "I listened, motionless and still"). Yet listen to the pure sound with which Rich's poem concludes: "when summer comes the ocean may," in perfectly regular iambics, opens the poem's final section. The final line of the poem—"takes naked and fiery forms"—is more irregular but is still within the metrical contract of ballad meter. The metrical echoes of Wordsworth, coupled with the falling rhythm, bring the poem to closure, despite the fact that the image of "naked and fiery forms" suggests a protean energy that resists closure. Whose music does Rich bear in her heart, "whate'er the theme"? As in Ashbery's somewhat different interrogations of his poetic heritage, it is as if no attempt to counter the traditional features of lyric poetry—whether tropes, thematic concerns, aural patterning, philosophical or critical presuppositions—can succeed without reinscribing at least some of these same features: after all, how else to mark what the conversation is about, except by repeating the terms of the argument? Moreover, as with Stevens's solitary singer, Rich's sisterhood of women who refuse to pose as poetic models returns us to Wordsworth's poem, which (as I've already argued) self-consciously acknowledges (even as it maintains for the purposes of his song) its distance from the female subject. "Stop here, or gently pass!" is already a warning against something like the very kind of transgression Rich's poem protests against.

However, what interests me most is less the thematic arguments about figures of women than the figure of song or resonance (and the "mimic motion" or repetition) used by all three American poets in their self-conscious explorations of the limits of lyric poetry, and how the terms used in these poems are already set by Wordsworth—terms that persist, if with salient differences, in the twentieth-century American lyric for reasons I have tried to sketch in both poetic and cultural contexts. This is neither influence (in the old-fashioned or in the Bloomian sense) nor purely intertextuality (although culturally circulating constructions of the literary certainly are involved). Nor is it quite Dimock's "resonance," although that term comes closest to capturing the ways in which the American poets hear and recirculate images of and questions about what kind of work poetry does, as well as about what makes linguistic creations count as poems.

If the reciprocal relationships I have traced among Wordsworth's, Stevens's, Ashbery's, and Rich's "Solitary Reapers" are not arbitrary, neither do they define anything like Wordsworth's chain of poets "each with each / Connected in a mighty scheme of truth" (*The Prelude* [1805], 12:301–2), which proposes an unchanging structure set either by history or by a transcendental ideal. Indeed, these relationships are not even captured by Eliot's image in "Tradition and the Individual Talent" of a canon that is retrospectively reconfigured when the shape of literary culture is refashioned by ensuing generations. Among other things, Eliot has in mind a single—and singular—series of poets and poems, while the connections I am discussing are only some among many possible kinds of poetic legacies. Certainly, if we are to imagine a chain formed by the poems treated here, it is one that appears less and less to constitute a "mighty scheme of truth" and one in which the individual links appear to have less and less obvious integrity (to use Ashbery's image). Acoustic waves—resonance, or re-sounding (in both the acoustic and the nautical sense)—seem a more appropriate figure for the articulations I have been characterizing, in which repetition becomes reverberation. Finally, to think in terms of poetic resonance is to acknowledge conversations between poetic generations that are ongoing—that have integrity—but are also at the same time critically astute and fluid.

Notes

1. John Ashbery, *Some Trees* (New York: Ecco, 1956).

2. Wai Chee Dimock, "A Theory of Resonance," *PMLA* 112 (1997): 1063.

3. All references to Stevens's poems are to *The Collected Poems of Wallace Stevens* (New York: Knopf, 1955).

4. *Romantic Bards and British Reviewers,* ed. John O. Hayden (Lincoln: University of Nebraska Press, 1976), 15.

5. Cited in Patrick Cruttwell, "Wordsworth, the Public, and the People," *Sewanee Review* 64 (1956): 71.

6. Lewis Leary, "Wordsworth in America: Addenda," *MLN* 58 (May 1943): 393.

7. *Poems, in Two Volumes, and Other Poems, 1800–1807,* ed. Jared Curtis (Ithaca: Cornell University Press, 1983), 415.

8. See Paul H. Fry, *The Poet's Calling in the English Ode* (New Haven: Yale University Press, 1980).

9. *Letters of Wallace Stevens,* ed. Holly Stevens (New York: Knopf, 1972), 86.

10. Douglas Mao, *Solid Objects: Modernism and the Test of Production* (Princeton: Princeton University Press, 1998), 218.

11. Stephen Gill, *William Wordsworth: A Life* (Oxford: Clarendon Press, 1989), 246.

12. *Complete Works of William Hazlitt,* ed. P. P. Howe (London: J. M. Dent, 1930–34), 19:10.

13. Bill Brown, *The Material Unconscious: American Amusement, Stephen Crane, and the Economics of Play* (Cambridge, MA: Harvard University Press, 1996), 4.

14. James Longenbach, *Wallace Stevens: The Plain Sense of Things* (New York: Oxford University Press, 1991), 158.

15. Harold Bloom, *Wallace Stevens: The Poems of Our Climate* (Ithaca: Cornell University Press, 1977), 104.

16. Ramon Fernandez, "I Came Near Being a Fascist," *Partisan Review* 1 (1934): 19.

17. William Empson, *English Pastoral Poetry* [first printed in the U.K. as *Some Versions of Pastoral*] (New York: Norton, 1938), 6.

18. *Sur Plusieurs Beaux Sujects: Wallace Stevens's Commonplace Book,* ed. Milton J. Bates (Stanford: Stanford University Press; San Marino: Huntington Library,

1989), 45–47. See Longenbach, *Wallace Stevens,* 164.

19. See John Hollander, in *Wallace Stevens: A Celebration,* ed. Frank Dogget and Robert Buttel (Princeton: Princeton University Press, 1980), 236.

20. See Barbara L. Packer, *Emerson's Fall: A New Interpretation of the Major Essays* (New York: Continuum 1982), 105–12, and Lisa M. Steinman, *Masters of Repetition: Poetry, Culture, and Work in Thomson, Wordsworth, Shelley, and Emerson* (New York: St. Martin's Press, 1998), 173–74.

21. See Motlu Konuk Blasing, *Politics and Form in Postmodern Poetry: O'Hara, Bishop, Ashbery, and Merrill* (Cambridge: Cambridge University Press, 1995).

22. Adrienne Rich, *Poems: Selected and New, 1950–1974* (New York: Norton, 1975), xv.

Coleridge, Ted Hughes, and Sylvia Plath:
Mythology and Identity

John Beer

At first sight, Ted Hughes might not seem to be a writer who would find Coleridge's work appealing. However, when *Winter Pollen,* a collection of his prose pieces, appeared in 1994, it included two recently published items displaying his enthusiasm for his Romantic precursor, one of which was titled "Myths, Metres, Rhythms" and the other "The Snake in the Oak." I had been reading Hughes's work at intervals for many years, but it was only when I came to read the *Winter Pollen* essays that I grasped how our interests during the period had run parallel, without ever quite touching one another. Our Cambridge careers overlapped by a few years, but I don't suppose that he ever came across my work and at that time I knew nothing of his promise as a poet or critic. Of course, after he had been in Cambridge for some time, he had the by now well-known experience that convinced him he was wasting his time studying for an English degree. According to one of his friends, he had "sweated late at night over the paper on Dr. Johnson et al.—things he did not want to read":

> One night, very late, very tired, he went to sleep. Saw the door open and someone like himself come in with a fox's head. The visitor went over to his desk, where an unfinished essay was lying, and put his paw on the papers, leaving a bloody mark; then he came over to the bed, looked down at Ted and said, "You're killing us," and went out the door.[1]

Following this, Hughes decided to read archaeology and anthropology for the final part of his course, which gave him a good deal of knowledge about forms of magic and ritual and about the very necessary part played by mythology in the experience of poetry.

In the same years, as it happened, I was coming to a similar interest, though from a quite different angle. I had noticed the extent to which Coleridge's interest in ancient mythology seemed to shape his poetry, and sensed that disparate ideas and images in the supernatural poems that Livingston Lowes had brought together under his own, imagist conception of poetry in *The Road to Xanadu* could be regarded as constituting not meaningless (if wonderful) reverie, as Lowes had thought, but an attempt on the part of Coleridge to shape his own mythological interpretation of human experience. My investigation had little in common with Hughes's later discussion of myth in *Shakespeare and the Goddess of Complete Being* (1992); but we both recognized the vital part that can be played in the development of poetic vision by a mythology that is shared between writer and audience, and we both realized how true this had been in previous centuries. As Hughes was later to write:

> By modern secular definition, myth is something not to be taken seriously. This is so rooted in the popular point of view, and this point of view has so thoroughly naturalized Shakespeare as a secular author, that it is almost impossible for a modern reader to consider the myth of Venus and Adonis, as Shakespeare adapts it, as anything but a picturesque fable, a Renaissance ornamental fantasy, sensationalized to amuse an idle lord. Forcibly desacralizing his poem in this way, we somehow exempt him, by a kind of arbitrary secular warrant, from the world of feeling in which he lived, where at his birth two-thirds of the country (including his mother and most probably his father too) had been worshippers of the cult of the sacrificed god and the Great Goddess, taking the myth absolutely seriously.[2]

Whether or not one accepts his point about the sacrificed god and the Great Goddess, he is clearly right about the value for poets of the superadded significance that was imparted to a work by the possession of a shared mythology. At the same time among Hughes's contemporaries, literary fashion rendered such ideas suspect. The scene was dominated by writers such as Philip Larkin, who deplored the predilection among authors for dipping into the "myth-kitty," and Kingsley Amis, who informed poets that they should "shut up about Orpheus."[3] In one sense, of course, they were perfectly right: the world of mythology, and still more of mythological reference, had so disappeared from ordinary life as to be no longer available to writers who wanted to reflect their contemporary culture, so that it became simply pretentious for them to go on writing as if it were still alive. But it was still legitimate to ask—as I did—what was lost when a meaningful mythology died, and an even more worthwhile, if quixotic, venture was to try and create a mythology fitted to the modern world that might restore to human beings a sense of the sacredness of their own existence, as Blake had done, and as Hughes was now doing.

In Hughes's world, as to a limited extent in Coleridge's, the importance of mythology, given the alienation of the modern poet from society, was twofold. On the one hand, it offered a way of interpreting one's own personal identity, since the poet might see him- or herself as a being set apart from society with a special calling, in which case it was possible to scrutinize all the mythological figures who corresponded to that sense of self. But it was also possible to look at all mythologies for their common elements, and to infer from them the existence of an original, shared mythology that had once been common to all humanity. In Coleridge's time, this had been a plausible goal, given the unscientific nature of philological inquiry; that all languages could be traced to a universal *Ursprache* was a commonly held belief. After Coleridge's time, that possibility more or less disappeared with the advent of the scientific study of etymology and the realization that languages were more numerous and widespread than had been supposed, and that the civilizations in which they had developed were much older than the six thousand years the biblical chronologies had posited. At the end of that particular road lay the monitory figure of George Eliot's Mr. Casaubon, still toiling away at the task of bringing the work of the eighteenth-century mythologists to fruition, oblivious to the fact that the world had moved on. But, of course, Mr. Casaubon's was a deadly presence in a very particular sense, since he had already decided in advance what the result of his researches would be. At the end of the road, he was certain, it would be proved that all mythologies were distortions of the original account of things in the Jewish and Christian sacred writings. Coleridge's interest in myth was informed, by contrast, by a more liberal ideology: his investigations would open out mythologies to reveal an ancient wisdom that would transcend particular religions and perhaps even comprehend the theories and discoveries of recent science.[4] In its boldest form, this dream did not, I think, survive his expedition to Germany (1798–99), though I also doubt whether he ever quite abandoned it. It was in many ways a doomed enterprise, particularly when he relied on the Bible for confirmation, but it was by no means as deathly as that of Eliot's Casaubon, since his mind was so much more open and exploratory. Even now, if one begins to examine ancient mythologies for the correspondences between them, it is striking to see how many links can be divined across a wide range of cultures. An alternative system to Casaubon's attempted to establish that all mythologies could be traced back to sun worship,[5] while even Sir James Fraser's later work, *The Golden Bough,* still offered a "key to all mythologies"—this time to be found in the ancient fertility cults. Coleridge's attempts to sketch out a universal mythology had its own particular attraction, even though its chief fruit was to become abbreviated and scrambled into the dream-work of "Kubla Khan," in which, as I have tried to show in various studies, its main lines of argument were still boldly visible. In composing the poem, he also demonstrated how the trajectory of such a project could become, at its deepest level, bound up with the question of the poet's own personality, so that in the concluding stanza the tyrannical genius of the Tartar emperor presented at the beginning of the poem could turn almost effortlessly into the first-person identity of the poet himself.

Ted Hughes's world was, of course, very different from Coleridge's. I have already indicated, however, Hughes's intense interest in mythology and in its enabling relationship to the poetic enterprise. The general mythology he endeavored to create changed in character over the years, but at its center was a sense of the crucial connection between human beings and nature, evidenced, among other things, in the part played by animals and other living creatures in religious rituals. This preoccupation meant that in addition to writing the brilliant and well-known poems about animals, Hughes was consciously developing his subject matter in order to take in these links. He was also devoting himself to elements in Coleridge's poetry drawn from his immediate observations of animals and related natural organisms.

This was not the only way in which mythology could be enlisted. Hughes was deeply fascinated by Robert Graves's book *The White Goddess: A Historical Grammar of Poetic Myth* (1948), which not only focused on traditional myth and ritual but emphasized the role of the female poetic muse as a necessary participant in poetic creation. As the years went by, this interest broadened and deepened. Hughes's upbringing in nonconformist Yorkshire was marked by what he felt to be restrained, joyless Sundays; this was a world whose heart had been ripped out by the First World War. His sense of the inhumanity of modern, mechanized warfare was deepened when he performed his National Service as a wireless operator and was forced to spend months in a small radio station in Yorkshire where, he said, he had "nothing to do but read and re-read Shakespeare and watch the grass grow."[6] In later life, of course, he would move in quite different circles. Being appointed Poet Laureate involved membership of the royal household and invitations to Balmoral. The extent to which he had previously reflected on the role of the monarchy is unclear, but he was certainly bound to do so now; this also entailed thinking about the mythology and ritual involved.

In later years, his mythological thinking developed on a wide front, which included a reading of Coleridge's poetic work, notably that of his great creative period. He gradually began to arrange the elements he found into a great mythological pattern, and even carried out some research on his own. Any references to plants and animals in Coleridge were immediately seized upon—particularly if they recurred in the poet's work, since it was then more possible to believe that they had strong symbolic significance. William Bartram's account of the great "alligator hole" in his *Travels through North and South Carolina* had so struck Coleridge in the 1790s that he copied it into his notebook and also introduced it as a detail into the prose draft for his "Wanderings of Cain." Hughes, in pursuit of what he considers to be the underlying symbols that link key Coleridge poems, is himself fascinated by Coleridge's evident fascination with Bartram's description of the alligator. Coleridge's notebook entries include the following:

The alligators' terrible roar, ["]like heavy distant thunder, not

> only shaking the air & waters, but causing the earth to tremble—& when hundreds & thousands are roaring at the same time, you can scarcely be persuaded but that the whole globe is dangerously agitated["]—
>
> The eggs are layed in layers between a compost of mud, grass, & herbage.—The female watches them—when born, she leads them about the shores, as a hen her chicken—["]and when she is basking on the warm banks, with her brood around, you may hear the young ones whining & a-barking, like young Puppies.["]
>
> 20 feet long—lizard-shaped, plated—head vulnerable—tusked—eyes ["]small["] & "sunk["]—

Coleridge's notebooks reveal that he was also struck by the description of the "old Champion" who, when in rut, gave an extraordinary display of roaring and twirling.

> [He] darts forth from the reedy coverts all at once on the surface of the water, in a right line; at first, seemingly as rapid as lightning, but gradually more slowly until he arrives at the center of the lake, where he stops; he now swells himself by drawing in wind & water thro' his mouth, which causes a loud sonorous rattling in the throat for near a minute; but it is immediately forced out again thro' his mouth & nostrils with a loud noise, brandishing his tail in the air, & the vapor ascending from his nostrils like smoke. At other times when swollen to an extent ready to burst, his head & tail lifted up, he twirls round on the surface of the water. He retires—& others, who dare, continue the exhibition—all to gain the attention of the favorite Female—
>
> The distant thunder sounds heavily—the crocodiles answer it like an echo—[7]

As an account of animal behavior this is marvelously vivid; it is not surprising that Hughes should have been seized by it or that he should have seen it, in his long essay on Coleridge, "The Snake in the Oak" (1993), as a key document for understanding Coleridge's poetic development at the time. He finds in Coleridge's interest in Bartram a crucial clue to "Kubla Khan"—one that lent a context of animal, orgasmic violence to the images of the woman wailing for her demon lover and of the destructive fountain erupting with tremendous subterranean force. To this primeval sexual roaring and powerful fountainous eruption, Hughes then brings Coleridge's contemporaneous lines about the nightingale that precipitates "with fast thick warble" the "delicious notes" of its love chant; he also points up the resemblance to the "fast thick pants" of the earth's breathing in "Kubla Khan." "A song of some kind is twisting into existence," he writes, "a 'mingled measure' like the braids of current in the Alph itself."[8] With such deft touches, Hughes creates what is something like a poetic canvas of his own, centered in the orgasmic, even orgiastic, energy of the scene at the center of the second stanza of "Kubla Khan," which he regards as Coleridge's expression of what he had repressed within himself.

When he came to interpret "The Rime of the Ancient Mariner," Hughes saw in it an element of traditional religion that could be interpreted in relation to Coleridge's knowledge of shamanic practices. According to Hughes in "Regenerations" (1964), the shaman is initiated by way of a dream:

> The central episode in this full-scale dream, just like the central episode in the rites where the transformation is effected forcibly by the tribe, is a magical death, then dismemberment, by a demon or equivalent powers, with all possible variants of boiling, devouring, burning, stripping to the bones. From this nadir, the shaman is resurrected, with new insides, a new body created for him by the spirits.[9]

Hughes saw a clear parallel between the voyage, desolation, and restoration of the Mariner and this process of stripping and re-creation in the shamanic dream-flight.

The mythological development in Coleridge's verse was also to be interpreted in relation to Shakespeare. Over the years, Hughes's interest in myth affected his readings of the poet who had so consumed his attention during his National Service days. Shakespeare was always for him a touchstone, the one great repository of literary value. Later on, he was to attempt a reconciliation of his mythological and literary interests by writing a long study based on the idea that Shakespeare had produced a mythology of his own, first adumbrated in the early poems *Venus and Adonis* and *The Rape of Lucrece.* To put it briefly, these poems were seen to involve an interrelationship between two principles that had been in conflict in English civilization, represented by the Great Goddess of the old religion and the incipient Puritanism that emerged after the Renaissance. In *Venus and Adonis,* the young, refusing man became the object of the Goddess's rage, and her anger was aroused in the form of the boar that slew him; in *The Rape of Lucrece,* that anger was further realized in the male violence of Tarquin, turned back now against the female.

Hughes went on to argue that when Shakespeare returned to writing plays after his early excursus into poetry, the pattern that emerged, particularly in the great tragedies, was dominated by this myth, and Hughes presented his thesis in considerable detail. Shakespeare repeatedly returned to the same symbolic elements at the center of the myth, namely the Goddess and the Puritan patriarchal culture that rejected her, which typified the struggle between the old Catholic Church and the new Protestantism.[10]

Like some of the first reviewers of the volume, I find this reading of Shakespeare difficult to accept in its entirety. It is, however, very suggestive in places, and when Hughes comes to Coleridge, it certainly provides a very useful guide to his view of the poet as someone torn between two ideals. Whereas Shakespeare is seen as having been totally true to his vocation, Coleridge, in this account, had lost his way at an early stage. Accordingly, Hughes traces in Coleridge's work two selves: the Christian self, shaped by Coleridge's upbringing as the son of the vicar of Ottery St. Mary, who forever afterward was trying to find his way back to a fulfillment of his earliest religious identity—a self that militated against his potentialities as a poet; and the primitive self, suppressed from earliest childhood when Coleridge's mother ceased to give him proper attention—neglect that left him always in flight from his deepest feelings. His ill-fated marriage to a young woman from a religious family was contracted under pressure; he began to discover his primitive self only on walks with the wild young woman Dorothy Wordsworth on the Quantock hills in 1797 and 1798—the period when he also wrote his three great visionary poems, "Kubla Khan," "The Ancient Mariner," and part 1 of "Christabel." He is seen as having come closer at this time to an acknowledgment of the other, truer side of his identity, figured particularly in two images: those of the "snake" and the "oak." In Hughes's account of the matter, Coleridge's failure to fulfill his poetic potential meant that he did not have the strength of identity that he found figured in the oak tree. Instead, he remained a weak figure, captive to the Puritan ideal of Christianity that had ensnared him from birth. Hughes finds a telling illustration of this in one of Coleridge's later notebook entries. Coleridge painfully records his difficulties in praying, and recounts an incident in which he confided his woes to a sympathetic friend:

> Poor—embarrassed—sick—unpatronized, unread— / But (replied the soft consoling Friend) *innocent.*—I felt only as one that recoils—& sinful dust and ashes that I am—groaning under self-reproached inproaches!—*I* innocent?—. —Be thankful still! (repeated the same so sweet Voice) you are an *innocent* man—Again I draw back but as a little child from a *kind* Stranger, but without letting go of the Stranger's hand / —"You have the child-like Heart."—Ah but even in boyhood there was a cold hollow spot, an aching in that heart, when I said my prayers—that prevented my entire union with God—that I could not *give up,* or that would not give *me* up—as if a snake had wreathed around my heart, and at this one spot its Mouth touched at & inbreathed a weak incapability of willing it away— / —Never did I more sadly & sinkingly prostrate myself in sense of my worthlessness—and yet, after all, it was a *comfort* to me— / My innocency was a comfort—a something, for which that was the name, there were [*sic*] which I would *not* resign for Wealth—Strength—Health—Reputation—Glory— / —Hence I learnt—that a sinful Being may *have* an innocence / I learnt, that the Skirt of Christ is nearer to a Man than his own Skin! For that *spot* in my heart even my <remaining &> unleavened *Self*—all else the Love of Christ in and thro' Christ's Love of me![11]

It was characteristic of Hughes's interest in myth that the central image he seized on in this paragraph was that of the snake, coiled round the heart and waiting to dart its poison on any generous impulse. He also fastened on Coleridge's reference to the "unleavened self" as a key to his personality. Coleridge makes interesting use of the Pauline phrase. St. Paul urged his correspondents in Corinth to put aside the "leaven of malice and wickedness" and to keep the feast with the "unleavened bread of sincerity and truth" (1 Cor. 5:6–8). Coleridge uses the metaphor rather differently, figuring human nature as something that can normally be leavened by true Christianity but may still retain an unleavened element of self-centeredness. Hughes takes the metaphor and gives it a further twist, assuming that Coleridge's despised unleavened self was in fact the true one, struggling to waken into activity and be "leavened" by the sincerity and truth of his animal nature. That this further development of the sense is what is in his mind becomes clear from subsequent references in "The Snake in the Oak" to Coleridge's "Unleavened Self."

From now on, Hughes's interpretation is more idiosyncratic, centering largely on "Kubla Khan." Coleridge becomes Marsyas, the rival to Apollo, who was defeated in their musical contest and skinned alive in consequence: "as one might metaphorically say," Hughes contends, "Coleridge was flayed by the official committee of the Orthodoxy."[12] It is assumed that at the beginning of the final verse paragraph of "Kubla Khan," Coleridge has "wakened up," and that the wailing woman is translated by the benevolently censoring imagination into "a quite different *memory* which is yet the same"—that of the damsel with a dulcimer. Hughes reads "Abora" as a pun on "A + B (= Alphabet) + 'ora,'" producing: "O Mountain of the Word, pray for us." Somewhere, too, he traces the vision of St. John the Divine dreaming of the River of Life and hearing a voice say, "I am Alpha and Omega, the beginning and the end." Mixed up with the doubtful wordplay and speculation of this interpretation are significant images of amorousness, streams, breathing, and song. Hughes is sufficiently stimulated by these images to create a poetic vision of his own, which still has as its starting point the presumed division between Coleridge's Christian self and an "unleavened" self of instinctual behavior and paganism that was never allowed to develop.

That there was a division of some such kind within Coleridge's personality is hard to deny. Much evidence can be adduced to support the contention that there existed a Christian, preaching self that was constantly undermined by the work of an imagination that led him into other paths of knowledge—from which Coleridge retreated unceremoniously when the full implications of these journeys became apparent. Hughes's own imaginative powers give him an unusually privileged entrée to this sphere. They are most fruitfully at work when he can enter the dance of imagery to create his own pattern; they also encourage him to concentrate on little regarded aspects of Coleridge's poetry, notably the contributions to Southey's *Joan of Arc* later incorporated into "The Destiny of Nations," a poem that displays Coleridge's strong interest in the 1790s in myths (notably those of the northern nations) and in mythmaking. It may well be, as Hughes suggests, that Coleridge would have been a better poet had he given freer rein to that mythmaking side of himself. But many of the details Hughes conjures are harder to accept.

Coleridge, like Sylvia Plath, was a poet of highly developed consciousness, like her, unballasted, by a strong sense of inner being. Indeed, I've elsewhere argued that there is an important parallel to be drawn between the Coleridge-Wordsworth and Plath-Hughes relationships—Hughes and Wordsworth being similar figures of monolithic self-confirming identity who were yet fascinated by their counterparts, needing their mercurial stimulus.[13] The dynamics of this symbiosis corresponds, in fact, to the two types of genius as described by Coleridge: the one, the Shakespearean, darts itself forth, passing into all forms of human character and passion, "the one Proteus of the fire and flood"; the other, the Miltonic, attracts all forms and things "into the unity of its own ideal."[14] In her journals, Plath returns more than once to her sense that she had no identity, showing less self-confidence even than Coleridge. Hughes, on the other hand, believed that he could help her build one by drawing her into a poetic mold more like his own; indeed, he believed that she had succeeded in her last years and sought to convince her of the fact.[15] Something of the same sort, I would argue, holds good of Wordsworth's attempts to guide his friend into a more "Wordsworthian" identity—one that would assist in balancing his impulses to affection against a firmer sense of duty.

Sylvia Plath, on this reading, was taking Coleridge's problems a stage further, involving an identity that was by no means nonexistent but constantly shifting. As it happened, she chose to represent this state of things in a poem that can be seen as strangely self-referential. "Snakecharmer" is, in my opinion, one of her best, in which the charmer is pictured bringing the energies of the snake to life—at first vegetative in form—until they shape themselves into a pattern that dissolves again only when he tires and ceases: "As the gods began one world, and man another," the poem begins, "So the snakecharmer begins a snaky sphere." And by the time he has finished, "nothing but snakes is visible":

The snake-scales have become
Leaf, become eyelid; snake-bodies, bough, breast
Of tree and human. And he within this snakedom

Rules the writhings which make manifest
His snakehood and his might with pliant tunes
From his thin pipe.[16]

"Moon-eye, mouth-pipe"—the whole poem relies on the interplay between the two as the charmer produces a snake-play so powerful that the scene and the verse describing it are one in their intricate interweaving of sinuosities. As he tires, what has been created subsides into its constituent elements: the interweaving snake forms become straightforward warp and weft, which in turn are seen as cloth, dissolving then into green waters, until only the charmer himself is left, silent and unseeing.

The fit of energies and form is superb throughout: no further meaning need intrude beyond the story of the charmer's enterprise and his eventual tiring, which precipitates the relapse of the snakes and the closing of his moony eye. Technically, Plath has touched perfection. And the tight intricacy of the threefold pattern—music, interplaying energies, and moonlight—reveals itself as one of the most important paradigms in her visionary imagery.

In the end, the only fixed identity is that of the charmer—and he has fallen asleep. The preceding mutations and metamorphoses perhaps help explain why those who look for settled form in poetry find Plath's poetic articulation of her identity so challenging: it shifts and changes its point of focus even as one looks. It was for the same reason, no doubt, that those who dealt with her personally found her equally elusive. Although Coleridge's poetry succeeded better in its formal content, there is something of the same evasiveness in his tendency to escape any particular net one tries to throw around him. Hughes, undaunted, continues to look for a firm pattern in what Coleridge is producing, only to fail once he tries to push his patternings too far. The sense at such points is less of the quietly magical than of the violent, with a reliance on strong physical impressions.

Above all, however, one is aware of the alertness and receptivity of Hughes's poetic imagination whenever it encounters something in Coleridge's text that ignites his interest in myth. Coleridge's ultimate achievement in the visionary poems is to write in a manner that awakens a sense in the reader of the text's concealed mythological power.

By the same token, Hughes's endeavor to make a pattern out of the images that Coleridge presents can at times lead him astray. A good example is his treatment of "The Ballad of the Dark Ladié," a poem that was written around the same time as the great works but is simple and fragmentary. The fragments concern a lady sitting in distress as she waits for her lover, whose name turns out to be Lord Falkland. When Hughes encounters the name, he immediately makes a connection with the well-known islands, which were fraught with political resonance at the time he was writing since the Falklands campaign had only recently ended; the imagery he draws on, however, is more general: "from the fringe of the Antarctic seas, the latitudes of the Albatross."[17] Of course, Coleridge's own readers would have been unlikely to see any geographical reference; if they did make a connection, it would have been with the aristocratic Falkland of Godwin's novel, *Things as They Are, or The Adventures of Caleb Williams,* published five or so years before, which might have alerted them to the possibility that Lord Falkland's nobility in Coleridge's ballad would turn out to be flawed. And this is a sound clue, since in the rest of the poem the lady begins to suspect just such a flaw, as Falkland proposes that they flee "through the dark." But she has no desire to elope, wishing instead to be married in the light of day:

"The dark? the dark? No! not the dark?
The twinkling stars? How, Henry? How?"
O God! 'twas in the eye of noon
　He pledged his sacred vow!

And in the eye of noon my love
Shall lead me from my mother's door,
Sweet boys and girls all clothed in white
　Strewing flowers before:

But first the nodding minstrels go

With music meet for lordly bowers,
The children next in snow-white vests,
Strewing buds and flowers!

And then my love and I shall pace,
My jet black hair in pearly braids,
Between our comely bachelors
And blushing bridal maids.[18]

We have no knowledge of Falkland's reaction to her speech, since the poem breaks off at this point, but his silence enables Hughes's imagination to take off:

> Lord Falkland, one imagines, is listening in dismay. Hoping to embrace a Geraldine, he finds his neck locked in the arms of a Christabel. His dream of converting her into an Abyssinian singing girl and going wild to her instrument, perhaps on the Susquehanna where the alligators roar, seems to have walked straight into a trap.[19]

Someone has walked into a trap here, but it is not necessarily Lord Falkland; and when Hughes goes as far out on a speculative limb as this, one turns with relief to the following admission:

> What I have to say here may be of use only to me. The only value of these remarks to some other reader may be—to prompt them to fill the vessel up themselves, from their own sources. Like the variety of potential readers the variety of potential interpretation is infinite.[20]

This is not altogether true either, of course. The variety of potential interpretation may be multiple but it is still finite, constrained by various factors of language and the legitimacy of evidence. Some of Hughes's interpretations are persuasive, some highly idiosyncratic. His eye is fixed firmly on images of nature in the visionary poems, and, as I have pointed out, the result of his focus is to draw attention, justly, to the unusual amount of interest shown in natural imagery during the Quantock period, and even more during Coleridge's early years in Cumbria. A good example of the second is Hughes's reading of a little-noticed poem, "The Knight's Tomb," which Coleridge described as "an experiment for a metre":

> Where is the grave of Sir Arthur O'Kellyn?
> Where may the grave of that good man be?--
> By the side of a spring, on the breast of Helvellyn,
> Under the twigs of a young birch tree!
> The oak that in summer was sweet to hear
> And rustled its leaves in the fall of the year,
> And whistled and roared in the winter alone,
> Is gone,—and the birch in its stead has grown.
> (Coleridge, *Poems,* 378)

Hughes's most immediate reaction to this was to respond to the meter, which he compared to the metrical experimentation of "Christabel"; he was happy to find that Walter Scott had been fascinated by it from the same point of view. But he was also struck by one of the images in it—that of the birch. Knowing that Coleridge had shown interest in northern mythology, he made a swift connection with the traditional sacredness of the birch in northern cultures, opposing it to the more secure rootedness of the oak, a rootedness Coleridge lacked. Hughes saw the oak as having a particular value for Coleridge:

> Coleridge's many references to the Oak are countered, here and there, by his delight in the Birch. The airy, showering light of the silvery Birch is opposite, in obvious ways, to the Oak—and yet in his mythos, though it does not belong to that rooted "strength" and truth of the heart's passions, it does offer a substitute happiness: the consoling pleasure of freedom from those passions: the promised pleasures of love not as it actually is, tragic and terrifying to him, but love as it ought to be—a nostalgia for an idealized love that might have been.[21]

Here again, we do not need to follow the detail of the statement to see the extent to which it catches Coleridge's quality as a poet: how he delights in the mobile beauty of a plant such as the birch while he can accord no more than respect to the strength of the oak. (The rhythmic innovation of "The Knight's Tomb," a work Hughes singles out for praise, strengthens the case for supposing that the rhythmically innovative poem, "The Barberry Tree," often attributed to Wordsworth, was in fact written by Coleridge.[22])

I have spoken of the contrast between Wordsworth and Coleridge, and as we know, their friendship declined in the subsequent decade into a painful breach, to be patched up in time but never completely redeemed. At the turn of the nineteenth century, however, the dialectic between them was a fruitful one, focused on their respective conceptions of the "One Life." For Coleridge, this awareness focused itself in relation to particular scenes—for example, his contemplation of the North Somerset sunset, as he gazed "till all doth seem / Less gross than bodily," and blessed in "This Lime-Tree Bower My Prison" the single homeward flying rook, which seemed a potent manifestation of the One Life. Just over a year later, on his way to Germany, he wrote to his wife:

> About 4 o'clock I saw a wild duck swimming on the waves—a single solitary wild duck—You cannot conceive how interesting a thing it looked in that round objectless desart of waters.[23]

Between the two—the single rook and the single wild duck—there had appeared the most curious of his creations: the single albatross that attached itself to the human beings on the ship bearing the Ancient Mariner. But in addition to the isolation of these living beings, Coleridge had evoked in that poem a different vision of the One Life, in the shape of the water-snakes:

> They moved in tracks of shining white,
> And when they rear'd, the elfish light
> Fell off in hoary flakes.
>
> . . . .
>
> Blue, glossy green, and velvet black
> They coil'd and swam; and every track
> Was a flash of golden fire.
>
> (Coleridge, *Poems*, 232)

This was the moment, perhaps, when Coleridge came closest to expressing his vision of the One Life in terms of its *energies*. Similarly, in his poem "That Morning," which describes an experience in Alaska when he and his son saw an overwhelming number of salmon moving instinctively together in a stream, Hughes's vision of existence achieved a rare moment of clarification. For him, the closest parallel to this epiphanic experience had, ironically, been the sight of Lancaster bombers moving in formation over Yorkshire, a mechanical menace that usurped the sky. In Alaska, the salmon now overwhelmed Hughes's sense of the whole landscape with their vision of apparently unending life:

> There the body
>
> Separated, golden and imperishable,
> From its doubting thought—a spirit beacon
> Lit by the power of the salmon
>
> That came on, and came on, and kept on coming
> As if we flew slowly, their formations
> Lifting us toward some dazzle of blessing
>
> One wrong thought might darken.[24]

In one of Shakespeare's darkest moments, Macbeth declares, "Light thickens; and the crow / Makes wing to th' rooky wood." The lines can be interpreted as a comment on the manner in which even nature's more equivocal creatures need companionship (just as Macbeth was also to be distressed by the absence of "troops of friends"). For Hughes, the vision of the salmon was evidently akin to Coleridge's experience of the sunset in "This Lime-Tree Bower My Prison," in which he confidently asserted that "No sound is dissonant that tells of Life"—an insight that prefigured the moment of unconscious blessing in "The Ancient Mariner." In 1798 there had been nothing to link the moment with any particular religion, though Coleridge would later gather it up into a Christian interpretation; in "The Ancient Mariner," it is presented as an existential act issuing from deep within the Mariner's being, a simple affirmation directed toward the luminous energies of the water-snakes as they "coil'd and swam." Potent beyond all particular manifestations, the same joy would be re-created in Coleridge's psyche when he beheld the luminous activity in the shadow of the boat at sea a few years later on his way to Malta, seeing the energies at work there as "Spirals, coiling, uncoiling, *being*."[25] At such moments, the Coleridge whose Mariner blessed the water-snakes and the Hughes who found himself blessing the myriad salmon seem to encounter each other most surely, in a moment of mutual recognition as "creatures of light."

Notes

I would like to acknowledge my debt to Graham Davidson, who first drew my attention to Hughes's interest. A shared locality was one reason for that interest. Hughes spent many of his later years in North Devon, Coleridge's home county, not far from the parts of Somerset where some of his most inspired poetry was written.

1. W. S. Merwin, quoted in Keith Sagar, *The Art of Ted Hughes* (Cambridge: Cambridge University Press, 1975), 8.
2. Ted Hughes, *Shakespeare and the Goddess of Complete Being* (London: Faber, 1992), 56.
3. Quoted by Frank Kermode in *Puzzles and Epiphanies: Essays and Reviews, 1958–61* (London: Routledge and Kegan Paul, 1962), 35.
4. This venture, which I discuss in *Coleridge the Visionary* (London: Chatto and Windus, 1959), has since been explored further by Ian Wylie in *Young Coleridge and the Philosophers of Nature* (Oxford: Clarendon Press, 1989).
5. For C. F. Dupuis and his *Origine de tous les cultes*, see Beer, *Coleridge the Visionary*, 109, 213, 241.
6. Sagar, *The Art of Ted Hughes*, 8.
7. *The Notebooks of Samuel Taylor Coleridge*, ed. Kathleen Coburn (London: Routledge and Kegan Paul, 1957–), vol. 1 (Text), #218 and #221.
8. Ted Hughes, *Winter Pollen: Occasional Prose*, ed. William Scammell (London: Faber and Faber, 1994), 394–96.
9. Ibid., 57.
10. The theory is set out in its most elaborate form in his *Shakespeare and the Goddess of Complete Being*.
11. *Notebooks*, vol. 4 (Text), #5275.
12. Hughes, *Winter Pollen*, 397.
13. See the last chapter of my *Post-Romantic Consciousness: Dickens to Ted Hughes* (Basingstoke: Palgrave, 2003).
14. See Coleridge, *Biographia Literaria*, ed. James Engell and Walter Jackson Bate (Princeton: Princeton University Press, 1983), 2:27–28.
15. Ted Hughes, foreword to *The Journals of Sylvia Plath*, ed. Frances McCullough (New York: Dial Press, 1982), xiv–xv. See also Hughes, *Winter Pollen*, 182–83.
16. Sylvia Plath, *Collected Poems* (London: Faber and Faber, 1981), 79.
17. Hughes, *Winter Pollen*, 448.
18. Coleridge, *Poems*, ed. John Beer (London: J. M. Dent, 1993), 198.
19. Hughes, *Winter Pollen*, 450.
20. Ibid., 394.

21. Ibid., 446.

22. A manuscript of this poem was discovered among papers at Christ Church Library, Oxford, in 1964. Jonathan Wordsworth believed it to be a strange self-parody by Wordsworth himself. Some years later, when it was found by Jim Mays to have been published in an 1807 Bristol journal, there was an argument in the pages of the *Review of English Studies* (new ser. 37 [1986]: 348–83), in which Jonathan Wordsworth defended his previous view, Mays examined further possibilities, and I noted that since Coleridge had been in the West Country in 1807 there was a good case for supposing it to have been his: a light skit on Wordsworth—and, as I now think, on his own poetry as well. I also felt that my case justified including it in my revised Everyman editions of the *Poems* (1993–), where anyone interested can most conveniently find it. It will be found to have distinct resemblances of rhythm to the lines quoted here.

23. Coleridge, *Collected Letters,* ed. E. L. Griggs (Oxford: Clarendon Press, 1956–71), 1:426.

24. Ted Hughes, *New Selected Poems, 1957–1994* (London: Faber and Faber, 1995), 265.

25. *Notebooks,* vol. 2 (Text), #2070.

"The All-Sustaining Air": Yeats, Stevens, Rich, Bishop—Responses to Romantic Poetry

Michael O'Neill

"Shakespearean fish swam the sea, far away from land; / Romantic fish swam in nets coming to the hand; / What are all those fish that lie gasping on the strand?"[1] The effect of Yeats's countdown triplet is not merely one of diminishment. The image of modern poems as fish out of water, gasping on the strand, suggests, too, a bracing austerity, the need to adapt to a new, harsh element, to vaporize past oceans into a breathable air. Certainly, though, Yeats's lines indicate the difficulty for a modern poem or poet of being "reborn as an idea, something intended, complete."[2] Few poems convey this difficulty as affectingly as Hart Crane's "The Broken Tower" does. The poem is interpretable as an elegiac celebration of Crane's poetic career, in particular his entrance as a latter-day American Romantic into "the broken world / To trace the visionary company of love, its voice / An instant in the wind."[3] "To trace the visionary company of love" means, as the verb and yearningly elongated rhythm intimate, a brave attempt to track, copy, or emulate a "company" of beckoning and dissolving shadows. In "the broken world," Crane is outside any Romantic "world to which the familiar world is a chaos," in Shelley's words from *A Defence of Poetry*,[4] and in search of a lost wholeness, a search made possible by the experience of fragmentation.

Crane's poem openly proclaims its anxiety of influence, thus severing any supposedly necessary link between poetry and repression: "My word I poured. But was it cognate, scored / Of that tribunal monarch of the air . . . ?" Here, the "tribunal monarch of the air," if allegorized as the Romantic tradition, suggests a Jupiter-like superego.

But the "poured" word hangs for more than "An instant in the wind" of inspiration by virtue of Crane's exalted, punishing sense of poetic vocation. Reliant on a "dynamics of inferential mention," his poem "scores" a new music that is in complex harmony with, say, Shelleyan figurative orchestrations (as in the earlier image of stars "caught and hived in the sun's ray").[5] More poignantly, it is "scored" (in the sense of marked or slashed) by its very ambition. At the same time, the capacity to be wounded has humanized the poet's soul and underpins the poem's trust in the "latent power" stirred by "sweet mortality" (l. 28).

Healed by the poet's capacity to be wounded, Crane's work exemplifies the intricacy of relations between Romantic and post-Romantic poetry. And yet, these relations occur within an "all-sustaining air." A pervasive, protean, and polysemous metaphor in this essay, the phrase occurs twice in Shelley's *Prometheus Unbound:* once when Ione beholds the final two Spirits of the Human Mind in act 1 (l. 744), and again when Asia says of "love" that "Like the wide Heaven, the all-sustaining air, / It makes the reptile equal to the God" (2.5.40, 42–43).[6] The air we breathe is a hackneyed phrase, revivified by Shelley for whom the "world-surrounding ether" (1.661) serves as an image of the way human beings are affected by, and affect, prevailing climates of thought and belief. Asia's words catalyze the near identification of "air" and "love" that her simile describes; a "*Voice (in the air, singing)*" (stage direction before 2.5.48) celebrates the way Asia is different and also inextricable from the "atmosphere divinest" (2.5.58) that surrounds her. In the lyric exchange between the Voice and Asia, Shelley affirms what in *A Defence of Poetry* he will call the capacity of poetry to "transmute" its materials, so that "every form moving within the radiance of its presence is changed by wondrous sympathy to an incarnation of the spirit which it breathes" (*Shelley's Poetry and Prose*, 533). So, Asia imagines "Realms where the air we breathe is Love" (2.5.95), near identification now becoming complete.

Prometheus Unbound is an exercise in deep breathing, an eco-utopian search for and journey into a transformed, no-longer-polluted ideological atmosphere. Inhalings and exhalings of "oracular vapour" (2.3.4), at once inspiringly and ambivalently Dionysian, gust through the awakening world of the second act.[7] Pollution vanishes in the utopian conditions of the last two acts, but the subliminal fear that "vapour" has turned—and therefore can again turn—pestilential is evident throughout the work. Shelleyan "air" is always ready to rhyme with "despair," as in Ione's lines, even if it is "despair / Mingled with love, and then dissolved in sound" (1.756–57). Shelley's lyrical airs alert us to the desirability of keeping a check on the air we metaphorically breathe. Indeed, his use of the word "air" is alert to the spectrum of quasi-symbolic suggestions that the word can imply. When in the fourth act of *Prometheus Unbound* Panthea hears "The music of the living grass and air" (l. 257), she verges on the pantheism of Wordsworth's "living air" (l. 99) in "Tintern Abbey" or "Lines Written in Early Spring" ("And 'tis my faith that every flower / Enjoys the air it breathes" [ll. 11–12]). But when the Poet in *Alastor,* contemplating the swan, laments that he is condemned to waste "these surpassing powers / In the deaf air" (ll. 288–89), the word anticipates the bleak reality that for Wallace Stevens challenges and provokes what his Ozymandias in *Notes toward a Supreme Fiction* ("It Must Change," sec. 8) calls "A fictive covering."[8] "How cold the vacancy," Stevens writes in section 8 of "Esthétique du Mal," echoing the Poet's plight in *Alastor,* "When the phantoms are gone and the shaken realist / First sees reality." Arguably, Shelley's Poet in *Alastor* elicits a mixture of blame and praise because of his refusal to accept that "vacancy" is "reality." For Stevens, "air" bodies forth the real, yet it is a reality that must be imagined for it to exist; "air" is the atmosphere that sustains the mind's fictions and a figure for the breath of inspiration. In many of his poems, "air" is a trope for spaces where new modes of being are fostered. "Esthétique du Mal" concludes with a question that gathers momentum and dispenses with a mark of interrogation:

> And out of what one sees and hears and out
> Of what one feels, who could have thought to make
> So many selves, so many sensuous worlds,
> As if the air, the mid-day air, was swarming
> With the metaphysical changes that occur,
> Merely in living as and where we live.

That meaning is invested in an endless reshaping—"So many selves, so many sensuous worlds"—of the everyday involves a radiant, if hard-won and conditional, post-Romantic illumination. The "air, the mid-day air," the noun repeated with something close to quiet amazement, swarms with revelations, bearing witness, as it does so, to Stevens's intricate engagement with Romanticism's own finding of new colors and words to do justice to ordinary sights.

Locating value in "the weather, the mere weather, the mere air," as *Notes toward a Supreme Fiction* ("It Must Be Abstract," sec. 6) has it, is a major task for Stevens. Here, the very repetition of "mere" paradoxically invests the "weather" with significance, even as "mere air" verges on a sense of "air" as emptied space, an image for loss of belief. Stevens may seem convinced of the need to leave behind the old mythologies, especially the myth of religious belief: "To see the gods dispelled in mid-air and dissolve like clouds is one of the great human experiences," he writes with sardonic tranquility in "Two or Three Ideas."[9] Yet the phrasing endows the dispelled gods with a presence in the act of repudiating the idea of such presence.

"The god approached dissolves into the air" is William Empson's starting point and equivalent assertion in his "Doctrinal Point." There, "dissolves" works to establish air as the illusory token as well as the destroyer of deity, and the poem concludes with a dark, ebullient flurry of rhymes on "air"—the last word—in lines that comprise a sardonic reworking of Shelley's dome image in *Adonais:*

> That over-all that Solomon should wear
> Gives these no cope who cannot know of care.
> They have no gap to spare that they should share
> The rare calyx we stare at in despair.
> They have no other that they should compare.
> Their arch of promise the wide Heaviside layer
> They rise above a vault into the air.

Empson's note to the poem suggests it is a tissue of analogies for coverings and layerings.[10] The passage teases jokily, yet builds powerfully, the "They" growing less specific as the rhymes mount until the line, "They have no other that they should compare," describes the predicament of a post-Romantic culture that has grown entirely skeptical of any transcendent "radiance of Eternity" (*Adonais,* l. 463; *Shelley's Poetry and Prose,* 426).

This may be a post-Romantic predicament. But it has its roots in Romantic culture, as does the troubled impulse to find a solution in the workings of desire, an impulse mocked yet elegized in

Empson's final line. At their most imaginatively daring and heterodox, the Romantics glimpse epiphany and loss in the same moment of vision; they foreshadow the dual outlook of many post-Romantic poets who at once see "the gods dispelled in mid-air" and "The god approached dissolve into the air." The shared experience of a dispossession that empowers a sense of possible sublimity links Romantic poems with many poems of a later climate. There is a side of Stevens that thrives on the attempt to assert, as he does in the elegant metaphysical spring cleaning performed by "A Clear Day and No Memories," that "Today the air is clear of everything . . . it flows over us without meanings." In this poem, "air" is the Romantic tradition and that which supplants such a tradition. Stevens adopts the tone of the letter writer who says, a shade misleadingly, "while . . . I come down from the past, the past is my own and not something marked Coleridge, Wordsworth, etc," or who would contend with Emerson that "there remains the indefeasible persistency of the individual to be himself" ("Quotation and Originality").[11] An inveterate "scholar," to use his word, of Romanticism, Stevens asserts in "Evening without Angels" that "Air is air, / Its vacancy glitters round us everywhere. / Its sounds are not angelic syllables / But our unfashioned spirits realised / More sharply in more furious selves." Manifesto here turns epiphanic, as "glitters" and the chiming "everywhere" reveal.

Stevens's serio-comic lecture goes on to remind us that we "repeat antiquest sounds of air / In an accord of repetitions." For all the antitranscendental drift of the writing (it is "light / That fosters seraphim"), the phrasing mimics "The gaiety of language" ("Esthétique du Mal," sec. 11) that Stevens uses to concede, and yet free himself from, allegiance to "antiquest sounds of air." If "we" repeat what the Romantics were saying (for example), it is because we are always making it new. This is one implication of Stevens's use of the very Romantic trope of the "wind / Encircling us" that "speaks always with our speech." Stevens contrives to make the word "air" serve a double purpose: to sustain our link with the past and shore up our trust in our ability to find fresh significances. In "Evening without Angels," the very sound of the word sponsors the trust that "Bare night is best. Bare earth is best. Bare, bare." The noise made by the poem imitates the way its "air" resonates with "the voice that is great within us." As so often in Stevens, the antitranscendent ("Air is air") coexists with a recognition of possibilities it seems right to call sublime. "Air," here, is "An abstraction blooded, as a man by thought," as Stevens will say in *Notes toward a Supreme Fiction* ("It Must Be Abstract," sec. 6): the imaginative "abstraction" is "blooded" by reentering the world that engages the mind and senses until an abstraction (such as the Supreme Fiction) and the "mere weather" blend, "making visible / The motions of the mind" ("Evening without Angels").

"I slowly start again in the open air," writes Philippe Jaccottet (in Derek Mahon's translation) at the close of an untitled poem about poetry. Mahon sees Jaccottet's "Airs" (the punning title of one of his collections) as dealing with an idea "familiar to us since the Romantics," and quotes Jaccottet: "The limitless is the breath which gives us life. . . . Poetry is the word which this breath sustains and carries, whence its power over us."[12] The "mere air" gives promise of origins, yet it does so by retaining a capacity to house the sublime, the limitless, to hint at traces of dispelled presence, as it does in Keats, elegist of an "air" that was once "haunted" (*Lamia,* 2:236) or "Holy" ("Ode to Psyche," l. 39) and is now in danger of being "emptied" by "Philosophy" (*Lamia,* 2:236, 234).[13] Mallarmé's "L'Azur" with its "serene irony" canopies the earth of much modernist and modern poetry: that "irony" takes the form of mocking the poet with an "absolute that is simultaneously perfection and nothingness," in Henry Weinfeld's words.[14] Even an apparently anti-Romantic poet such as Larkin is haunted in "High Windows" by the thought of "deep blue air, that shows / Nothing, and is nowhere, and is endless," much as Mallarmé asserts at the end of "L'Azur": "*Je suis hanté.* L'Azur! L'Azur! L'Azur! L'Azur!"

"I made it out of a mouthful of air," Yeats asserts in an alliterative compacting of poetry's newness and capacity to last. "He Thinks of Those Who Have Spoken Evil of His Beloved," the poem from which the line comes, finds that a song made of air will "weigh" more than "the great and their pride," a phrase that loses air like a deflated balloon when Yeats rhymes it with itself. For the youthful Yeats, *Prometheus Unbound* was "among the sacred books of the world," and his own poetic breathings are sustained by his lifelong engagement with Shelley's poetry and Romantic poetry more generally.[15] In later work, he relishes pungent variations on Shelleyan themes. The swan of *Alastor* and Asia's lyric in *Prometheus Unbound,* where the soul is "like a sleeping swan" (2.5.73), transmogrifies into the terrifying swan who assaults Leda in a poem that is concerned, like *Prometheus*

Unbound, with the inauguration of a fresh cycle. Unlike *Prometheus Unbound,* however, "Leda and the Swan" tramples utopian dreams into the dust. "The brute blood of the air" (l. 12) is Jupiter returned to take revenge on the Shelleyan creed of redemption through love and forgiveness. Against and yet in subtle accord with the "dragon-ridden" destruction of civil war, Yeats sets the Romantic Image of Loie Fuller's Chinese dancers unwinding their "shining web" until it seemed "a dragon of air / Had fallen among dancers" ("Nineteen Hundred and Nineteen," ll. 3–4): art has the power to find an image for turbulent chaos. But "Nineteen Hundred and Nineteen" opens itself to such chaos at its close when what emerges from the air, from "the labyrinth of the wind," is the lurching image of "That insolent fiend Robert Artisson." "The disentangled Doom," in Shelley's phrase, is well and truly out of the "pit" (*Prometheus Unbound,* 4:569, 564).

Yeats, the self-styled last Romantic (in "Coole and Ballylee, 1931"), is led to exalt art, yet, as in the Keatsian odes that lie behind his Byzantium poems, he discovers the limits of seeking to exist in a world "All breathing human passion far above" (Keats, "Ode on a Grecian Urn," l. 28). His Byzantium, a place that disdains "All that man is" ("Byzantium," l. 6), in a terse, contempt-filled line, turns out to be a place too ghostly, too virtual, a place where "Breathless mouths" (l. 14) are too at home, and a series of trance-wrecking images leaps to the defense of the "unpurged" (l. 1) in the final stanza, in which "bitter furies of complexity" (l. 37) flood back into the poem with a vengeance. Indeed, Yeats is sensitized by Romantic poetry to an inescapable war of contraries.

Two quotations will help show his involvement in such a war. The first is from "Blood and the Moon": "And Shelley had his towers, thought's crowned powers he called them once" (2.3); the second comes from the end of the final poem in "Meditations in Time of Civil War": "The abstract joy, / The half-read wisdom of daemonic images, / Suffice the ageing man as once the growing boy" (7.38–40). The allusion to Shelley in the first quotation is to *Prometheus Unbound,* act 4, where the Chorus of Spirits sings of how they have come "From those skiey towers / Where Thought's crowned Powers / Sit watching your dance, ye happy Hours" (ll. 102–4). The second passage echoes Wordsworth's "Ode: Intimations of Immortality," in which the poet laments that "Shades of the prison-house begin to close / Upon the growing Boy" (ll. 67–68). Yeats quotes Shelley in support of a defiantly idealist and Anglo-Irish perspective and a consciously arrogant "mockery of a time / Half dead at the top" ("Blood and the Moon," 1.11–12); Wordsworth's phrase serves a deeply plangent dying fall. In both cases, Yeats uses the Romantic poem for his own ends. Shelley's phrase, snatched from its Promethean context, is made to serve a vision that is powerfully if dangerously contemptuous of the present; "Meditations" finishes with Wordsworth's phrase, as though Yeats were denying the Romantic poet's narrative of growth through loss. Yet it is the bitterness of Yeats's self-characterization that keeps his poetry alive: "A poet, when he is growing old," Yeats writes in "Anima Hominis," "will ask himself if he cannot keep his mask and his vision without new bitterness, new disappointment." But "new bitterness, new disappointment" is what, for Yeats, creates, in Stevens's words from one of his *Adagia,* "a romantic that is potent" (*Opus Posthumous,* 180), and in "Anima Hominis," as in the poem, he turns on his dreams of escaping bitterness: "Then he will remember Wordsworth withering into eighty years, honoured and empty-witted, and climb to some waste room and find, forgotten there by youth, some bitter crust."[16] Wordsworth's supposed failure sustains Yeats's new lease of imaginative life.

In both Yeats poems, a Romantic poem serves as a point of light, however ironized, that enables the later poet's imagination to assert its presence. Harold Bloom, the hierophant of such assertions and the tortuous misprisions they may involve, has made us familiar with the notion that post-Enlightenment poetry traces a curve of quasi-inevitable decline: "it seems just to assume," he writes, "that poetry in our tradition, when it dies, will be self-slain, murdered by its own past strength."[17] As its title suggests, the present essay swerves from Bloom's work in seeing Romantic poetry as often "sustaining" a supply of imaginative oxygen to later poems. To put the point differently, Bloom's generous shrewdness emerges most persuasively when he contends that the imagination is always making a final reckoning, that every new poem battles to bring something original into being, and that possibilities other than the ironic or the diminished are forever luring poets. Hence he ends *Poetry and Repression* with the fascinating claim that Wallace Stevens, for all his limitations, is "the authentic twentieth-century poet of the Sublime" and rejects the view of Stevens as "an ironist, as a wry celebrant of a diminished version of Romantic or Transcendental selfhood."[18] This is well said and brings out why George Bornstein's unmelodramatic term—"transformations"—is as helpful as any in describing uses made of the Romantic legacy by twentieth-century poets.[19]

The effort to imagine such transformations is among Wallace Stevens's major concerns. His great gift is not only to talk about the need for poetry to "be living, to learn the speech of the place," but, as he does in "Of Modern Poetry," to create a poetry that persuades us that "the act of finding / What will suffice" is at work. In the poem's words, such a poetry "has / To construct a new stage" and "be on that stage." The poem enacts its theme, especially through the workings of a quirkily, even comically, inventive diction and an adroitly complex syntax that gives the air of inspecting its unfurlings. As the poem takes possession of "the delicatest ear of the mind," the reader grows conscious of "Sounds passing through sudden rightnesses": sounds that have at and as their center the word "mind." Near the end, Stevens modulates from the vehement "It must / Be the finding of a satisfaction" to the relatively playful "and may / Be of a man skating, a woman dancing, a woman / Combing." As at the close of Yeats's "Among School Children," these images seek to express the "satisfaction" that occurs when analysis is defeated and we cannot distinguish between "dancer" and dance," or agent and act, or poem and the mind. Yet the poem's satisfactions are neither complacent nor repeatable, and are distinctly provisional: a hallmark of Stevens's "new romanticism."[20]

Stevens argues that "For the sensitive poet, conscious of negations, nothing is more difficult than the affirmations of nobility, and yet there is nothing that he requires of himself more persistently." "Nobility," apparently "false and dead and ugly," is, in fact, "a force and not the manifestations of which it is composed." It shows itself wherever we are conscious of "a violence from within that protects us from a violence without."[21] This fraught defense of "nobility" comes close to explaining the continual hold of Romantic poetry over twentieth-century poets, however strong the urge to jettison the past. Recapturing the "almost disbelieving wonder" she felt at encountering the poetry of Adrienne Rich, Helen Vendler echoes Stevens's plea for poetry to be "living" when she writes, "I had not known till then how much I had wanted a contemporary and a woman as a speaking voice of life." She goes on to quote Wordsworth's *Prelude* (1805, 4:145–46): "Strength came where weakness was not known to be, /

At least not felt."[22] The tribute expresses the continuity between Romantic poet, twentieth-century poet, and twentieth-century critic. In her recent *Midnight Salvage: Poems, 1995–1998,* Rich has a poem made up of flayed units of prose and poetry called "A Long Conversation," and the title points up the protracted dialogue between Romantic and twentieth-century poets. More immediately, Rich's conversation is between poetry and politics, poet and reader, and moves toward a "nerve-driven" defense of poetry. At the core of this defense is the belief that "All kinds of language fly into poetry" (60), a belief that is in direct, if distant, descent from the Preface to *Lyrical Ballads,* and a conviction—enabling for Rich as for Shelley—that "the words have barely begun to match the desire" (63). Rich's stance in this poem is that of a tough-minded, modern-day Romantic, her economical, intense style catching the force of "desire," and her eloquent, principled refusal to settle for an illusion of aesthetic mastery. She organizes her poem through allusions: to Marx, Nixon, and Mandelstam, and, vitally, to Blake and Coleridge. The first poem in the unnumbered and unsectioned sequence (hence the provision of page numbers) elliptically sets the "warm bloom of blood in the child's arterial tree" against the parental warning against catching "*your death of cold*" (53). She finishes this first section of the poem with the bracketed phrase "energy: Eternal Delight," referring to Blake's *Marriage of Heaven and Hell.* Amid the war of feeling in the poem, the phrase serves as a beacon of revolutionary purpose. Later, she quotes a famous letter from Coleridge to Wordsworth, in which Coleridge anticipates the very terms used about him by hostile critics in his day and ours: "I wish," he says to Wordsworth, as lineated by Rich, "*you would write a poem / addressed to those who, in consequence / of the complete failure of the French Revolution / have thrown up all hopes / of the amelioration of mankind / and are sinking into an almost epicurean / selfishness, disguising the same / under the soft titles of domestic attachment / and contempt for visionary philosophes*" (63). In subsequent lines, failure, rebuff, and repetition are Rich's emphases, yet it is when "the cold fog blows back in" that the chances of a new imaginative breathing present themselves in the dense, suggestive, and generously mocking lines that follow: "Your lashes, visionary! screening / in sudden rushes this / shocked, abraded crystal" (63). The visionary "screens" a reality tinged with possibilities, "this / shocked, abraded crystal," and in the twinned meanings of "screens" (covering and showing),

Rich obliquely frames a double response to Romanticism's visionary quest.

Many twentieth-century writers wear bifocal lenses as they contemplate the legacy of Romanticism. In Elizabeth Bishop's "Sandpiper," the poet chooses as her hapless, obsessive surrogate a bird who "runs to the south, finical, awkward, / in a state of controlled panic, a student of Blake." Here, a Blakean distillation gives way to a "finical" condition. The opening lines of the Romantic poet's "Auguries of Innocence"—"To see a world in a grain of sand, / And a heaven in a wild flower, / Hold infinity in the palm of your hand, / And eternity in an hour"—ironically ghost Bishop's poem, a poem much concerned with whether it is possible "To see a world" at all, let alone "in a grain of sand."[23] The sandpiper is "a student of Blake," knows about the possible significance of "minute particulars," but is in a panicky state, however controlled the panic, because the particulars seem to open into nothing more than themselves. As "he stares at the dragging grains," meaning seems to be chance-ridden and fortuitous: "The world is a mist. And then the world is / minute and vast and clear." There, the clarification, across the line ending, promises the double vision ("minute and vast") previously eluding the bird, but the subsequent, "He couldn't tell you which," touchingly and astringently mimics a collapsing back into uncertainty.

The bird's problem is that of the poet for whom particulars are all that can be trusted, yet merely amount to a heap of disconnected objects. He is less oblivious to history—if one so allegorizes the Atlantic beside which he runs—than uncurious about it: "The roaring alongside he takes for granted, / and that every so often the world is bound to shake." But while Bishop may stand at a laconic, severely charitable arm's length from her surrogate ("Poor bird"), she does not deny the residual post-Romantic ardor of his search: "he is preoccupied, // looking for something, something, something." Romantic "somethings"—one thinks of Wordsworth's "something far more deeply interfused" or "something evermore about to be"—cloak themselves in an aura of sublime indeterminacy.[24] Bishop's triple repetition catches more the twitchy routine of obsessive compulsion. Yet, as though she had taken to heart another maxim from Blake's "Auguries of Innocence"—"If the sun and moon should doubt / They'd immediately go out" (ll. 109–10)—Bishop concludes with a forceful and transformative vision that half justifies the bird's obsession: "The millions of grains are black, white, tan, and gray, / mixed with quartz grains, rose and amethyst." Half justifies: the bird may be missing what is under his eyes, and that final off-rhyme ("obsessed" and "amethyst") may be saying as much. Or the "rose and amethyst" vision may sanction the obsession, even as "millions of grains" implies a potentially nightmarish infinity of particulars, the opposite of that "effect of reducing multitude to unity" Coleridge saw as a proof of original genius in the use of images.[25]

In her perceptive study of Bishop's perceptions, Bonnie Costello claims that the poet "dismantles the transcendent gaze of Romanticism." But Costello also quotes the poet's letter to Robert Lowell in which she says wryly, "I find I'm really a minor female Wordsworth."[26] Her subtle, agnostic poetry refuses to be neatly corralled and is finely attuned to the way Romantic poetry itself resists easy categorizing. Wordsworth, read through lenses supplied by Bishop, seems as much a poet of disconcerting juxtaposition as visionary climax. "Crusoe in England" depicts Crusoe recollecting emotion once taken off the island, but tranquility eludes him. Bishop has her character say, "I tried / reciting to my iris-beds, / 'They flash upon that inward eye, / which is the bliss . . .' The bliss of what? / One of the first things that I did / when I got back was look it up." The bliss of solitude eludes Crusoe trapped in a post-Darwinian nature that had no particular care of him; he suffers nightmares, breeding across the line ending, of "infinities / of islands, islands spawning islands." Still, the recollecting, isolated self of the poem, who remarks of waterspouts, "Beautiful, yes, but not much company," is a sardonic heir of the Coleridge who, in "Dejection: An Ode," saw, not felt, how beautiful the natural scene was.

In "The Unbeliever," Bishop produces a parable of types of poet: the unbeliever, who "sleeps on the top of a mast / with his eyes fast closed"; the cloud, "Secure in introspection"; and the gull, who "remarked that the air / was 'like marble.'" A discernible but sympathetic irony governs the poem. Bishop is concerned with stances and strategies associated with Romantic poetry and implicitly mocks the buoyancy of Shelley's speaker in "The Cloud." At the same time, the fear experienced by the unbeliever is as subjective as the confidence of cloud and gull, and when the gull decodes the unbeliever's "dream," what opens up is a post-Romantic abyss in which the solitary "I" battles with a malevolent other: "'I must not fall. / The spangled sea below wants me to fall. / It is as hard as diamonds; it wants to destroy us all.'" Metaphoric projection has turned paranoid; Urizen's "unseen conflictions with shapes / Bred from his forsaken wilderness" (*The First Book of Urizen*, ll. 14–15) may come to mind, and his desire—"a solid without fluctuation" (l. 55)—is the unbeliever's terror.

Bishop's poem, like Blake's, empathizes even as it critiques. It is one thing to satirize the gull's figurative impulse to see "the air" as "like marble," another to forsake the poem as a space where "before unapprehended relations of things" can come into being (*Shelley's Poetry and Prose*, 512). Bishop's self-reflexive poetry composes an observer's skeptical *ars poetica*. For a Romantic belief in the One Life, she substitutes her own "one art" in a villanelle of that title. In this poem, "the art of losing" is available both to author and to things. Dualism gives way, not to some Heideggerean condition of dwelling but to a unifying capacity for loss. For such loss, there is always the recompense that Bishop finds in her imperative at the close: "It's evident / the art of losing's not too hard to master / though it may look like (*Write* it!) like disaster." "In the Waiting Room" also ironically invokes oneness: "What similarities," the young girl thinks, fascinated by photos of "naked women" in "the *National Geographic*," "held us all together / or made us all just one." Costello asserts that in the poem "Bishop clearly separates herself from Wordsworth, whose 'Ode: Intimations of Immortality' decries the fall into difference and social definition and takes comfort in the promise of spiritual oneness derived from recollections of childhood."[27] Still, if Wordsworthian intimations dissolve into a sense of identity as appallingly inexplicable ("Why should I be my aunt, / or me, or anyone?"), the Romantic poet's "obstinate questionings / Of sense and outward things" (ll. 144–45) help shape Bishop's poem. Her search for a language adequate to negative wonder ("How—I didn't know any / word for it—") results in the self-consciously inadequate "how 'unlikely,'" a low-key replay of Wordsworth's "Fallings from us, vanishings" (l. 146). Bishop's lines pass into another "how," this time an obstinate questioning: "How had I come to be here, / like them, and overhear / a cry of pain that could have / got loud and worse but hadn't?" Involving in both cases repetition of the same sound that has, when repeated, a different meaning, the half echo of Keats's "Here, where men sit and hear each other groan" ("Ode to a Nightingale," l. 24) reminds us again that the Romantics cannot be turned into poets of transcendent flight. Theirs is also a poetry of "The weariness, the fever, and the fret" ("Ode to a Nightingale," l. 23).

In "The Monument," Bishop rewrites for a later age the drama of artistic creation enacted in Coleridge's "Kubla Khan." At one stage in Bishop's poem, an imagined voice asks, commenting on the ramshackle monument, "Why did you bring me here to see it? / A temple of crates in cramped and crated scenery, / what can it prove? / I am tired of breathing this eroded air, / this dryness in which the monument is cracking." "Tired of breathing this eroded air" articulates one response to the sense of belatedness, of coming after the Romantics. But Bishop finds a way out of anxiety and exhaustion. Coleridge's poem is brought in when Bishop speaks of an "artist-prince," who might have wanted, looking at the seascape running behind the monument, to "make / a melancholy or romantic scene of it." And yet her monument resists the decree of any such artist-prince; no stately pleasure-dome, it is more a matter of "piled-up boxes," a wooden, box-like structure with warped poles at the top, a makeshift installation that emphasizes its materiality. It is a shape, though, and here Bishop begins her surreptitious rediscovery of purpose, that teases the viewer in and out of thought. Art has ceased to be iconic or symbolic of unaging intellect. The monument, rather, is "the beginning of a painting, / a piece of sculpture, or poem, or monument, / and all of wood." It is subject to and made out of the contingent and requires the observer's wary involvement: "Watch it closely" is how the poem ends. Yet for all its deflation of "Kubla Khan," the poem's cunning insertion of the phrase "or poem" reminds us that Bishop has written a monument and has, in her own unshowy way, fulfilled Coleridge's desire to "build a dome in air" ("Kubla Khan," l. 46).[28]

Poems about art bring poetic responses to the Romantic legacy sharply into focus. Stevens's "Anecdote of the Jar" works its ambiguous way to what he himself calls "the American Sublime" by replacing Keats's Grecian Urn with a "jar" that is not only comically "round upon the ground" but is also unignorably if awkwardly present, "tall and of a port in air." Its uncomfortable dominion is marked by the sudden outbreak of rhymes on "air": "It took dominion everywhere. / The jar was gray and bare." Here, art's nonsense pierces us with strange relation. Of all post-Romantic poets, Stevens is the most concerned, in his relations with the Romantic, to make the air breathed by his poems uneroded, unstale, not filled with spent images. The weather, especially air, however much they may stand for "reality"—that troublesome term in Stevens—imply the workings of that equally troublesome term "imagination." When in a complex passage in *Notes toward a Supreme Fiction* Stevens asserts, "The air is not a mirror but bare board" ("It Must Be Abstract," sec. 4), he is building on his existential conviction that "we live in a place / That is not our own and, much more, not ourselves." The distinction between "mirror" and "bare board" both holds and collapses: if the air were a mirror, it would merely give us back our reflections; as a bare board or stage it serves as a place where plots not of our devising can unfold. Yet the fact that Stevens uses one metaphor to discredit another may mean that the strongest impression conveyed by the line and the passage is of support for one of the *Adagia:* "Reality is a cliché from which we escape by metaphor."[29] When Stevens rejects the air, as in "Poem with Rhythms," he sculpts a post-Romantic rhetoric of the sublime that verges on solipsism; here the mind's figurations emerge as clothing the mind "*in the powerful mirror of my wish and will,*" "*Not as in air, bright-blue-resembling air.*" The italicized assertion sways between the grand and the grandiloquent, and seems vulnerable to skepticism about the final power of the doubled "*wish and will.*"

As James Longenbach has shown, Stevens articulates the friction between the claims of politics and poetry.[30] It is at once a Romantic and post-Romantic dilemma but one which, treated by Stevens, turns quickly into metapoetic commentary. In "Mozart 1935," Stevens feels the lure of "That lucid souvenir of the past, / The divertimento; / That airy dream of the future, / The unclouded concerto." With calculated airiness, the word "airy" undercuts itself, and Stevens instructs his poet, by way of Shelley's "Ode to the West Wind": "Be thou, be thou / The voice of angry fear, / The voice of this besieging pain." In the "Bethou" section of *Notes toward a Supreme Fiction* ("It Must Change," sec. 6), however, Stevens ironizes Shelley's urgent prayer to the wind: "Be thou, Spirit fierce, / My spirit! Be thou me, impetuous one!" (ll. 60–61; *Shelley's Poetry and Prose,* 300). The prayer's failure is tacitly conceded by the very form of the plea. Stevens's canto concludes, "Bethou him, you / And you, bethou him and bethou. It is / A sound like any other. It will end." The sparrow's "Bethou" is spoken against the "ké-ké" of the other birds, but the attempt to assert an original sound and the significance of the self fades as all voices turn into "A single text, granite monotony." It is a typical and sardonic Stevensian parable about poetry, about its continual capacity for entropy.

Stevens's later imagining of a supreme fiction, "the fiction of an absolute" as he calls it in *Notes toward a Supreme Fiction* ("It Must Give Pleasure," sec. 7), shows the mind in the act of finding what will suffice. In this section of the poem, Stevens takes to an elaborated extreme a fictive impulse in Shelley. True, he does not say, as Shelley does in the conclusion to "The Sensitive-Plant," "It is a modest creed, and yet / Pleasant if one considers it" (ll. 13–14; *Shelley's Poetry and Prose*, 295). But after he asks, in section 8 of "It Must Give Pleasure," "Am I that imagine this angel less satisfied? / Are the wings his, the lapis-haunted air?" he implies that he is the creator of the "air" his poem breathes: "I have not but I am and as I am, I am." "I have not" lets go of ownership (of the fictions of angel and lapis-haunted air) in order to assert identity: "I am." Having asserted identity, the poet is able to reach out beyond the self at the section's close. "Cinderella fulfilling herself beneath the roof" may seem autoerotic to a damaging degree, yet "external regions," the poem makes us aware, are sustained by poetic "reflections."

Fortuitously, the end of Stevens's late poem "The Course of a Particular" read, in its original printing in *Opus Posthumous*, "It is the cry of leaves that do not transcend themselves, // In the absence of fantasia, without meaning more / Than they are in the final finding of the air, in the thing / Itself, until, at last the cry concerns no one at all." Subsequent printings have "the final finding of the ear," but the misprint is peculiarly suggestive. The poem dramatizes in miniature Stevens's response to his own "fantasia" and to that of Romanticism: in this response, "There is a conflict, there is a resistance involved." Stevens appears to want to capture, in the poem, a step-by-step withdrawal from imaginative projection, to reach a state in which the cry of the leaves "concerns no one at all." "Final finding of the ear," in a sense, wants to be "final finding of the air": "air" would imply that the mind has been subsumed by "the thing itself." As it is, we are left with that mind as it subtly rehearses what has been a major theme in Stevens since "The Snow Man": the wish to behold "Nothing that is not there and the nothing that is." But this wish is never quite realized. Stevens's leaves may refuse the metaphoric transformations undergone by Shelley's leaves in "Ode to the West Wind," and yet there is conflict in the American poet's project. For one thing, his negations reveal him to be necessarily involved in a mode of thinking officially outlawed by the poem: "It is not a cry of divine attention, / Nor the smoke-drift of puffed-out heroes, no human cry." For another, the sentence "The leaves cry" will not divest itself, despite the poem's best efforts, of the associations—desire, torment, and longing—produced by the verb.

In "The Noble Rider and the Sound of Word," Stevens distinguishes between a pejorative sense of the word "escapism" ("where the imagination does not adhere to reality") and a nobler sense of the word where poetry is a way of "resisting or evading the pressure of reality." Stevens's "syntactic provisionality" and use of metaphor are forms of such resistance and evasion.[31] Instead of accepting "blank space," a Lockean void, poetry can re-shape reality, as in Wordsworth's sonnet on Westminster Bridge, quoted by Stevens to show how the poet "creates the world to which we turn incessantly and without knowing it." And it is intriguing that the Wordsworthian lines, as quoted by Stevens, conclude with a vision of London "All bright and glittering in the smokeless air."[32] That "smokeless air" is object and medium of Wordsworth's vision of what is "bright and glittering," and it is such an expansion into supra-sensuous transparency that is often signaled by Stevens's images of air. Wordsworth's lines are freshly romantic, as Stevens wants his lines to be, and as he claims Marianne Moore's are in "A Poet That Matters." Moore's ways of making it new are the reverse of "the sense in which the romantic is a relic of the imagination." By contrast, she "hybridizes by association," disconcerts expectation, and is "romantic" in the positive sense, "meaning always the living and at the same time the imaginative." The "romantic" in this sense "is a process of cross-fertilisation, an immense process . . . of hybridization."[33]

Hybridization, in Stevens's sense, is a fitting image for the way in which many twentieth-century poets enter into sustaining dialogue with the great Romantic poets. Mrs. Alfred Uruguay may wipe away the romantic moonlight like mud, but Stevens's sympathies are always with the figure of capable imagination who passes her. In his "Final Soliloquy of the Interior Paramour," Stevens offers a conversation as well as a monologue. So, Coleridge's "The Eolian Harp" and his near-pantheist affirmation in chapter 13 of *Biographia Literaria* appear to be alluded to, in lines that compare poetry's warmth to "A light, a power, the miraculous influence" and assert, albeit tentatively, "We say God and the imagination are one."[34] At the same time,

Stevens concedes that his own reassertion of Romantic hope coexists with awareness that hope is created from its own very possible wreckage: it is "for small reason" that we think "The world imagined is the ultimate good"; it is because of our poverty that we wrap ourselves in "the miraculous influence"; "We say" is a phrase that reminds us that our words are sounds that will end like any other; our candles light up an immense darkness. Yet, at the last, "We make a dwelling in the evening air." Here Stevens makes poetry "the song that names the earth," in Jonathan Bate's words;[35] but it is such a song, the poetry suggests, because post-Romantic poetry is often, and at its greatest, concerned, as Ezra Pound has it, "To have gathered from the air a live tradition."[36]

Notes

1. W. B. Yeats, "The Nineteenth Century and After," in *W. B. Yeats: The Poems*, ed. Daniel Albright (London: Dent, 1994), 290. The poem is cited by Bate in *The Burden of Past and the English Poet* (Cambridge, MA: Belknap Press/Harvard University Press, 1970), 61, as one of four examples of authorial fear that "poetry has been cultivating progressively smaller plots or concentrating on less general interests."

2. W. B. Yeats, "A General Introduction for My Work," in *W. B. Yeats: Selected Criticism and Prose*, ed. A. Norman Jeffares (London: Pan/Macmillan, 1970), 255.

3. *The Complete Poems and Selected Letters and Prose of Hart Crane*, ed. Brom Weber (London: Oxford University Press, 1968), 193.

4. *Shelley's Poetry and Prose*, ed. Donald H. Reiman and Neil Fraistat (New York: Norton, 2002), 533.

5. "General Aims and Theories," in *Complete Poems*, ed. Weber, 222. The image of starlight fading into sunlight is a favorite of Shelley's. See *Prometheus Unbound*, 2.1.17–25; "To a Sky-Lark," ll. 18–20; and *The Triumph of Life*, ll. 77–79.

6. *The Poems of Shelley*, vol. 2, 1817–1819, ed. Kelvin Everest and Geoffrey Matthews (Harlow: Longman, 2000), 521, 571. This Longman edition, including vol. 1, 1804–1817 (1989), is used for quotations of Shelley's poetry where possible. Later poems are quoted from *Shelley's Poetry and Prose*.

7. See Kelvin Everest's notes, especially to 2.3, in *The Poems of Shelley*.

8. *The Collected Poems of Wallace Stevens* (London: Faber, 1955), 396. Stevens's poetry is quoted from this edition, except for "A Clear Day and No Memories" and "The Course of a Particular," which are quoted from *The Palm at the End of the Mind: Selected Poems and a Play by Wallace Stevens*, ed. Holly Stevens (New York: Vintage, 1990).

9. Wallace Stevens, *Opus Posthumous*, ed. Samuel French Morse (New York: Vintage, 1982), 206.

10. William Empson, *Collected Poems* (London: Hogarth Press, 1984). For Empson's note, see 103–4.

11. *Letters of Wallace Stevens,* ed. Holly Stevens (New York: Knopf, 1966), 292. *Emerson's Prose and Poetry,* ed. Joel Porte and Saundra Morris (New York: Norton, 2001), 329.

12. *Selected Poems: Philippe Jaccottet,* trans. Derek Mahon (London: Penguin, 1988), 9.

13. *The Poems of John Keats,* ed. Jack Stillinger (London: Heinemann, 1978).

14. Stéphane Mallarmé, *Collected Poems,* trans. Henry Weinfeld (Berkeley: University of California Press, 1994).

15. "The Philosophy of Shelley's Poetry," in *Yeats: Selected Criticism and Prose,* ed. Jeffares, 53. For discussion of Shelley and Yeats, see (among other studies) Harold Bloom, *Yeats* (New York: Oxford University Press, 1970); George Bornstein, *Yeats and Shelley* (Chicago: University of Chicago Press, 1970); and Carlos Baker, *The Echoing Green: Romanticism, Modernism, and the Phenomena of Transference in Poetry* (Princeton: Princeton University Press, 1984).

16. *Yeats: Selected Criticism and Prose,* ed. Jeffares, 179, 180.

17. Harold Bloom, *The Anxiety of Influence: A Theory of Poetry,* 2nd ed. (Oxford: Oxford University Press, 1997), 10.

18. Harold Bloom, *Poetry and Repression: Revisionism from Blake to Stevens* (New Haven: Yale University Press, 1976), 282.

19. See George Bornstein, *Transformations of Romanticism in Yeats, Eliot, and Stevens* (Chicago: University of Chicago Press, 1976).

20. For Stevens's use of the phrase "new romantic," see *Letters of Wallace Stevens,* ed. H. Stevens, 277.

21. See "The Noble Rider and the Sound of Words," in Wallace Stevens, *The Necessary Angel: Essays on Reality and the Imagination* (London: Faber, 1960), 35–36.

22. Helen Vendler, "Ghostlier Demarcations, Keener Sounds," in *Adrienne Rich: Poetry and Prose,* ed. Barbara Charlesworth Gelpi and Albert Gelpi (New York: Norton, 1993), 300.

23. For searching commentary on this poem and Bishop's work more generally, see Jamie McKendrick, "Bishop's Birds," in *Elizabeth Bishop: Poet of the Periphery,* ed. Linda Anderson and Jo Shapcott (Newcastle upon Tyne: Bloodaxe, 2002), 123–42.

24. "Tintern Abbey," l. 99; *The Prelude* (1805), 6:542.

25. *Biographia Literaria,* ed. Engell and Bate, 2:23.

26. Bonnie Costello, *Elizabeth Bishop: Questions of Mastery* (Cambridge, MA: Harvard University Press, 1991), 6, 8.

27. Ibid., 123–24.

28. See ibid., 218, for a comparison between "The Monument" and "Kubla Khan."

29. Stevens, *Opus Posthumous,* 171.

30. See Longenbach, *Wallace Stevens.*

31. See Stevens, *The Necessary Angel,* 31, 30, and Bornstein, *Transformations of Romanticism,* 205.

32. Stevens, *The Necessary Angel,* 31.

33. Stevens, *Opus Posthumous,* 248, 249.

34. Compare "The Eolian Harp," l. 28 ("A light in sound, a sound-like power

in light"), and *Biographia Literaria,* 1:304 (where the "primary IMAGINATION" is said to be "a repetition in the finite mind of the eternal act of creation in the infinite I AM").

35. Jonathan Bate, *The Song of the Earth* (London: Picador, 2000), 282.

36. Canto 81, in Ezra Pound, *The Cantos* (London: Faber, 1975).

John Keats and Tony Harrison:
The Burden of History

John Whale

In this essay, I want to consider some of the ways in which poetry is informed by history and is able to articulate its own historical self-consciousness. My starting point is Tony Harrison's "A Kumquat for John Keats," an avowed and explicit gift exchange from one poet to another. On the surface at least, the poem seems relatively free from the agonized anxiety of influence that is often thought to haunt such exchanges. What I found most interesting in Harrison's gift, however, was the burden of history it contained. Harrison's poem assumes, as we might expect from a poet whose very aesthetic has been described as post-holocaustal,[1] an innocence on Keats's part that tends only to reify the ways in which Keats's life and art have been turned into a "life of allegory"—a voyage of the spirit, a purifying martyrdom that transcends suffering and, strangely, places the poet beyond the reach of history. And so, before proceeding to an analysis of "A Kumquat for John Keats," it is necessary to inquire briefly into two other distinctive twentieth-century reimaginings of Keats which, in their different ways, focus on the problematic nature of his legacy: namely, what is perceived as his linguistic excess and his removal from the business of history through various forms of biographical and aesthetic transcendence.

Amy Clampitt provides one of the most celebrated and explicit reimaginings of Keats in twentieth-century poetry. Clampitt hears the echoes of Milton and Keats, and admits to never quite being able to shake them off. In her essay "Robert Frost and the Better Part of Poetry," which focuses on the importance of the auditory imagination, she shows how much Keats is her touchstone.[2] And in her explicit poetic homage to Keats, "Voyages"—a sequence of eight poems published in *What the Light Was Like* (1985)—she maps out an American lineage from Keats through Hart Crane to herself. The sequence charts a voyage of the soul performed by the imagination. Though most of the poems' titles ("Margate," "Teignmouth," "Chichester," "The Isle of Wight," "Winchester: the Autumn Equinox") are rooted in place, the sequence in fact articulates a profound dislocation, an exile of spirit in which place is actually only an uncongenial limit, even blank incarceration, that must be transcended along with the particularity of relationship. The allegory of a life illustrated in Clampitt's voyage is one of spiritual transcendence and liberation performed by the imagination. Keats moves beyond the limit of place and romance to an inner freedom that can be experienced only as anticipation. The imagination is already elsewhere in these poems. Through imaginative anticipation, Keats is in the New World with his brother George and his sister-in-law, Georgiana—something of obvious importance for Clampitt—and he has already experienced the "warm South": "the Italy he'd never seen, though in / imagination he already lived there: / his mind's America. Bright star."[3] Keats's martyrdom, for Clampitt, is a peculiarly poetic and spiritual one: the state of the artist, as the final powerful title poem in the sequence makes clear, is an exile, a martyrdom to one's alienating creativity, which is also one's true home. In this way, Clampitt is able to link Crane, Mandelstam, and Keats. All three are displaced and susceptible to the kind of paradoxical sense of belonging that haunts the American poetic imagination.

The success of Clampitt's reimagining of Keats is achieved more through the letters than through the poetry. Keats's epistolary style renders its subject accessible to the demands of the twentieth-century imagination in a way that the poetry itself—except in broken phrases—cannot. Clampitt illustrates the need to transcend Keats's poetic style with a pared-down, late twentieth-century poetic idiom that deftly negotiates between the quiddity of things and the understated yearning of the idealizing imagination.

In the case of Keats's other most famous reworker in twentieth-century poetry—Wilfred Owen—the problem has largely been how to transcend the predecessor's dangerously lush style. In Owen's case, the disciplining of the Keatsian excess is, in part at least, thought of as having been performed by war. Douglas Kerr puts it starkly and aggressively. After referring to the "Romantic afflatus of Wordsworth and Coleridge, Scott, Keats and Shelley," he offers the following account of Owen's poetic development:

> Everyone knows that Owen's war writings eventually came to take a challenging and sometimes hostile posture toward that tradition, but it took first-hand experience of warfare to expose what came to seem its inadequacies and dishonesties. The war was the bleak unforgiving critic that caused the foliage of Romanticism to wither for Owen; without that experience, he might have been as content to sport in its comfortable shade as his cousin, and fellow poet, Leslie Gunston.[4]

And in support of this supposition of the incompatibility of a Keatsian aesthetic and the subject of war, there is in Owen's correspondence a letter to Leslie Gunston of 25 July 1915 that tantalizingly broaches the question of Keats's own apparent elision of the Napoleonic wars from his poetry, a question hauntingly reminiscent of the one often leveled against Jane Austen:

> I wonder that you don't ply me with this argument; that Keats remained absolutely indifferent to Waterloo and that commotion. Well, I *have* passed a year of fine-contemptuous nonchalance: but having now some increase of physical strength I feel proportionately useful and proportionately lacking in sense if I don't use it in the best way—The Only Way.[5]

If, in this instance, we can assume that Owen's entry into a useful, physically strong, and martial masculinity is set against a figure of the indolent, feminized Keatsian aesthete, we could read this as an exit from his complex romance with Keats as he prepares himself physically for war: a physical preparation soon to be matched by a linguistic one in the poetry. Although Kerr goes on to suggest that the terms of Owen's "feverish" biographical response to Keats—another version of what we might think of as Keatsian sensuousness—were to reappear in such poems as "Dulce et Decorum Est," "S.I.W," "Greater Love," and "The Kind Ghosts,"[6] the poetic progress he maps out assumes the replacement of feverishness with a more safely masculinized and healthy resolve. What I would like to question here is not the truth of this development for Owen as a poet, but the assumption by his critics, including Kerr, of the inevitability of this "progress." It is true that for the young Owen, Keats represented an ideal of beauty and friendship bordering on holiness, to the extent that he was surprised and relieved after reading the *Letters* to find that his idolized young Romantic poet actually had a sense of humor. As he put it, much in the manner of Keats himself, "he didn't lack humour, narrabitavit."[7] But even the terms of Owen's romance with Keats—"To be in love with a youth and a dead 'un,"[8] as he had once described it in a letter—are capable of mixing romance with a gritty realism. And, even at his most "feverish," Owen's agonized and ecstatic, though book-learned, intimacy with the dead poet might have served him well in verse to come. Keatsian sensuousness might actually get to the heart of the thing. After reading W. M. Rossetti's *Life of Keats,* Owen wrote, "Rossetti guided my groping hand right into the wound, and I touched, for one moment the incandescent Heart of Keats."[9]

Recent Keats criticism has expended a great deal of energy tracing and uncovering the complex ways in which his poetry addresses political and social issues.[10] The Victorian construction of an aesthete Keats has been replaced, in the new orthodoxy, by a radical liberal, dissenting, and thoroughly politicized consciousness that manifests itself obliquely, indirectly, but nevertheless powerfully in the poems. "To Autumn" is now assumed quite confidently to be a political poem dealing with social unrest. This kind of sociologically explicit and political referencing of Keats's poetry interests me less—for the purposes of this essay—than the way in which Keats's "style" might have been thought to stand outside history rather than being conceived of as symptomatic of it. The more long-standing critical question of Keats's "stylistic badness" offers, I think, a more productive way of linking Keats with one of contemporary English poetry's more conspicuous and disturbing talents, Tony Harrison.

Marjorie Levinson's provocative and iconoclastic 1988 study, *Keats's Life of Allegory: The Origins of a Style,* returned critical attention to the embarrassing awkwardness of style that had first been addressed in the hostile reception afforded to Keats's poems in contemporary reviews. The problem of "stylistically self-indulgent verse: prolix, repetitive, metrically and lexically licentious, overwrought" is brought by Levinson into the domain of class and history. She mobilizes the language of sexual abuse deployed by the early reviewers and turns it to historical account so that what she calls Keats's "masturbatory exhibitionism" can be seen in a class context as part of "the self-fashioning gestures of the petty bourgeoisie." What Christopher Ricks had previously described as Keats's "conscious discomforture"—a poetry not simply about but creatively engaged with embarrassment—can now be viewed as symptomatic of Keats's quest to be legitimized by the Establishment culture. But what Keats produces from his position of anxious exclusion is a poetry that is "aggressively literary and therefore not just 'not Literature,' but, in effect, *anti*-Literature: a parody."[11] Even if one might, quite reasonably, disagree that there is a straightforward relationship between "parody" and "anti-Literature," the suggestion here that Keats's "overwrought" style might be read as an agonized and creative marker of his precarious status as a writer, that the excess of Keats's poetic language might be seen as dialectical and historically informed, seems to me to be liberating and suggestive for the way in which we might think of poetic style's relationship to history. Too often, perhaps, the assumption—following the prefaces to *Lyrical Ballads* and the watchwords of American Modernism—has been on the side of simplicity and purity, of a paring down. The possibility of excess or "overwroughtness" being a sign of historical self-consciousness in poetry seems worth exploring, especially when one encounters the poetry of Tony Harrison where an aggressively deployed literariness allows the deracinated poet to speak subversively and disconcertingly from behind the lines of English poetry. Although we have swapped the lower-middle-class, precarious Keats for Harrison, the fraught working-class classicist, the latter's self-proclaimed militant "occupation" of "lease-hold poetry" pushes the sign of poetry to an excess and often, as we shall see, to the limit of its historical vulnerability.

In the preface to his 1975 translations of "that gloomy epigrammatist of the fourth century AD, Palladas of Alexandria,"[12] Harrison provides an interesting account of a historically determined "bitterness." According to Harrison, Palladas manifests "a bitterness compounded of historical pessimism."[13] This brief preface is eager to locate Palladas in a violent, sectarian society in which the last vestiges of the poet's pagan culture are being swept away by the brutality of an emergent Christianity. Palladas's chosen poetic modes—his "mordant wit," his "point," and his "strong sense of form," as well as his embarrassing "railing against the dying of the light"—are thus, for Harrison, conjured by the poet in the face of an uncongenial epochal shift. History impinges on poetry and manifests itself in form. Poetry itself, it is suggested, is marked by the historical process but contains the embarrassing capacity to speak out. Palladas's classicism is anything but dignified stoicism; its "point" contains a disturbing refusal to shut up. Harrison's preface ends, as one might expect from him, with a contraction—perhaps one had better say a concentration—of the historical and metaphysical consciousness to the question of poetic form:

> There is a strong sense of form in Palladas and it is something which barely seems able to contain the apoplectic energy of his nihilistic scorn. It is as if the formal endeavor and metrical tension were all that stood between Palladas and the choking silence, sheer cosmic exasperation and what Beckett's Lucky calls "divine aphasia."[14]

Harrison conjures the figure of Beckett's Lucky not only to alert us to the silence around all poetry but, inversely, to that character's hauntingly maimed logorrhea: a ritual, excessive flow of language emanating from one previously assumed to be dumb. The figure of Beckett's Lucky joins a well-developed litany of maimed speakers throughout the corpus of Harrison's work whose apparent incapacity with language is uncannily associated with the flow of poetry. Even Harrison's uncles, "one a stammerer, the other dumb,"[15] stand in some genealogical relationship to his own poetic prowess. In the paradox best exemplified by Demosthenes, the stammerer who filled his mouth with pebbles to give himself the power of fluent oratory, those whose mouths are apparently empty because silent, turn out to have "gobs" productively full of an almost divine eloquence.

Harrison's terse reflections on Palladas might tempt one into making a simple connection between the fourth-century epigrammatist and the early 1970s translator and sonneteer. To many prominent reviewers of his work in the late 1970s and early 1980s, Harrison's own strongly developed sense of form was something that engendered, in them, an embarrassed awkwardness.[16] Certainly, the subjects of Harrison's translations, even if they do not provide a straightforward substitute or alter ego for the translator, seem to act as a catalyst for his fascination with pessimism. One might even go as far as to suggest that Harrison's translations manifest a relish for Palladas's poetic bitterness. What I wish to identify in Harrison's "versions" of Palladas's poems is his concern for historical self-consciousness and an awareness of the manifestation of historical pressure within the form of a poem: the idea that form itself might stand as a historical marker, particularly when seen as a sign of "excess." Its very excess, then, is capable of being seen as a register of historical pressure. Harrison's point about "pointedness" is that it stands out. There is always a worrying aspect, in the sense of being overdetermined, about this sticking to form. Palladas the pagan poet under siege from a militant Christianity also enables Harrison to explore his own embattled humanism, something on which he has spoken very eloquently and something that lies at the heart of his poetry. The example of Palladas suggests how, in Harrison, poetry and humanism operate in tandem. In—or, should one say, because of—the silence that surrounds it, poetry is the marker of our mortality. In respect of its suggestions about the relationship between history and poetry, silence and humanism, and, most particularly, in its articulation of the necessary creativity of bitterness, Palladas's work, then, provides an interesting point of departure for understanding Harrison's verse epistle to John Keats, written at the very end of the 1970s.[17]

"A Kumquat for John Keats" represents Harrison's most sustained engagement with the Romantic poet. Two other poems invoke Keats. "Viewless Wings," one of his "Curtain Sonnets," takes its title and its figuring of Aurora from Keats, as Harrison situates himself on "England's northern edge for nightingales";[18] the poem explores the historical difference, based on military threat, that separates "Keats's age" and "ours." Keats figures briefly, along with Milton and Wordsworth, in "Them & [uz]," one of the more prominent poems in the sonnet sequence *Continuous*, as part of the poet's complex cultural deracination: Harrison has been cut off from his working-class roots because of his education and engagement in literary scholarship and, as a working-class scholarship boy, from poetry because of his accent. Keats, along with Wordsworth, is mustered as support in Harrison's knowledgeable revenge against former teachers and their investment in "Received Pronunciation." Just as Harrison is delighted to announce, in retrospect, that the Cumbrian Wordsworth rhymes "chatters" with "waters" so the pupil, remembering having been interrupted by his grammar school teacher in his reading aloud of Keats's

"Ode to a Nightingale," now responds with a knowing parenthesis:

Poetry's the speech of kings. You're one of those
Shakespeare gives the comic bits to: prose!
All poetry (even Cockney Keats?) you see
's been dubbed by [^s] into RP.[19]

Keats, like Wordsworth, then, has been enlisted conveniently by Harrison to figure English class conflict focused through language, although most scholars might take a very different view of the respective social rank or class positions of the two Romantic poets, neither of whom would usually be thought of as "working class," even if social unease is a significant aspect of Keats's poetry and of the response it generated among his contemporaries. In "A Kumquat for John Keats," Harrison leaves the issue of class behind—or at least unspoken—as he assumes a fraternal bond with a fellow male poet. Beyond that, the grounds of the camaraderie that allows for the gift exchange of a poem, culminating, as we shall see, in a meeting of poetic souls, are fairly straightforward: Keats is the poet of love, beauty, and death—and, more particularly, a poet of sensory, specifically oral, relish.

When "A Kumquat for John Keats" appeared (it was first published in *PN Review* in 1979 and subsequently as an illustrated pamphlet by Bloodaxe in 1981), it seemed to be part of a new flowering of Harrison's talent, in some ways constituting a release or break from the tight Meredithian sonnets that had composed most of his original output (as against his translations) throughout the previous ten years in the sequences *From the School of Eloquence* and *Continuous*. In this new group of poems written in Florida (which includes the closely related "The Fire-Gap," "Cypress and Cedar," and "The Lords of Life"), a new creative surge and inventive playfulness is evident as Harrison finds poetic ways of exploring the immediate present of his life.[20] These poems exploit his prodigious talent as a translator of classical satire—from the ancients through to Molière—to harness the power of occasional poetry; at their best, they couple this ceremonializing of the present tense with an anguished sense of romance. The poem, I think, with the strongest affinity to "A Kumquat for John Keats" is "The Fire-Gap: A Poem with Two Tales."[21] This iconic or emblematic poem (which was also published in pamphlet form by Bloodaxe in

1983) offers an interesting example of how, at this stage of his career, Harrison's commitment to the present and to his immediate locale is more than mere convenience. In a process reminiscent of Lawrence's "Snake," Harrison, in "The Fire-Gap," addresses a rattler across the divide—the fire-gap of the title—between the wild and the cultured. From an initial position of fear, the poet ends up sympathetically accommodating the snake in the gap between the two, unlike his aggressively disposed Bible-belt neighbors. The very form of the poem, as designed by Michael Christopher Caine, exploits this characteristically Harrisonian dichotomy by presenting the image of the rattler in the gap between the parallel verses. The conflict laid out and epitomized by the snake—between light and dark, the wild and the cultured or cultivated—is dramatically measured against a violently offensive masculine alter ego. (This is also true of "The Lords of Life," where Harrison's poem self-consciously expresses the impasse of communication between himself and his macho, redneck neighbor.) In its bold address, alternate rhymes, and confident assumption of a flexible verse epistle, "The Fire-Gap" is unafraid of its local detail, its happy inclusion, and its quiet assumption of the biographical. In its conclusion, it provides a fitting end for this immediacy: "the only real eternity is a tale (like your tail) in the mouth." This subscription to a material image of eternity, the Greek *Ouroboros*[22] (an image that refutes the harmful metaphysics of religion), permeates Harrison's work—in the circles of fire he conjures from Dante; in the scorched rings on the cobbles on VE Day; in the image of his mother's ring, imagined in the white heat of the crematorium; in the sign of nuclear holocaust; in the circles inhabiting his ideas of "continuous" cinema programs and the "looped tape" of his most famous antiwar poem, "A Cold Coming"; and in his insistent inquiry into "Nothingness."

"A Kumquat for John Keats" opens with gleeful confidence about the aptness of the poet's newly discovered kumquat: "Today I found the right fruit for my prime" (though "prime" seems somewhat misplaced). For all its relish of things savored orally and its abiding awareness of mortality, the poem is also a poetic exchange between souls. Harrison sees the kumquat in line 42 as the "best . . . metaphor, to fit the soul / of one in Florida at 42"; and refers in line 78 in a suitably ambivalent way to his "grudging but glad spirit." In the gustatory climax of the poem he claims, "My spirit greets / the kumquat with the spirit of John Keats." The tenor of the opening paragraph and the measured perspective of the poem as a whole, however, are better gauged by Harrison's presentation of himself as "a man of doubt." The poetic confidence, linguistic facility, and imaginative aptness are accompanied by—and are in the service of—a profound metaphysical skepticism. Harrison proceeds to put words (as well as a kumquat) in Keats's mouth. Harrison's imagined "gift" is rendered, through Milton, into one of metaphysical bitterness—a dubious gift of the fallen knowledge of the modern historical condition. The kumquat thus enables Harrison to challenge Keats while exploring the grounds of his own skepticism—a skepticism prompted by his savoring of the mutually defining bittersweet quality of the fruit:

he'd bite just once and then apostrophize
and pen one stanza how the fruit had all
the qualities of fruit before the Fall,
but in the next few lines be forced to write
how Eve's apple tasted at the second bite. . . .

I'd offer Keats some kumquats and I'd say:
You'll find that one part's sweet and one part's tart:
say where the sweetness or the sourness start.

As the paragraph reaches its conclusion, it suddenly moves out of straight couplets into alternate rhymes in order to articulate the meaning of the kumquat:

Then it's the kumquat fruit expresses best
how days have darkness round them like a rind,
life has a skin of death that keeps its zest.

The middle line introduces another metaphorical and quasi-autobiographical strand to the poem to which Harrison will return in a later paragraph but which, until this point, has been signaled only by a tense parenthesis at the opening: "(though last year full of bile and self-defeat / I wanted to believe that no life was sweet)." The pressure of this more personal bitterness, as opposed to the pressure of history or metaphysical doubt, is allowed to break in to the poem in order to provide the grim frame for its current romantic zest for life, much as the poem's ending sets the "bleak cries" of buzzards overhead against its slightly coy reference to sexual pleasure evident in the sound of the bedsprings.

This sense of measured ambivalence, which is evident in the opening phase of the poem, is suddenly ruptured by the introduction of the following couplet at the beginning of a new verse paragraph: "History, a life, the heart, the brain / Flow to the taste buds and flow back again." This jarring couplet effects a break from the initial fancy of the opening section in which Harrison, the self-consciously apostrophizing poet, alights on the kumquat as the fruit most fit to stand as a poetic bond between himself and his Romantic predecessor. (Something of the exotic flavor of the poem has been lost with the now relatively common sight of kumquats in supermarkets, but when the poem first appeared, Harrison was obviously justified in relishing the incongruity and excess of the kumquat in the same way that Keats reaches beyond apple, quince, and plum for "gourd" in *The Eve of St Agnes.*) Keats, dead at twenty-five; Harrison, reanimated by romance at forty-two: history now introduces the sourer note of a more significant, unbridgeable difference. The couplet quoted above, however, still meets Keats on the shared ground of the oral imagination. As if to reinforce this connection, Harrison's public readings of the poem in the 1980s were usually accompanied by accurately remembered and vibrantly performed quotations from Keats's letters, including the letter of 28 August 1819 to his sister Fanny, where he professes his desire to promenade around her gardens "apple tasting—pear-tasting—plumb-judging—apricot nibbling—peach sc[r]unching—Nectarine-sucking and Melon carving,"[23] and his letter to Dilke of 22 December of that same year where he reveals that "this moment I was writing with one hand, and with the other holding to my Mouth a Nectarine—good god how fine—It went down soft pulpy, slushy, oozy—all its delicious enbonpoint melted down my throat like a large beatified Strawberry" (*Letters of John Keats,* 2:179).

Not simply common mortality then but "History" informs the very organs of sense perception, just as in the preface to Palladas it had been seen by Harrison to inform the very organism of the poem. Harrison's substitution of his recently encountered kumquat in place of "the grape John Keats thought fit to be Joy's fruit" in "Ode on Melancholy" further emphasizes the burden of historical consciousness.

In what is still in many ways a celebratory love poem, Harrison introduces the burden of history, the better to appreciate the nature of human joy. Harrison's humanism allies itself with Keats's own more obviously agnostic brand of humanism to celebrate love and life within limits. The "full life" conjured at life's midway by forty-two-year-old Harrison—much like Keats's "full-grown lambs" reeking of mortality and the implied onset of slaughter in his elegiac "To Autumn"—must be measured by the surrounding emptiness, just as poetry is measured by its surrounding silence.

As Harrison's paragraph on "History" proceeds, it leads to a decentering, abstracted core to the poem:

That decade or more past Keats's span
makes me an older not a wiser man,
who knows that it's too late for dying young,
but since youth leaves some sweetnesses unsung,
he's granted days and kumquats to express
Man's Being ripened by his Nothingness.
And it isn't just the gap of sixteen years,
a bigger crop of terrors, hopes and fears,
but a century of history on this earth
between John Keats's death and my own birth—
years like an open crater, gory, grim,
with bloody bubbles leering at the rim;
a thing no bigger than an urn explodes
and ravishes all silence, and all odes,
Flora asphyxiated by foul air
unknown to either Keats or Lemprière,
dehydrated Naiads, Dryad amputees
dragging themselves through slagscapes with no trees,
a shirt of Nessus fire that gnaws and eats
children half the age of dying Keats.

Far from claiming superior wisdom, Harrison's poem is founded on the problem of the historical burden. As it moves from biographical to historical difference it confronts the full force of the paradox of bitterness it has set in motion with its choice of the kumquat: "Man's Being ripened by his Nothingness." There is perhaps a gritty humanism here, but one that does not find it easy to dissociate itself completely from a competing idea of despairing nihilism. This is confirmed in what is perhaps the most devastating and worrying image in the poem, one that is in danger of undercutting the abiding image of the fruit: "a thing no bigger than an urn explodes / and ravishes all silence, and all odes." The full force of the nuclear threat as articulated in this poem is not only its capacity to "explode" Keats's poetry, poetry more generally, and culture beyond that, but also its capability of "ravish[ing] all silence." Here, Harrison's language pushes against the ineffable. The use of the Keatsian verb "to ravish" makes all too clear the ruination of romance. The dreadful comparisons that follow between Keatsian classical figures and the realm of twentieth-century warfare seem almost redundant after this. It is therefore not surprising that the verse paragraph reaches no syntactical conclusion and remains fragmented and unresolved in a series of ellipses.

The rupture provided by "History" is complemented by one which, in an equally daring way, wrenches the poem back to a grim autobiographical scene of family suffering. Harrison's lines on "Days" are as disconcerting and potentially disruptive as the lines on history:

> Each evening when I reach to draw the blind
> stars seem the light zest squeezed through night's black rind;
> the night's peeled fruit the sun, juiced of its rays,
> first stains, then streaks, then floods the world with days,
> days, when the very sunlight made me weep,
> days, spent like the nights in deep, drugged sleep,
> days in Newcastle by my daughter's bed,
> wondering if she, or I, weren't better dead,
> days in Leeds, grey days, my first dark suit,
> my mother's wreaths stacked next to Christmas fruit,
> and days, like this in Micanopy. Days!

What begins as an extended and slightly forced comparison between the two sides of the poem—the dark and light, the fruit both bitter and sweet—ends up as a dangerously inexplicable and stalled apostrophe from which the poem has to recover itself in its problematic return to an intensely realized and located present.

This concern with "Nothingness" posed against the consolation of human love is evident in Harrison's first book, *The Loiners,* published in 1970.[24] In two poems situated toward the end of that collection—"Newcastle Is Peru" and "Ghosts: Some Words before Breakfast"—Harrison bravely articulates the tough-minded reality of his humanism. In the former poem, a return to the desolate hearth, as center of the home, leads to a raking over of the ashes of the poet's past, which culminates in the kind of disturbing disorientation promised in its title:

> I lay down, dizzy, drunk, alone,
> life circling life like the Eddystone
> dark sea, but lighting nothing; sense
> nor center, nor circumference.[25]

In the manner of a latter-day John Donne, Harrison turns to the heroics of an intimate and domesticated love besieged by the wasting energies of history. In terse, epigrammatic understatement, he proclaims, "we brave / harsh opposition when we love," and goes on to offer up the specifics of "this cluttered room" in a rhetoric of a heroic, metaphysical conceit:

> this poor, embattled fortress, this strong-
> hold of love, that can't last long
> against the world's bold cannonade
> of loveless warfare and cold trade,
> this bed, this fire, and lastly us,
> naked, bold, adventurous.[26]

This image of love striving against the odds, the boldness of sexual love set to match the bold cannonade of the world, does not provide the final scene of the poem, however. There, the isolated male poet confronts his own besmirched and besmirching identity as his coal-dusted, whorled fingerprints "press onwards into nothingness," while the fire, kindled with a newspaper supplement dealing with breast cancer, presents him with a gruesome and disturbing image of a woman's body.

In the poem that forms the moving final section of *The Loiners,* "Ghosts: Some Words before Breakfast," Harrison moves from heterosexual love to paternal and maternal love in a poem dedicated to his daughter, Jane. Once again, Harrison is concerned to measure love against "Nothingness," but in this instance he pushes further with an idea of the limited transcendence of love embodied in the physical contact of a kiss. The choice of the word "trophallaxis" from the scientific discourse of natural history (the exchange of food between adult insects and their larvae) is but one disturbing facet of these interesting lines that hinge problematically on the words "brave" and "scent," where the latter can be a verb as well as a noun. Harrison focuses with searing realism on the inefficacy of love, insistent on its inability to transcend time. He characteristically denies transcendence, but offers in its stead a short circuit, a humanist circling back on mortality—his own distinctive version of the classical *Ouroboros:*

> but my kiss can't make you less
> the helpless prey of Nothingness—
> *ring-a-ring-a-roses* . . . love
> goes gravewards but does move.
> Love's not something you can hoard
> against the geriatric ward.
> Mother, all, *all,* of us in this
> brave trophallaxis of a kiss
> that short-circuits generations scent
> mortality's rich nutriment.[27]

The sixth and final poem in the "Art & Extinction" section of *Continuous,* "t'Ark," contains a quatrain that comes closest to encapsulating this paradoxical basis of Harrison's poetry. Precisely because of its liminal, precarious status on the brink of collapse, poetry displays the essence, the cultural fingerprinting, of our humanity:

> Silence and poetry have their own reserves.
> The numbered creatures flourish less and less.
> A language near extinction best preserves
> the deepest grammar of our nothingness.[28]

For Harrison, the grammar school boy, there is a moving irony in his apparently vengeful statement of intent to "occupy" the "lousy leasehold Poetry" ("Them and [uz]") of the cultural establishment. It is because of its decayed and diminished status, its temporality rather than its permanence, its "leasehold" rather than eternal values, that poetry can best articulate the human spirit. All and the most that it can do, from Harrison's perspective, is to pose historically structured form—"deepest grammar"—against prevailing "nothingness."[29]

In his encounter with fellow poet John Keats, the "trophallaxis" of the kumquat does not, of course, take the form of a kiss, though it is focused on the male poet's experience of a kiss. The nature of the exchange is, however, somewhat ambivalent and forlorn: the kumquat brings with it a taste of the Fall or, at least, a taste of history's lost innocence. The fruit that suits Harrison, but not Keats, carries the bitter burden of history. It is the fruit John Keats cannot possibly eat. Keats's historical innocence is posed against the terrible difference of twentieth-century experience. The objects of Keats's classical and pastoral imagination are now blown apart, violated or fragmented in the face of Harrison's grimmer late twentieth-century reality. Harrison the classicist deploys Keats's classical world in order to reveal its inadequacy for his own contemporaneity. His agenda here differs somewhat from that of his translations, which, far from conjuring the classical past as an age of polished innocence, seek to release the classics from such a falsifying aesthetic. In his versions of Palladas, Harrison creatively gives voice to the Alexandrian poet's capacity to deal with unspeakable atrocity and nihilism. Harrison seems, however, uninterested in exploring, even allowing for, how Keats might be deploying the classical pastoral in order to deal with, rather than shy away from, the harsh realities of death, disease, pain, and oppression. In equating Keats with a historical innocence, Harrison seems to be subscribing to a Victorian, post-Romantic vision of Keats that combines the innocence of early death with an innocent aesthetic, rather than to a vision that views Keats's search for excess, for sensation, as a deliberate foray into the dangerously disfiguring conjunction of poetic form and historical self-consciousness.

Notes

1. See Antony Rowland, *Tony Harrison and the Holocaust* (Liverpool: Liverpool University Press, 2001); Rick Rylance, "Doomsongs: Tony Harrison and War," in *Tony Harrison: Loiner*, ed. Sandie Byrne (Oxford: Clarendon Press, 1997).

2. Amy Clampitt, *Predecessors, Et Cetera* (Ann Arbor: University of Michigan Press, 1991), 160, 147–53.

3. Amy Clampitt, *Collected Poems* (London: Faber and Faber, 1998), 170.

4. Douglas Kerr, *Wilfred Owen's Voices: Language and Community* (Oxford: Clarendon Press, 1993), 240.

5. Wilfred Owen, *Collected Letters,* ed. Harold Owen and John Bell (London: Oxford University Press, 1967), 349.

6. Kerr, *Wilfred Owen's Voices,* 249.

7. Owen, *Collected Letters,* 129.

8. Ibid., 187.

9. Ibid., 161.

10. See, e.g., Nicholas Roe, *John Keats and the Culture of Dissent* (Oxford: Clarendon Press, 1997); James Chandler, *England in 1819: The Politics of Literary Culture and the Case of Romantic Historicism* (Chicago: University of Chicago Press, 1998); Alan Bewell, "The Political Implications of Keats's Classicist Aesthetics," *Studies in Romanticism* 25 (1986): 220–29; Jerome McGann, "Keats and the Historical Method in Literary Criticism," *Modern Language Notes* 94 (1979): 988–1032; Daniel P. Watkins, *Keats's Poetry and the Politics of the Imagination* (Madison, NJ: Fairleigh Dickinson University Press, 1989).

11. Marjorie Levinson, *Keats's Life of Allegory: The Origins of a Style* (Oxford: Basil Blackwell, 1988), 3, 4, 5.

12. Tony Harrison, *Palladas: Poems, a Selection in Versions* (London: Anvil, 1975), i.

13. Ibid., iii.

14. Ibid., iv.

15. Tony Harrison, epigraph to *Continuous: 50 Sonnets from the School of Eloquence* (London: Rex Collings, 1981).

16. See, e.g., Christopher Reid, "Articulating the Awkwardness," *Times Literary Supplement,* 15 January 1982, 49.

17. For brief considerations of this poem, see N. S. Thompson, "Book Ends: Public and Private in Tony Harrison's Poetry," in *Tony Harrison: Loiner,* ed. Byrne, 129–31; and Rylance, "Doomsongs," 143–44.

18. Tony Harrison, *Selected Poems* (Harmondsworth: Penguin, 1984), 56.

19. Ibid., 122.

20. For a consideration of this group of poems, see Luke Spencer, *The Poetry of Tony Harrison* (New York: Harvester Wheatsheaf, 1994), 100–113.

21. Tony Harrison, *The Fire-Gap: A Poem with Two Tails* (Newcastle upon Tyne: Bloodaxe, 1985).

22. For a consideration of the letter "o" in Harrison's poetry, see Sandie Byrne, *H, V, & O: The Poetry of Tony Harrison* (Manchester: Manchester University Press, 1998).

23. *The Letters of John Keats, 1814–1821,* ed. Hyder Edward Rollins (Cambridge, MA: Harvard University Press, 1958), 2:149.

24. Tony Harrison, *The Loiners* (London: London Magazine Editions, 1970).

25. Harrison, *Selected Poems,* 64.

26. Ibid., 66.

27. Ibid., 73.

28. "t'Ark," in Harrison, *Selected Poems,* 178.

29. For a brief consideration of Harrison's juxtaposition of poetry and history, see Damian Grant, "Poetry versus History: Voices Off in the Poetry of Tony Harrison," in *Tony Harrison,* ed. Neil Astley (Newcastle upon Tyne: Bloodaxe, 1991), 105–13.

"Johnny's in the Basement": Keats, Bob Dylan, and the End of Influence

Richard Marggraf Turley

This essay is not pitched—has no desire to pitch in—as a contribution to the "John Keats versus Bob Dylan" debate. Attentive to the nature of Dylan's relationship with Keats, my discussion is not however detained by questions of relative literary merit, perhaps *the* chestnut of the "high" versus "low" culture debates of the 1990s. While the agon of the Keats-Dylan opposition has made for compelling reading, these figures are too diverse, too representative of different *types* of authorship, for meaningful evaluative comparison. Indeed, the essential *dis*parity between Keats and Dylan is what is at issue in this essay. I wish to suggest that the crucial aspect separating the two men as "types" of writer is their attitude toward influence, their respective poise in the presence of the precursor. Keats's poetic forebears included Milton, of whom he famously declared, "Life to him would be death to me."[1] In turn, John(ny) Keats is a prominent figure in Dylan's literary basement. But whereas the "overpowering idea of our dead poets" (Keats's formulation in a letter dated 9 June 1819) inspires and unsettles the Romantic poet in equal measure, Keats's bearing on Dylan is less psychologically corrosive. While the precursor poems used by Dylan to generate "new" lyrics might well be, and often are, paradigmatically anxious themselves, the new works, I would contend, emerge largely untroubled by any original Romantic disquietude. Dylan, then, effectively steps out of Bloomian paradigms, demonstrating an end to influence as we have been encouraged to understand it as an essentially parricidal engagement.

Richard Marggraf Turley

Forever/For Ever Young

Howard Sounes is not the first critic to draw attention to conjunctions between the title and refrain of Bob Dylan's 1974 song "Forever Young" and stanza 3 of "Ode on a Grecian Urn":[2]

> happy love!
> For ever warm and still to be enjoy'd,
> For ever panting, and for ever young.[3]

But apart from the verbal similitude, what do the two texts have in common? Keats's famously troubled ode records a poetic life-and-death struggle with an artifact of classical culture. The superlative precursor aesthetic, like the lovers on the urn's "leaf-fring'd" legend, remains "forever young," taunting Keats with its perfection and giving rise to a textual dialectic exemplarily illustrative of the anxiety of influence as outlined by Bloom in *The Anxiety of Influence,* which appeared in 1973. In contrast to Keats's and Bloom's meditations on anxiety, Dylan's "Forever Young," a simple prayer for the artist's son, is (outwardly, at least) free from the anxieties and contestations that demoralize Keats's narrative persona. "May you stay forever young," Dylan intercedes tenderly on his son's behalf. In Dylan's song, the idea of a permanently youthful aesthetic, oppressive to Keats in "Ode on a Grecian Urn," has diminished into a mere figure of speech, a harmless piece of rhetoric: after all, it's hardly to be supposed that Dylan is requesting actual immortality. On the face of it, then, the notion of eternal youth has been drained of the unease that accompanied it in the Ode.

It may not be *quite* as clear-cut as all that, of course. I began by stating that Dylan's songs are largely untroubled by Bloomian anxiety. From one perspective, though, "Forever Young," a lyric addressed by a father to a son, could also be understood as ruminating on the theme of comparative achievement. Apparent deep-level disjunctures between "Ode on a Grecian Urn" and "Forever Young" actually begin to look rather less decisive or even disappear altogether in lines 5–6 of the song:

> May you build a ladder to the stars
> And climb on every rung.

"Like I've done," does Dylan mean? After all, one might expect the Dylan of 1974, aggressively asserting his achievements to date, to be different from the more mature, at times apparently resigned Dylan of 2006, who looks for closure and who senses the "mercy of God must be near" ("Not Dark Yet," 1999). Or is the pleasure of accomplishment sought here—climbing on every rung—vicarious and disinterested? It's difficult to say, since all texts involving sons and fathers are potentially vulnerable to competitive tensions, to family romances. We should certainly consider the possibility that while Dylan may have intended to take only the phrase "for ever young" from Keats's poem, some of the patrifilial struggles centered on it might have been transferred, too.[4] That is to say, the phrase "forever young" in Dylan's song may be freighted with Keats's original anxiety.

The question interestingly is not simply whether Dylan is engaged in a family romance with his son in "Forever Young" but whether Dylan is engaged in a family romance with Keats. Two archetypes offer themselves as a basis for determining the nature of the relationship's dialectic. In the first, Dylan's attitude toward Keats is benevolent, a reversal of "Forever Young," the son looking down kindly on the father now. Echoes of Keats in Dylan's work—even the repetition on which "Forever Young" could be said to depend absolutely, since the title phrase occurs twelve times within the space of twenty-seven lines—are acts of good faith and constitute fond remembrances. Dylan's use of Keats is thus consummately pragmatic, Dylan finding in his precursor a gift of words that he is happy to accept. As he puts it in 1999's "Things Have Changed"—the bookend to 1963's "The Times They Are A-Changing"—"Only a fool in here would think he's got anything to prove."

The second version of the relationship is distinctly agonistic. Here the strong predecessor disables any ephebe who follows, as Keats is disabled by his overpowering sense of the urn's ageless perfection. Dylan worries, even as he "cites" Keats in his own work, that echoes of a once beautiful sound return weaker than the original report, always slightly diminished. It would be better not to allow Keats's voice to be heard at all, Dylan mutters, while accepting that he has little choice in the matter. At best, he recognizes, intonations of the precursor impart a secondhand glory to the new, yet always old, work of art. But they might also function to confirm the effortless superiority of the precursor aesthetic. Resentfully, then, Dylan endeavors to empty Keats's phrase of Keats. For if Dylan's title *is* a quotation from the Ode, then the capitalization of "for ever young" (three words in Keats), its contraction into "*Forever* Young" (two words in Dylan)—which remains, however, a grasping or squeezing together, not a creative squeezing out, or new birth—and enclosure in title quotation marks are acts of appropriation, signaling transferred ownership. In this reading, when Dylan says of his child/precursor, "May your song always be sung" (l. 24), he is really saying, "May *my* song always be sung," at the same time fearing that his art will prove less durable. Bloom formulates this sentiment in *The Anxiety of Influence* as, "Where it, the precursor's poem, is there let my poem be" (80).

Which of these two archetypes more accurately describes Dylan's demeanor toward Keats? The latter, essentially Bloomian in outlook? Or the former, approaching Shakespearean levels of pragmatism regarding sources and its relaxed—though in no way *lax*—bearing toward "originality"? The proposition I will be elaborating in this essay is that Dylan does not fit comfortably within the parameters of Bloom's classic study, which asserts that anxiety before the "Great Original" intensifies through Romanticism and Modernism to the present day. Dylan's attitude toward influence and originality, I wish to suggest, is radically at variance with the Bloomian model and marks a significant juncture in the psychology of late twentieth-century authorship. Indeed, my contention is that while Keats often appears to us as a tremulous poet, prototypically anxious in the manner Bloom outlines, Dylan enacts a return to the days "Before the Flood"—the title of his 1974 live album, as well as the phrase Bloom uses to designate writers (Shakespeare being the supreme example) who lived before the age of influence anxiety.[5] Dylan may very well be the greatest living writer; but he may also be one of the least original, originality no longer being, because it *can no longer be* so late in the day, the sine qua non of genius it was for Keats and his peers. While for Keats the condition of great literature was originality—and the 1810s was already too late safely to adopt that position—for Dylan it has become influence, or rather indifference to the ineluctability of influence. A punctilious stance on originality doomed Keats and other Romantics to a crisis of influence; and in one sense Keats's work is permanently "in crisis." By contrast, what I will be arguing is Dylan's extraordinary degree of freedom from anxiety—the condition of being in love with theft, to paraphrase the title of his most recent collection of songs—marks the end of the era of influence, the age after the flood in Bloom's terminology, at least as we have been urged to understand it. Since the bearing of Keats on Dylan cannot be fitted within the contours of Bloom's study, a retheorization of the relationship may prove instructive.

"To Live outside the Law You Must Be Honest"

Keats's "presence" in Dylan's work is extensive; in terms of concrete references, allusions, and verbal parallels more extensive perhaps than has been hitherto acknowledged. I want to begin by considering "Love Minus Zero/No Limit" from *Bringing It All Back Home* (1965). Once again we hear echoes of "Ode on a Grecian Urn":

> My love she speaks like silence
> Without ideals or violence
> She doesn't have to say she's faithful,
> Yet she's true like ice and fire.
> ("Love Minus Zero/No Limit," ll. 1–4)

Compare the above lines with the opening of Keats's Ode:

> Thou still unravish'd bride of quietness,
> Thou foster-child of silence and slow time
> ("Ode on a Grecian Urn," ll. 1–2)

Both texts—Dylan's "Love Minus Zero/No Limit," and Keats's best example of writing degree zero, whose "leaf-fring'd" legend, without beginning or end, points up the temporal limits of Keats's own end-stopped aesthetic—begin by contemplating a muse: Keats's urn, Dylan's lover. Each work addresses self-reflexively the mystery of composition, the text's coming into being as text.[6] Dylan's lover, like Keats's silent, unravished urn, is a bride of quietness and silence, similarly disassociated from "violence." In addition, neither muse is wholly tractable. The urn refuses to answer Keats's questions about the "leaf-fring'd legend"; indeed, the urn's only utterance, held back until the end of the poem, is a cryptic pronouncement as circular as the urn's leafy legend:

"Beauty is truth, truth beauty,"—that is all
Ye know on earth, and all ye need to know.
(ll. 49–50)[7]

Dylan's lover is equally enigmatic, since the words she speaks are reported as being "like silence."

There are further correspondences. Lines 15–16 of "Love Minus Zero/No Limit" powerfully evoke the aphoristic tone of lines 49–50 of "Ode on a Grecian Urn," as well as intriguingly mimicking their famous chiastic structure:

She knows there's no success like failure
And that failure's no success at all.
(ll. 15–16)

These lines offer a rare instance of chiasmus in Dylan's oeuvre.[8] But the point to emphasize is that they occur in a lyric attentively and distinctively involved in "Ode on a Grecian Urn." Incidentally—and perhaps not coincidentally—the Ode appears to have continued to preoccupy Dylan. The Ode's penultimate line is echoed in the penultimate line of *Masked and Anonymous* (2004), the notoriously inscrutable film coscripted by and starring Dylan:

> The one thing I've learned is that beauty and truth are in the eye of the beholder.

Here Dylan changes a common idiom into a knowing allusion.

What, then, is the precise nature of the relationship between "Love Minus Zero" and "Ode on a Grecian Urn"? Vitally, Dylan has not simply rewritten Keats or fallen headlong into his aesthetic. Rather, the precursor's high Romanticism, mindful of the importance of the marketplace even as it seeks to disguise its knowledge in Romantic ideology, has been updated into the late twentieth-century logic of literary production, into the world of marketing, tour managers, and sales figures—a world where, as Dylan sings in "Subterranean Homesick Blues," it's "hard to tell / If anything's going to sell" (ll. 39–40), although everything *is* for sale. In place of transcendent ideals such as "beauty" or "truth" (or, for the purposes of my argument, "originality"), Dylan substitutes new absolutes: "success" and "failure." Succumbing to the anxiety of influence signals failure. On the other hand, using the predecessor's text to enable one's own work of art counts as success in Dylan's book, and in the most literal sense. Dylan effectively circumvents the anxieties that torment Keats, since within this new dispensation "influence" itself is revealed as commodity, as something that can be bought and sold, or stolen, just like everything else. Maintain a steady trade in those most available and valuable of secondhand items, words and phrases, Dylan advises in "Love Minus Zero." The important thing is to make a sale, to succeed. Keats might frown on this new economy; by the terms of his idealistic and self-punishingly uncompromising aesthetic, unoriginality is synonymous with failure. But answering him is Dylan's equally insistent credo, "There's no success like failure." Dylan's work succeeds precisely because it fails in Romantic terms.[9] As Groucho Marx put it, "If you aim to fail, and succeed, which have you done?"

We might look back at those muses in "Love Minus Zero" and "Ode on a Grecian Urn." The key difference is that Keats's muse, the urn, exists primarily to awaken the poet to the problem of influence. "Without ideals," on the other hand (l. 2), Dylan's muse is *be*mused by the importance Keats attaches to his ideal (originality), wholly indifferent to the uses to which she will be put. Why reinvent the wheel, she asks, genuinely perplexed? Dylan's cheerful recycling of elements from Keats's ode in the upbeat, major-keyed "Love Minus Zero" is neither a resentful *clinamen* in Bloom's terms, nor a violent appropriation along the lines of the second paradigm I outlined at the beginning of this essay. We find no "correction" of Keats, no ill-willed misprisioning. Keats simply belongs to the inexhaustible literary community chest. In commodity terms, he's a resource. Most important of all, he's out of copyright. Although Bloom identifies the modern text in virtual paralysis before the "Great Original," Dylan's work is remarkably composed, in both senses of the word, in the presence of Keats's poem. At lines 9–12, "Love Minus Zero" even blithely draws attention to its dependence on such sources as the Ode, articulating a poetics explicitly founded on textual circulation:

In the dime stores and bus stations,
People talk of situations,
Read books, repeat quotations,[10]
Draw conclusions on the wall.
(ll. 9–12)[11]

The idea of *repeating* quotations at line 11 is arresting. It implies a multilayered or self-recessive dimension to influence, since quotations are *already* repetitions, have already been retailed as part of an endlessly regressive sequence. With regard to Keats's famous dictum "Beauty is truth, truth beauty" in "Ode on a Grecian Urn," one of the poet's most often repeated—most apparently original, *Keatsian*—lines, this is certainly the case, the phrase actually originating in Condillac's *Essay on the Origin of Human Knowledge*, a conclusion I drew a couple of years ago when I came across Thomas Nugent's 1756 translation of the French philosopher's book. In chapter 10, among other soon-to-be Keatsian phrases, we find the statement, "Nothing is beautiful that is not true: and yet every truth is not always beautiful."[12] Keats has appropriated Condillac's formulation, altered it slightly to suit his needs (doing away with the unpalatable notion of ugly truths), and sold it on. A repeated quotation par excellence. The phrase has been literally sold on, since Keats's poems were composed with sales in mind. One of Keats's primary aspirations was to make a living solely by writing. Likewise, Dylan draws on—and calls on—Keats in his lyrics in "Forever Young" and "Love Minus Zero." The decisive difference between the two borrowers is that Keats's debt to the French philosopher causes anxiety, evident in the fact that nowhere does or can Keats admit to reading Condillac, who in the view of key Romantic figures such as Hazlitt, Coleridge, and Wordsworth was a Continental bugbear, an "infra-bestial metaphysician," a purveyor of "pestilential pellets of logic." Despite borrowing heavily from Condillac, Keats is chary of paying his demon all the monstrous debt. Dylan's borrowing, by stark contrast, is a routine affair, a matter of both love *and* theft, with no apprehension attached to it. Like the eponymous hero of "Arthur McBride," the traditional song sung by Dylan on his album *Good As I Been to You,* he "pays all his debts without sorrow or strife." At any rate, Dylan makes no attempt to conceal familiarity with *his* Romantic precursor in the way Keats does with Condillac. The following is taken from a 1985 interview in which Dylan talks directly about influence:

> To the aspiring songwriter and singer I say disregard all the current stuff, forget it, you're better off, read John Keats.[13]

Beautiful and true.

"Crying Like a Fire in the Sun"

It would be misleading to suggest that Bloomian moments of anxiety are *wholly* absent from Dylan, whose writing career, we should remember, is fast approaching Wordsworth's in length. In "Going, Going, Gone," from 1974's *Planet Waves,* Dylan worries that "There's not much more to be said." He even senses the end of composition, adding, "I'm closin' the book / On the pages and the text / And I don't really care / What happens next." At the end of 1989's "Tweeter and the Monkey Man," we find Dylan in despondent mood: "Think I'll go to Florida, / Get myself some sun, / There ain't no more opportunities here, / Everything's been done."[14] It's tempting—although in "It's Alright, Ma (I'm Only Bleeding)," "Temptation's page flies out the door"—to interpret this as a powerful endorsement of Bloom's dictum that "the covert subject of most poetry for the last three centuries has been the anxiety of influence, each poet's fear that no proper work remains for him to perform" (*Anxiety of Influence,* 148). Then again, in "Hero Blues," Dylan reminds us that it is possible to read "too many books." To be sure, literature is full of these moments, Keats providing several memorable examples. In canto 1 of *The Fall of Hyperion* (1819)—a poem that is all about getting oneself some sun—the poet/dreamer discovers that he has arrived at the feast (of the poets) too late. Only the "refuse of a meal" remains:

> Turning around,
> I saw an arbour with a drooping roof
> Of trellis vines, and bells, and larger blooms,
> Like floral-censers swinging light in air;
> Before its wreathed doorway, on a mound
> Of moss, was spread a feast of summer fruits,
> Which, nearer seen, seem'd refuse of a meal
> By angel tasted, or our mother Eve;
> For empty shells were scattered on the grass,
> And grape stalks but half bare, and remnants more,
> Sweet smelling, whose pure kinds I could not know.
> Still was more plenty than the fabled horn
> Thrice emptied could pour forth, at banqueting
> For Proserpine return'd to her own fields,
> Where the white heifers low. And appetite

More yearning than on earth I ever felt
Growing within, I ate deliciously;
And, after not long, thirsted, for thereby
Stood a cool vessel of transparent juice,
Sipp'd by the wander'd bee, the which I took,
And, pledging all the mortals of the world,
And all the dead whose names are in our lips,
Drank. That full draught is parent of my theme.
(ll. 24–46)

The reference to lowing heifers at line 38 links this passage to the heightened anxieties of "Ode on a Grecian Urn," with its heifer lowing famously at the skies, offering an insight into the real nature of Keats's "theme" in *The Fall of Hyperion:* originality, influence, and parricidal contest—as well as ruminating on the theme of the sun, the poem is also concerned with sons. Sure enough, sixty lines further on in the first canto, the poem's "I" narrator is about to be confronted with the "image, huge" of Saturn, the titanically proportioned, anxiety-inducing poetic Father. Although the manifest concern of *The Fall of Hyperion* is the patrifilial struggle between Titans and Olympians—between Saturn the father and Jupiter the son, the old sun god Hyperion (who not only turns out to be not forever young but also, like Tweeter, fast running out of opportunities) and the young pretender, Apollo—the poem is thus also patrifilial for Keats's dreamer, the anxious, would-be poet of canto 1, lines 11–18.

Who alive can say,
"Thou art no Poet; may'st not tell thy dreams"?
Since every man whose soul is not a clod
Hath visions, and would speak, if he had lov'd
And been well nurtured in his mother tongue.
Whether the dream now purposed to rehearse
Be poet's or fanatic's will be known
When this warm scribe my hand is in the grave.

So deeply has Keats internalized the father-son model of precedence that he is prepared to accept that only when he is himself a "dead poet," only when that "warm scribe" his hand is "in the grave," will—

can—his always precarious claim to the status of poet be settled. Having already abandoned the first *Hyperion,* Keats finds the intonations of *über* dead-poet Milton vexing his second, initially optimistic attempt at an epic narrative.[15] At this demoralizing juncture, Keats confronts the hopelessness of his entire literary enterprise, as defined according to its basis in originality. In simple terms, Keats arrives too late in the day. There may still be sweets to be gathered at the feast; the husks, empty shells, and other remnants may represent "more plenty than the fabled horn / Thrice emptied could pour forth" (*The Fall of Hyperion,* ll. 35–36). But the crucial factor raising anxiety in Keats is the recognition that he is not the first to eat at the table. Others have already tasted the poetic banquet, leaving only scraps and "remnants," however "sweet smelling" (ll. 33–34).

If Keats is on the side of the Olympians, those figurative modern poets, his text is irresistibly drawn to the plight of the literary Fathers. *The Fall of Hyperion's* narrative arc stops short of the Olympian's entrance; and in Keats's first attempt at the tale, even the brief presence in book 3 of Apollo, youngest of the gods, provokes an aposiopesis so catastrophic that the poem breaks off altogether amid celestial shrieks. Keats may yearn to forget the Titans, the great men of history (see *Hyperion,* 3, 3: "O leave them, Muse! O leave them to their woes"), yet his medium—poetic discourse itself—insists on and, what is more, demonstrates the impossibility of this ambition. Apollo hardly gets a look in. The weight of history proves too much for the modern writer, who is always unable to complete the task of leaving past poets behind.

While "Tweeter and the Monkey Man" strikes a clear note of resignation, by and large Dylan shows few signs of succumbing to Bloomian anxiety. Keats may be intolerably burdened by "all the dead whose names are in our lips," as he concedes in canto 1 (l. 45) of *The Fall of Hyperion,* but the dead are precisely what motivate and enable Dylan's aesthetic. Nicholas Roe memorably calls Dylan a "cultural ragman" who "draws a circle around the entire Western literary tradition."[16] In 2001 Dylan released a new album, *Love and Theft.* It shares a title with a book written by Eric Lott on the origin of blackface minstrelsy. The correspondence points up the "borrowed" nature of Dylan's lyrics on this album, which constitute a patchwork of quotations, allusions, echoes, and lifted phrases. These are mostly unacknowledged, though not at all, it would appear, in an attempt to obscure debt. On the contrary, Dylan's borrowings tend to be obvious, deployed in ways that seem calculated to aid recognition (as opposed, say, to Coleridge's practice, where traces of "enabling" authors are typically disguised or obscured). As Sean Wilentz explains,

> One needn't know much more about the songs of Robert Johnson and the rest of the Delta blues players than the versions copped by the Rolling Stones in order to recognize the po' boy prodigal son or the line in "Tweedle Dee and Tweedle Dum" about someone's love being "all in vain." . . . Dylan has been committing this kind of theft all of his working life, right down to swiping his own surname. . . . Now, as then, Dylan is a minstrel, filching other people's diction and mannerisms and melodies and lyrics and transforming them and making them his own.[17]

Time Out of Mind, 1997's hypersentient bricolage (the title of which is possibly an allusion to act 1, scene 4 of *Romeo and Juliet*—significantly, since this is where Mercutio discusses Queen Mab, pregnancy, and conception: that is, the creative force), is also stitched together out of echoes, adaptations, and direct quotations from blues songs, vaudeville, minstrelsy, and the folk tradition. Where Keats, pondering fame, declares, "How fevered is the man who cannot look / Upon his mortal days with temperate blood" ("On Fame *(I)*," ll. 1–2), Dylan seems to reply, "How fevered is the man who cannot look *back*." The title of D. A. Pennebaker's documentary of Dylan's 1965 tour of Britain, *Dont Look Back,* need not be read as contradictory here. We ought simply to understand it in the way Dylan evidently does: "Take what you need from the past, and stop worrying!" After all, as Dylan points out in "It's All Over Now, Baby Blue," a song included on *Bringing It All Back Home* (1965)—whose title alludes to the problem of influence—other writers will have no compunctions when it comes to taking what they need from you: "The vagabond who's rapping at your door / Is standing in the clothes that you once wore" (ll. 21–22).

Dylan hardly shrinks from playing the role of scavenging vagabond himself in this song. As Aidan Day points out, lines 19–20 are in close dialogue with section 1, lines 1–4, of Tennyson's *In Memoriam*.[18] First Dylan:

> Leave your stepping stones behind, something calls for you,
> Forget the dead you've left, they will not follow you.

Now the "source" text in Tennyson:

> I held it truth, with him who sings
> To one clear harp in divers tones,
> That men may rise on stepping-stones
> Of their dead selves to higher things.[19]

In Day's elegant analysis "the voice of the lyric . . . incites Baby Blue to respond to a call away from the safely plotted course, away from constricting definition by extinct modes of being" (*Jokerman*, 80). Here we can read modes of *poetic* being. The alternative to taking what you need is to submit to the anxiety of influence, obsessively rehearsing self-deprecation in the ever-presence of the Great Original. (Incidentally, "It's All Over Now, Baby Blue" provides an apt image for this condition, too, in the figure of the orphan "crying like a fire in the sun" [l. 3]). There may be little in collections like *Time Out of Mind* or *Love and Theft* that Dylan can call his own, but even less reason, in Dylan's eyes, why he should want to in the first place. You might say that Dylan succeeds in "linking all perplexèd meanings / Into one perfect peace," like the Lost Chord, to quote from the poem of that name by Adelaide Anne Procter, daughter of Keats's literary rival, Bryan Waller Procter (alias "Barry Cornwall"). There are no lost chords in Dylan—everything is out on bootleg these days—but his best pieces certainly attain a "peace" that is conspicuously absent from Keats's relentlessly self-questioning work.

To offer a coda to this section, "It's All Over Now, Baby Blue" contains the injunction: "Strike another match, go start anew." This could be read in two ways. If we take "match" as an allusion *to* allusions (to words or phrases that match), then Dylan is either saying "make another match"—a sentiment allied to his earlier endorsement of stealing from the dead but at odds with his demand that we "start anew"—or he is saying "strike *out* the match," that is, remove the allusion (write it from scratch, start anew). The lyric is double-voiced; it has not made up its mind. Or it appreciates there are two sides to the question, two right roads to walk down. Seen as a whole, the final stanza's double-mindedness on the theme of creative originality is presented in vivid terms:

Leave your stepping stones behind, something calls for you.
Forget the dead you've left, they will not follow you.
The vagabond who's rapping at your door
Is standing in the clothes that you once wore.
Strike another match, go start anew
And it's all over now, Baby Blue.

Bloom's analysis of influence fits Keats very well but fails in an important respect to accommodate Dylan's achievement. Dylan makes an impression of being virtually impervious to anxiety; or, more precisely, he fosters a paradigmatically different attitude toward influence than his Romantic precursors, enabling him to avert moments of crisis. There is no evident compulsion in Dylan to purge his texts of influential voices as Keats attempted to do in *The Fall of Hyperion.* Where Keats strives for originality, abandoning projects that contained tones too obviously carried over from other poets, Dylan *assumes* that his work will sound like an assemblage of repeated quotations. This even includes quotations from his own songs—acts of self-quotation, something that Pennebaker's film comments on humorously. The famous opening sequence reveals Dylan standing at the end of a row of brick buildings, holding a sheaf of placards. Scribbled on each is a quotation (sometimes a misquotation), from "Subterranean Homesick Blues" (again from *Bringing It All Back Home*). Allen Ginsberg, another of Dylan's poetic precursors, watches on amused as the song starts playing, and Dylan, looking bored, as if the point were too obvious to need making, lets the placards fall in sequence (mostly, but not always, in sync with the music). It becomes difficult to be certain whether the placards are quoting, or misquoting, the song or vice versa. Whatever the case, Dylan seems to insist, text is simply repeated quotation.

In the preface to the second edition of *The Anxiety of Influence* (1997), Bloom contends that Shakespeare "fully resolved" his struggle with anxiety in *As You Like It,* the point at which the ghost of

Christopher Marlowe, hitherto a wounding presence in the plays, was finally exorcized (xlv). After that, Shakespeare was able to write unburdened. No great poet, Bloom continues, "ever has journeyed as far from his origins as Shakespeare" (xxxiv). This may or may not be true. Certainly no great poet has journeyed as far *in* his origins as Dylan. Uncovering and repeating quotations is the foundational premise of Dylan's work—and I don't simply mean this in the nebulous sense that *all* literature is a flimsy tissue of quotations (a familiar post-structuralist mantra). As we have seen, there is a concreteness, a specific traceability, to quotations in Dylan that would satisfy even the "source hunters" so despised by Bloom, who makes withering reference to the "wearisome industry of source-hunting, of allusion-counting" (31). Bloom's antipathy to library work is only partially warranted. Precisely what makes "allusion-counting" so interesting in the Romantic period, and arguably so pointless in the modern, is that writers like Keats and Coleridge often deployed quotations furtively, tremulously, or unconsciously. After T. S. Eliot, by contrast, allusions are knowing, carefully placed, and entirely what one expects to find—indeed, in the case of Eliot, entirely what the reader is *expected* to find. They hold no secrets since there is no longer a genuine family romance to be excavated from them. In a sense, Dylan, who remarks in "Things Have Changed" that he's "Gonna take dancing lessons do the jitterbug rag" (l. 15), simply substitutes the "jitterbug rag" for Eliot's Shakesperian Rag as part of his cultural ragbag. There may be no "shortcuts," but there are plenty of short circuits—or short walks down the street—by both authors as a means of avoiding influence anxiety. If Eliot can't help asking, "What shall I do now?" ("The Waste Land," 2:131), he banishes anxious thoughts by deciding to "rush out as I am, and walk the street / With my hair down" (2:132–33). When it comes to rushing into things, Dylan ups the ante, announcing that he "Feel[s] like falling in love with the first woman I meet / Putting her in a wheel barrow and wheeling her down the street" (ll. 26–27). But for Eliot, today is just a way of delaying tomorrow. The question "What shall we do tomorrow?" remains. Dylan may not be immune to influence anxiety, but at least for him, tomorrow is always such a long time.

It's misleading to speak of Keats's "influence" on Dylan in a Bloomian sense. Dylan certainly *engages* his precursor but in an entirely knowing manner that cannot be considered either an effect or function of influence. Consider for a moment Bloom's unanxious Shakespeare, whose relationship with his predecessors goes some way toward providing the model for Dylan's relationship with Keats. We'd be unlikely, I think, to claim that William Strachey's letter of 15 July 1610, known now as *A True Reportory of the Wracke,* influenced *The Tempest,* where "influence" signifies in a Bloomian manner as something that occurs against one's will, even though we perceive a close relationship between the two texts. *A True Reportory* is quite possibly indispensable to *The Tempest's* textual ontology; that is to say, the play, or at least its opening scene, would have been radically different without Strachey. Nonetheless, we do not think of Strachey's idiom haunting Shakespeare's narrative, even if words and phrases from *A True Reportory* do seem to make dramatic reappearances in *The Tempest.* It's not simply that Strachey has a "low" status alongside Shakespeare (after all, which author doesn't?). Nor can our intuition of the absence of the psychology of influence be resolved into the generic distance between a letter or travelogue and a play. In Dylan's terms, Shakespeare has taken what he needs from the past and has not looked back. This has a major bearing on how we might think about anxiety: Strachey does not unsettle the pragmatic Shakespeare, just as Keats does not unsettle Dylan. In sharp contrast, Milton unnerved Keats, who was right to see that his precursor's idiom had to all intents and purposes commandeered the second *Hyperion.* There Milton returned with his voice intact, whereas Strachey's voice in *A True Reportory* is just one of several that are audible in *The Tempest.*

"Silhouettes in the Window"

In a BBC Radio 3 lecture titled "Dylan among the Poets," now included as part of his excellent book *Dylan's Visions of Sin,* Christopher Ricks showed how one of Dylan's late masterpieces, "Not Dark Yet" from *Time Out of Mind,* engages in creative colloquy with "Ode to a Nightingale." Even the title of Dylan's song, Ricks argued, can be viewed as a response to Keats's observation in stanza 4 of the Ode: "But here there is no light." As exhilarating as the lecture certainly is, and as wary as Ricks appears to be elsewhere of Bloom's notion of *anxious* debt (see Ricks's 2002 study, *Allusion to the Poets*), his view of Keats's and Dylan's relationship is, it seems to me, founded on fairly traditional Bloomian paradigms. For Ricks, even more so perhaps than for Bloom, unconscious echoes are the important thing, as if each new proof of how closely "Not Dark Yet" is preoccupied without knowing it directly by "Ode to a Nightingale" helps establish by increments Dylan's status as a writer worthy of serious attention. Dylan's stature swells with each Keatsian allusion unearthed, since a precursor as impressive as Keats, it is assumed, must exert an ennobling influence on those who follow. I do not believe Dylan's relationship with Keats, or for that matter any other precursor, can be adequately explained within this framework. In fact, *Time Out of Mind* tells us in precise terms how we are to understand Keats's bearing on Dylan.

"Love Sick," the album's opening song, is a secular companion piece to "Man in the Long Black Coat" from 1989's *Oh Mercy,* an album Richard Brown refers to as "designer Dylan," with its glassy sound effects, its at times glib deployment of eschatological register, and general atmosphere of fashionable brooding menace.[20] But if we think of designer culture as slick and obsessed with surface (and some would say that Daniel Lanois's production of *Oh Mercy* is just that), then there's a lot of different, multilayered things in motion in "Love Sick." We might note the humorous word painting, the reggae guitar mimicking on the album the ticking of the clock at line 16, further underlining Dylan's magpie approach to his art. If the ballad "Love Sick" looks back to a song on *Oh Mercy,* it looks back once again, and further, to "La Belle Dame sans Merci: A Ballad." I want to end this essay by picking up some intriguing textual associations between the two pieces.[21]

In "La Belle Dame sans Merci," Keats's knight, living a posthumous existence, sees everything around him either dead or dying. The rose on the loitering knight's cheeks "fast withereth" (l. 12) and the sedge has already "wither'd from the lake" (l. 3). In a similar daze, or deathly haze, Dylan's narrative persona wanders "through streets that are dead"; like the knight, thoughts of a mysterious Lady are "running around in [his] head" (l. 2). The Lady's "light" feet in Keats's poem (l. 15) have become "tired" feet in "Love Sick" (l. 3). Where the knight meets his lover "in the meads" (l. 13), Dylan's speaker "see[s] lovers in the meadow" (l. 11). Where the Lady is described as a "fairy's child" (l. 14), the narrator of "Love Sick" is said to speak "like a child" (l. 7). Here the central image of guileless immaturity in "La Belle Dame sans Merci" has been latched onto by Dylan, who transfers it to his narrator. And just as the knight is "lullèd asleep" and apparently betrayed at line 33, Dylan's speaker protests of his lady:

You destroyed me with a smile
While I was sleeping.
(ll. 7–8)

Where the knight has a dream-vision of "pale kings, and princes" (l. 37), the speaker in "Love Sick" sees "silhouettes in the window" and is haunted by a "shadow" (ll. 12, 15). The rhetorical parallels are especially compelling at this point: Keats's repeated use of *I see*—"I see a lily on thy brow" (l. 9), "I saw pale kings, and princes" (l. 37), "I saw their starv'd lips" (l. 41)—is echoed by Dylan:

I see, I see lovers in the meadow
I see, I see silhouettes in the window.
(ll. 11–12)

Additionally, the questions asked by Dylan's narrator, "Did I hear someone tell a lie?" (l. 5), "Could you ever be true?" (l. 19), seem to allude to La Belle Dame's precarious statement of fidelity, "I love thee true" (l. 28).

There is, then, a fascinating degree of congruence linking "Love Sick" and "La Belle Dame sans Merci." Again we find ourselves asking whether Keats has imposed himself and his poem upon a resentful Dylan or, to phrase it slightly differently, whether Dylan, against his will, has rewritten Keats's ballad? I would argue that "Love Sick" is no return of the dead, no *apophrades,* to use Bloom's term, in which precursors return with their voices intact to deprive the modern poet of his or her strength (*Anxiety of Influence*, 141–42). Neither are we presented with *clinamen,* where the belated writer feels compelled to "swerve" from and "correct" the precursor text. Dylan has certainly used "La Belle Dame sans Merci"; or, more properly speaking, Keats's ballad has enabled Dylan's song. We could even say that vital aspects of "La Belle Dame sans Merci" are contained within "Love Sick." However, we do not sense in Dylan's lyric any real sense of agonistic scuffling. Things look rather different in this respect, however, in "La Belle Dame sans Merci"—a poem demonstrably haunted by the memory of the patrifilial struggle with Milton that ruined the first *Hyperion* (and would shortly ruin the second). Keats encodes his sense of struggle with his poetic fathers in the tenth stanza:

> I saw pale kings and princes too,
> Pale warriors, death-pale were they all;
> They cried—"La Belle Dame sans Merci
> Hath thee in thrall!"
> (ll. 37–40)

The pale kings and princes, literature's patriarchs, claim that the Lady has the knight/Keats in thrall. The truth of the situation, of course, is that *they* do. We could say that stanza 10 instantiates prefiguratively the antagonism Dylan describes in "Floater" on *Love and Theft:* "The old men 'round here, sometimes they get / On bad terms with the younger men." But as Dylan concludes, "Old, young, age don't carry weight / It doesn't matter in the end." As the historically "younger" man Dylan explains in the next verse, when his boss tries to "bully" him, "strong arm" him, or "inspire" him "with fear," it simply has "the opposite effect."

The overriding issue here—as in *The Fall of Hyperion*—is primacy. The knight-at-arms learns the terrible truth that *he is not the first.* Others, the pale kings and princes, the spectral presences of past writers—the "overpowering idea of our dead poets," as Keats puts it memorably in a letter to Mary-Ann Jeffery six weeks after writing his ballad (*Letters,* 2:216)—have already encountered La Belle Dame, the muse whom Keats desires exclusively for himself.

"La Belle Dame sans Merci," like canto 1 of *The Fall of Hyperion,* tropes the moment of coming too late to the (poetic) feast—in this case, comprising "roots of relish sweet," "honey wild," and "manna-dew." At line 41, Keats discovers—as the poet/dreamer will discover in *The Fall of Hyperion*—that his poetic predecessors have already eaten, even if their "starved lips" testify that the meal has not been sustaining (they, too, are caught in cycles of anxiety; they, too, were not the first). Dylan comes to the meal still later; but where the anxious ghosts, the pale kings and princes of "La Belle Dame sans Merci," manifest themselves directly to the knight, engendering further anxiety, only the "shadow" (l. 15) of an original crisis remains in "Love Sick." Dylan sees mere "silhouettes in the window," or ghosts at two removes. The pale kings have lost their ability to disturb. As Dylan sings in *Street Legal*'s "Is Your Love in Vain," "I have dined with kings, I've been offered wings / And I've never been too impressed." At the close of "Love Sick" the speaker may be depressed, but he is not *op*pressed like the knight. He may be sick *now*, but as we know from "Subterranean Homesick Blues," he is going to "get well" again. And he will go back to "hanging around the inkwell," to writing. Dylan uses Keats's ballad as a template for his lyric, but the deeper, encoded issues of "La Belle Dame sans Merci" (influence and originality) are no longer at stake. That is to say, they have not been transported into the song along with elements of Keats's narrative and stylistic patina.

Drawing Conclusions on the Wall

In *The Anxiety of Influence*, Bloom invokes Freud's theory of the child who wishes to be the father of himself:

> Rescuing the mother [as repayment for her having given the child life] acquires the significance of giving her a child or making one for her. . . . All the instincts, the loving, the grateful, the sensual, the defiant, the self-assertive and independent—all are gratified in the wish to be *the father of himself*. (64)

Bloom suggests that "all quest-romances of the post-Enlightenment, meaning all Romanticisms whatsoever, are quests to re-beget one's own self, to become one's own Great Original" (64). This, it seems to me, is precisely to put a finger on the overriding disparity between Keats and Dylan (and ironically enough to account for the breakdown of the Bloomian model where Keats's and Dylan's relationship is concerned). In short, Keats aspires to be his own begetter, his own "Great Original" in Bloom's terms, while Dylan is content to make—or, rather, is resigned to the necessity of making—his voice the voice of others. For precisely what is "Dylanesque" about Dylan's idiom, that rich, ideolectic, aphoristic, many-voiced mix of styles, syntactic ranges, and verbal textures, is quarried from the Bible, French Symbolist poets, street jive, 1930s novels, blues songs, Tennyson, the folk tradition, and Keats poems.[22] Unlike Dylan, Keats obsessively sought to purge his texts of paternal presences (notably Milton's) and fantasized narratives about Saturn and Jupiter, Hyperion and Apollo, in which the son or figurative son deposes the father, that is, vies to *become* the father. It is impossible to say what Keats would have done had he lived. Perhaps he would have succeeded in transcending all other English poets and found a style that was uni-voiced and wholly individual. Alternatively, appalled at the cost in terms of abandoned poems, he may have chosen to adopt other voices, as he did Byron's in his last long poem, *The Cap and Bells; or, the Jealousies* (which is as preoccupied with Keats's jealousy toward/anxiety regarding Byron as it is, intradiegetically, with its characters' vexed interpersonal dynamics).

The psychology motivating Keats's desire in 1819 to eradicate the precursor can be partially elucidated in historical terms. In the early nineteenth century, the idea of a lofty literary and cultural heritage that right-thinking writers ought to mine and quote begins to confront Romantic theories of hermetic genius and individuality.[23] On the one hand, citing great forerunners is necessary to sanction the current project. Yet the practice is at the same time intricately bound up with questions of authenticity and originality. Thrown in for good measure, certain writers are barred from participating in the approved heritage altogether due to low social background or indifferent education. For figures like Keats, "vulgar Cockneys" whom the reviewer "Z" ridiculed in *Blackwood's* for deigning to emulate the classical tradition of Virgil and Homer—for having the temerity to aspire to poetry in the first place—the mere act of speaking, of attempting to be heard in an elite cultural arena, is a challenge in itself. Keats's response is self-quotation (a version of Bloom's self-begetting, memorably parodied by Dylan and Pennebaker in *Dont Look Back*, as we have seen)—the production of lines that through curious formulation and inventive, often challenging diction consciously quote or reiterate stylistic aspects of the poet that represent (or come to represent) for audiences the essence of that writer. For instance, a line such as "O what can ail thee, knight at arms / Alone and palely loitering?" arguably seems aware that it is uniquely formulated and "quotable" in a way that different, that *in*different, Keats lines—"O let me lead her gently o'er the brook," for example—are not.[24] Keats could be said to quote from an authorizing *ur*-text of his own devising, a text in which his style and idiom have already come to fruition. By "predating" himself in this manner, Keats can offer himself as his own authorizing precursor; he can be in "monstrous debt" to himself. The problem, as he discovers time and again, is that Milton, Shakespeare, and Spenser have already taken up lodgings in the supposedly original text.

At the end of history where every writer always finds him- or herself, there can be no triumphant, final return to the unified text, the never-before-uttered. Discourse *is* repeated quotation, as Dylan points out at the beginning of *Dont Look Back*. Dylan's style, his entire aesthetic, is predicated on this recognition. He is resolutely not the "worried man" from "Things Have Changed" who wishes to see "No one in front of me and nothing behind." By contrast, what is most *Keatsian* about Keats is his determination to find a way back to a time when there was only one voice or, best of all, no voices. "That which is creative, must create itself," Keats utters in his most famous poetic credo. Dylan retorts, "That which is creative, must use others creatively." The unbridgeable gap between these two dispositions helps explain why Keats spent much of his writing career in crisis, while Dylan appears to be able to work largely unconstrained by Bloomian anxiety.

Notes

1. *The Letters of John Keats, 1814–1821,* ed. Hyder Edward Rollins (Cambridge, MA: Harvard University Press, 1958), 2:212.

2. Howard Sounes, *Down the Highway: The Life of Bob Dylan* (New York: Grove Press, 2001), 27.

3. "Ode on a Grecian Urn" (ll. 25–27), in *The Poems of John Keats,* ed. Jack Stillinger (London: Heinemann, 1978).

4. In the same way, some of Milton's own anxieties of influence—centered in *Paradise Lost* on the relationship between Satan and God (see Bloom, *The Anxiety of Influence,* 19–23)—enter Keats's *Hyperion* along with Milton's idiom, as I will be discussing.

5. Bloom excluded Shakespeare from his discussion in the first edition of *The Anxiety of Influence: A Theory of Poetry* (New York: Oxford University Press, 1973), arguing that he "belongs to the giant age before the flood, before the anxiety of influence became central to poetic consciousness" (11).

6. Aidan Day interprets "Love Minus Zero/No Limit" as an exploration of Dylan's "vision of the processes of artistic creation." Day, *Jokerman: Reading the Lyrics of Bob Dylan* (Oxford: Blackwell, 1988), 35.

7. Two key words from lines 49–50 of "Ode on a Grecian Urn"—"know" and

"truth"—reappear in "Love Minus Zero": Dylan's lover "*knows* too much to argue or to judge" and is "*true* like ice and fire" (my emphases). "Like ice," moreover, conceivably alludes to the ode's "cold Pastoral" (l. 45).

8. For another example, in the Basement Tape version of "Open the Door, Homer," Dylan sings: "And that is that ev'ryone / Must always flush out his house / If he don't expect to be / Goin' 'round housing flushes." This occurs in a song in whose refrain Dylan repeatedly reminds us that he's heard it (all) said before, while worrying that he "ain't gonna hear it said no more."

9. Dylan gently satirizes Keats's compunctions about originality and obsessive self-comparisons with the mighty works of the past. Where Keats cowers self-effacingly before the urn, which he perceives as a monument of eloquent antiquity that can "express / A flowery tale more sweetly than our rhyme" (ll. 3–4), Dylan's muse "laughs like the flowers" (l. 7). In *like,* we surely hear *at* (where "flowers" are figures of speech in every sense).

10. As far as repeating *Dylan's* quotations goes, the not inconsiderable cost of securing permissions to reproduce full texts of individual lyrics means that readers are directed to the official and excellent Bob Dylan site, http://www.bobdylan.com. Here, all lyrics can be retrieved free of charge.

11. If Dylan has been "read[ing] books," there is good reason to suppose that an edition of Keats's poems was among them.

12. For a fuller discussion of this and other borrowings from the *Essay,* and for the reasons why Condillac, rather than Plato or Hazlitt, is the most likely source for Keats's chiasmus, see chapter 4 of my book, *The Politics of Language in Romantic Literature* (London: Palgrave, 2002). Keats also found in Condillac's *Essay* the sentence "suppose some sudden fit of melancholy seizes our minds," which he spun into lines 11–12 of "Ode on Melancholy": "But when the melancholy fit shall fall / Sudden from heaven."

13. Bob Dylan, *Bob Dylan: In His Own Words* (London: Omnibus, 1983), 110.

14. *Travelling Wilburys,* vol. 1 (1988). One could also cite "Blind Willie McTell" as an instance of a song in which Dylan compares himself nervously to great artists of the past.

15. See Keats's letter to Reynolds, 21 September 1819, in *Letters of John Keats,* 2:167.

16. Nicholas Roe, "Playing Time," in *Do You Mr. Jones?: Bob Dylan with the Poets and Professors,* ed. Neil Corcoran (London: Chatto and Windus, 2002), 86.

17. Sean Wilentz, "American Recordings: On *Love and Theft* and the Minstrel Boy," http://www.bobdylan.com/etc/wilentz.html (accessed 11 August 2002). Nicholas Roe makes a similar point equally well: "Unlike nearly every other writer, for whom 'finding a voice' or unique verbal identity may be an imperative, Bob Dylan is apparently most himself as a sublimely capable alias, merged into a babel of others' voices." Roe, "Playing Time," 85.

18. A love of Tennyson's poetry inspired Dylan to perform on the Isle of Wight in August 1969. Tennyson began a long association with the isle in 1853, when he first rented a house at Freshwater. See Robert Cook, *Wish You Were Here: Isle of Wight* (London: Buckingham Colour Press, 1997), 36. At the Isle of Wight Press Conference, Ronnie Burns from BBC TV South asked Dylan, "Why did you come to the Isle

of Wight?" Dylan replied, "I wanted to see the home of Alfred, Lord Tennyson." (To Burns's inquiry "Why?" Dylan answered: "Just curious.")

19. Christopher Ricks, *The Poems of Tennyson,* 2nd ed. (Harlow: Longman, 1987), 2:318.

20. Corcoran, *Bob Dylan with the Poets and Professors,* 194.

21. "Love Sick" is not the first Dylan song to engage "La Belle Dame sans Merci." "As I Went Out One Morning" from *John Wesley Hardin* (1967) is also closely involved with the themes and atmosphere of Keats's ballad.

22. In *The Western Canon,* Bloom slightly modifies the position maintained in *The Anxiety of Influence* concerning the immobilizing effects of influence on belated writers, suggesting that the really strong modern author "knows *how* to borrow." This insight—though not, of course, directed at Dylan—is particularly apposite in relation to Dylan's art. See *The Western Canon* (New York: Harcourt Brace, 1994), 11.

23. For a stimulating discussion of the legal and economic conditions underpinning the emergence of Romantic notions of autonomous literary genius, see Andrew Bennett, *Romantic Poets and the Culture of Posterity* (Cambridge: Cambridge University Press, 1999), 38–43.

24. "I stood tip-toe upon a little hill" (l. 101). Michael O'Neill has explored the unique level of self-reflexivity found in Romantic poetry in *Romanticism and the Self-Conscious Poem* (Oxford: Clarendon Press, 1997).

"Love's the burning boy":
Hemans's Critical Legacy

Emma Mason

To betray an admiration for or aesthetic appreciation of Felicia Hemans's poetry immediately invokes suspicion among twentieth-century critics and readers. For many, she confirms even the most liberal critic's reservations regarding "women's" poetry: that it is emotive, too full of feeling, and unashamedly gushy. T. E. Hulme's notorious attack on Romanticism as "spilt religion"—"It is like pouring a pot of treacle over the dinner table"—is considered doubly applicable to many of Hemans's sticky effusions.[1] The generation following Hulme remembered Hemans for the boy who stood on the burning deck, but considered her domestic patriotism overdone: while the complex bravado of Tennyson's "Charge of the Light Brigade" (1854) was palatable, the strains of "Casabianca" (1826) were deemed disquieting and excessive. Indeed, the latter poem provoked hundreds of parodies, which led to further satire on other familiar verses by Hemans, such as Noël Coward's "Stately Homes of England" (1938). While one-dimensional and limited in scope—droll at best, snide at worst—these parodies, constructing Hemans as a proud jingoist, were deaf to her complex, satirical voice. As the canon opened up during the 1980s and 1990s, critics became concerned that certain acts of literary recuperation might simply backfire: Wendall V. Harris worried that validating Hemans ran the risk of becoming a vague defense of sentimental storytelling, and Virgil Nemoianu feared for the sanity of readers exposed to the melodies of her trivial verses. As recently as 2000, Anne Mellor relegated Hemans to a maudlin "poetess" tradition, thus separating her from the more rational and political "female poet" tradition represented by hardier women like Anna Barbauld and Hannah More.[2] Like Charlotte Smith and Letitia Landon,

Hemans has been quickly slotted into a de Stäelean "Corinne" model of the female poet, which fashions the author as one who offers her reader verbose improvisations framed by a demonstratively emotive rhetoric. Nanora Sweet's work on Hemans and Louise Bogan confirms this analysis, conveying as it does how the two women "celebrated feeling as the distinctive legacy of the woman poet."[3]

Yet Sweet is also astutely aware that Hemans, like Bogan, sought a convergence of a "line of feeling" with which they were associated with a "line of thought," tempering emotive expression through poetic form. Hemans's efforts to express and encourage a kind of feeling that was already moderated by reason and thought were perhaps the very thing that secured her popularity throughout the nineteenth century. Her model of affect was inclusive, communal, and philanthropic, a form of reciprocal and interpersonal feeling developed in the eighteenth century by theologians such as Isaac Watts and Jonathan Edwards, and by philosophers like Francis Hutcheson and Adam Smith.[4] In the twentieth century, however, Hemans seems to have been entirely reconfigured as a poet of a gushy and saccharine individualism open to ridicule and derision. Why this shift occurred is the subject of this essay, which offers a discussion of modern views of poetic feeling. Intensely affectionate and christianized, concerned to draw attention to the feeling of the poem through the feeling of the poem's form, Hemans's poetry is an especially instructive body of work through which to explore this question.[5] Three twentieth-century writers who seem particularly aware of the issues involved are T. S. Eliot, whose indictments of Romanticism, I will suggest, are wrapped up in his childhood reading of Hemans; Alan Liu, whose recent work on modern definitions of "cool" as a kind of modish yet manic feeling is bound up with his work on Hemans; and Elizabeth Bishop, whose own take on "Casabianca" avoids parody to focus on Hemans's endorsement of feeling and love. My argument here is that Hemans's representation of feeling in her poetry can be rehabilitated when understood through Liu's and Bishop's reading of it as restorative. Hemans, they show, writes always "for feeling" (rather than about it) by privileging the reading experience as one of consolation and repair in a less than reassuring society. The issue of whether she is a "good" or "bad" poet is a potentially endless, and surely pointless, debate in that it elides her central project: namely to unite her readers through emotion and produce a collective benevolence on which society can be (re)built.[6] This essay argues that read from the post-cool perspective of Liu and Bishop, rather than from a position of Eliotian skepticism, Hemans's poems invoke a feeling which, far from being trivial or prattling, is consistent and curative.

Hemans and "the Ideal Poetry"

The role of feeling in Hemans's poetry has attracted commentators' attention from the Romantic period to the present. In 1891, Mackenzie Bell argued that Hemans would easily top any study of the "rise and fall of the sentimental in English poetry," recalling the judgment of Frederic Rowton, whose commentaries on the poet elevated her "delicacy," "softness," "pureness," "quick observant vision," and "ready sensibility."[7] Eric Robertson also drew attention to her investment in "subjective feeling" in his important *English Poetesses* (1883); and Arthur Symons championed Hemans's capacity to write with "genuine feeling and . . . easy spontaneity."[8] Yet Symons also recognized that feeling was at the heart of both her considerable popularity in the Romantic era and her dwindling status in the twentieth century:

> If poetry were really what the average person thinks it to be, an idealisation of the feelings, at those moments when the mind is open to every passing impression, ready to catch at similitudes and call up associations, but not in the grip of a strong thought or vital passion, then the verse of Felicia Hemans would be, as people once thought it was, the ideal poetry.[9]

Her excellence, Symons intimates, derives from her deployment of a particular kind of feeling that opens up the mind by freeing it from the extremes of strong passion and cold thought. Yet such moderation spurred Hemans's decline, even if she did remain popular with Victorian critics like Robertson and Rowton.[10] In 1933, for example, Janet E. Courtney declared that "we do not go to Mrs Hemans for profundity of thought," echoing the poet's late nineteenth-century biographer, Charles William Sutton, when he stated that "her poetry lacks deep thought or subtle emotion," and that "although it had immense popularity in its day, its sweetness and fluency have long palled upon the taste of thoughtful readers."[11] Exhibiting similarities with the Georgian strains of poets like Rupert Brooke, it ultimately could not be accommodated within the modernist vision of poetry—as part of a world in which feeling was vaguely embarrassing and seemingly irrevocably severed from thought.[12]

In response to critics like Courtney and Sutton, several critics, myself included, have argued that Hemans's work does not lack insight and that her representation of feeling is always sharply focused.[13] The question here is why the favorable opinions of Rowton, Robertson, and Symons were so quickly displaced by the negative judgments of Courtney and Sutton. Hemans's currency today is that of a poetic sound bite—the opening line of the endlessly parodied "Casabianca." The poem tells the story of the ten-year-old son of the French naval commander Giacomo Jocante Casabianca. The commander's ship, *L'Orient,* was part of the French fleet destroyed by Nelson at the Battle of the Nile (1798), a British victory whose meaning the poem destabilizes by depicting the French boy as a child martyr. As Susan Wolfson argues, the year of Nelson's triumph witnessed the publication of countless gloating, jingoistic war poems in British magazines, and Nelson was even presented with a coffin made from *L'Orient*'s mainmast (to which the boy clings in the poem) so that he could be buried in an object signifying victory.[14] That Hemans writes so sympathetically of the French child's plight, however, complicates any (popular) reading of the poem as jingoistic: to interpret the poem as patriotic, then, involves misreading the nationality of the child, "naturalizing" him as British:

The boy stood on the burning deck
  Whence all but he had fled;
The flame that lit the battle's wreck
  Shone round him o'er the dead.

Yet beautiful and bright he stood,
  As born to rule the storm;
A creature of heroic blood,
  A proud, though child-like form.

The flames rolled on—he would not go
  Without his father's word;
That father, faint in death below,
  His voice no longer heard.

He called aloud—"say, father, say
  If yet my task is done?"
He knew not that the chieftain lay
  Unconscious of his son.

"Speak, father!" once again he cried,
  "If I may yet be gone!"
And but the booming shots replied,
  And fast the flames rolled on.

Upon his brow he felt their breath,
  And in his waving hair,
And looked from that lone post of death
  In still yet brave despair.

And shouted but once more aloud,
  "My father! must I stay?"
While o'er him fast, through sail and shroud,
  The wreathing fires made way.

They wrapt the ship in splendour wild,
  They caught the flag on high,
And streamed above the gallant child,
  Like banners in the sky.

There came a burst of thunder sound—
  The boy—oh! where was he?
Ask of the winds that far around
  With fragments strewed the sea!—

With mast, and helm, and pennon fair,
  That well had borne their part—
But the noblest thing which perished there
  Was that young faithful heart.[15]

Patriotism is still regarded as the keynote to the poem by many critics, partly because of the way Hemans was filtered through the Victorian period to become a feminized model of British values. Yet, as Wolfson points out, as a "grim meditation on patriotic and patriarchal obligations" the poem touches on the ideological implications of warfare in a manner that reflected the mixed feelings of an early nineteenth-century reading public regarding conflict.[16] Moreover, as Myra Cottingham and Tricia Lootens argue, the Victorianized Hemans—nationalistic, imperialistic, jingoistic—does not accord with the Romantic Hemans who wrote war poetry "during a period of national threat rather than national imperialism."[17] In fact, the Romantic Hemans challenges masculinized military values by constantly laying bare the intense grief that warfare occasions, and "Casabianca" asks many more questions than it answers regarding conflict and national loyalty. As Cottingham asks, why does the boy stay on the burning deck when the rest of the naval officers have fled, leaving him behind, unprotected?[18] Hemans suggests we address these instabilities through attention to the poem's economy of feeling: the drama reveals the boy's emotional connection to his father, rather than a sense of duty to his country. The private, emotive theme of the boy's death is rendered far more significant than the public, historical event that readers and critics have reconstructed around him. The boy's "child-like form" is echoed in the very form of the poem; both, however, belie a greater power. The boy waits for adult instruction from his father, the captain of the ship, to say the "word" so that he might leave the sinking vessel (l. 8), yet it is the boy who voices the word here; his father, "faint in death" below deck, is unable to hear his son's prominent call (l. 11). Though he has been stripped of all physical power, the captain interestingly, emphatically, retains his hold over his son.

As the flames "breathe" upon his brow, wrap around the ship's sails, and finally explode with a "burst of thunder," readers are pushed to confront their roles as witnesses to a scene in which a boy burns alive (ll. 21, 33). That his "faithful heart" is consumed by external forces (the fire), rather than broken by internal anxiety, is a testimony to the strength of his feeling throughout this ordeal. Hemans carefully highlights his loyalty in order to pull this devoted feeling out of the flames and evoke empathy and affection in her readers.[19]

Eliot and the New Criticism

Certainly Hemans's capacity for writing a poetry able to evoke emotion in the reader is at the heart of Bell's, Robertson's, and Symons's fervent admiration, whatever they made of her politics. Yet late nineteenth- and twentieth-century critics turned on Hemans and her burning boy. As Mary F. Robinson wrote in 1880: "Fifty years ago few poets were more popular than Mrs Hemans; her verses were familiar to all hearts"; yet, she continues, "now they are chiefly forgotten and without injustice," since they emerge from "a talent expressive, not creative."[20] That this earnestness was considered distasteful in part for its Christian content is clear; Robinson laments the fact that the "inspiring genius of Mrs Hemans is neither personal nor artistic passion, but a mild Anglican variety of Christianity."[21] The modernist flight from emotion within an increasingly secular criticism, impelled by fin-de-siècle commentaries such as Robinson's, is fueled by a sense of discomfort with Victorian sentimentality evident in the pragmatic literary criticism that dominated the early twentieth century. In *Revaluation* (1936), for example, F. R. Leavis specifically dismisses nineteenth-century poets because they "do not lend themselves readily to the critical method of this book; and that it should be so is, I will risk suggesting, a reflection upon them rather than upon the method."[22] New criticism notoriously treats only the "concrete" or material elements of a poem, aesthetic experience being primarily an immaterial "mental activity," as I. A. Richards calls it in *Principles of Literary Criticism* (1924), depending "far less upon the nature of the external stimulus than upon the general internal circumstances of the individual's life at the time the stimulus occurs."[23]

Both Leavis and Richards are, of course, concerned to build an academic discipline out of what they perceived as the literary debris of the preceding period. Richards, for example, reminds us at the end of *Principles* that "to be seriously interested in art" at all in his era was "to be thought an oddity."[24] Consequently, new criticism gets very worried about the role of emotion in criticism, more so than the critical methodologies that immediately followed it. Richards, for example, spends a lot of time worrying that readers might misconstrue emotion as simply standing "for any noteworthy 'goings on' in the mind almost regardless of their nature." The emotional experiences Hemans's burning boy undergoes become meaningless, Richards warns, if regarded as "mere" sentimentality, patriotism, hysteria. Anticipating neurological theory, Richards instead configures emotional experience as inclusive of visceral, bodily sensation as well as an impulsive element of consciousness.[25] Leavis, too, is concerned about feeling, valuing Wordsworth for successfully illustrating "a relation between thinking and feeling," but argues that such a relation is rigorously regulated by the eighteenth-century context from which it emerges: Wordsworth's verse cannot be seen freely to emote. For Leavis, such regulating Enlightenment rationalism reaches a breaking point in Shelley, who "represents pre-eminently the divorce between thought and feeling, intelligence and sensibility," a divorce "characteristic of the nineteenth century."[26]

The harsh resonances of the word "divorce" here underline Leavis's mournful sense that something once harmonious and united has been torn apart. T. S. Eliot was acutely aware of the serious implications the act of dividing thought from feeling in poetry might occasion, both aesthetically and socially. He declared in "The Metaphysical Poets" (1921), for example, that no poet had truly expressed contemplative feeling since John Donne, for whom "a thought was an experience; it modified his sensibility."[27] For Eliot, the seventeenth century was a period in which "a dissociation of sensibility set in, from which we have never recovered"; poets since Donne, he claims, simply "do not feel their thought."[28] As the linguistic expression of feeling is refined, the "actual" feeling represented becomes "more crude": eighteenth-century sensibility, Eliot implies, is not about feeling at all but serves only to provoke nervous reactions in readers in an age in which people "thought and felt by fits, unbalanced."[29]

Eliot is concerned here that those who read to experience feeling in poetry written since Donne will engage only in an excessively sentimental nervousness: such verse is not regulated by any kind of reason or logic. Such a sweeping generalization is tendentious; Eliot is suspicious of poetry that is too emotional or, put another way, too feminine and affecting. Feminine feeling of the kind associated with Romantic lyric poetry is "crude" feeling for Eliot, a form of emotion that anyone could experience, regardless of class, gender, or education—all that was needed to feel was a "human heart," as Wordsworth suggested in *The Prelude*. The danger here, as perceived by Eliot, was that anyone who could feel could write, which enabled the most maudlin of versifiers, balladeers, and poetesses to style themselves poets.[30] If Eliot thought that Wordsworth had strayed into crude feeling, a poet like Hemans would have appeared to him to have drowned in it, and thus was not even worth mentioning in his critical prose. As Suzanne Clark argues in *Sentimental Mod-*

ernism, early twentieth-century intellectual life was precisely gender coded in terms of (masculine) rigor and meticulousness as opposed to (feminine) openness and sympathy.[31] During his childhood, Eliot certainly read Hemans's poetry. His local public library in St. Louis, Missouri, stocked many of her titles, and his school was driven by a New England Unitarianism with which Hemans's religious poetry was associated at the end of the century.[32] Moreover, Eliot's very community had been shaped by the ideals of Andrews Norton, father of Charles Eliot Norton, Hemans's friend and publisher in Boston.[33] Hemans's poetry, like Wordsworth's, had proved a successful export to America, in part owing to its apparently moralizing, christianizing, and sensitizing agenda.[34] As an essayist, Eliot was obsessed with Modernism's debt to Romanticism in general, seeming almost to resent Romanticism's formulation of a new poetic agenda founded on subjective feeling. In "Tradition and the Individual Talent," for example, Eliot claims:

> The business of the poet is not to find new emotions, but to use the ordinary ones and, in working them up into poetry, to express feelings which are not in actual emotions at all. And emotions which he has never experienced will serve his turn as well as those familiar to him. Consequently, we must believe that "emotion recollected in tranquillity" is an inexact formula. For it is neither emotion, nor recollection, nor, without distortion of meaning, tranquillity. . . . Poetry is not a turning loose of emotion, but an escape from emotion; it is not the expression of personality, but an escape from personality.[35]

This critique of Wordsworth might equally refer to Hemans's work, known for its gushiness and popular for creating an arena in which to indulge in emotion rather than escape from it. Hemans writes for feeling, moving toward rather than away from it, and this is partly why Eliot chooses to edit her out of his prose, constantly challenging her without naming her. One might argue that Eliot refrains from any discussion of Hemans in order to initiate a new poetics that escapes from the kind of emotion the poetess puts awkwardly on display. What he misses, however, is the way in which Hemans liberates feeling into a community of readers rather than pulling it back into a privatized reading space. As Harriet Monroe, an early reviewer of

The Waste Land (1922), claimed, Eliot was an "indoor thinker," being more concerned with theories of impersonality that distanced readers from personal sentiment than with experiences of "outdoor" shared emotion.[36] Indeed, Eliot's fear that his own lyric *Poems* (1920) were like female "discharge," coupled with his statement "I distrust the Feminine in literature," might account for the absence of explicit discussion of any women's poetry in his prose.[37] Hemans's poetry embodied the very sentimentality Eliot's poetry works to contain.[38]

Liu and the New "Cool"

If Eliot's theories of feeling were written against Hemans, Alan Liu's work on feeling emerges from a closer and more sympathetic consideration of her poetry. His landmark book, *The Laws of Cool: Knowledge Work and the Culture of Information* (2004), a study of contemporary Western culture's obsession with what is "cool," a discourse Liu is both attracted to and repelled by in that he perceives it to be at once excitingly au courant as well as detached and unfeeling. The book echoes his seminal contributions to "Reading Hemans, Aesthetics, and the Canon," an often cited online discussion convened by *Romantic Circles* in 1997 that focuses on the problems of teaching a poet whom many students dismiss as clichéd and melodramatic.[39] Liu underlines how our often negative critical responses to Hemansian feeling betray more about "us" than about the "Romantics"; he ironically declares:

> "We" do not like "schmaltz" because "we" in our successive recent generations are "cool" à la jazz, beat, rock, punk, etc. Or more accurately, we intellectuals (going back at least as far as the Hulme, Pound, Eliot, Ransom era . . .) *wish* to be cool in the manner of the various subcultures and vanguards that have staked their identity on aesthetic sensibilities antithetical to middle-class "lifestyle" or "leisure."[40]

Educated intellectuals, then, demarcate their "cool" taste for "good" poetry by cynically detaching themselves from the kind of schmaltzy, sentimental verse hegemonically valued in Western culture. Such readers may appreciate Hemans only for her poetic skill and extreme dexterity with form, not for her "soft" romanticism. Yet even when

Hemans is read as a skilled rather than sentimental poet, she is still frowned upon, Liu suggests, because she is concerned to make the poem a location from which emotion might be released and contemplated, rather than a space that contains and scrutinizes emotion. The reader cannot get around the fact that Hemans writes about feeling. By elevating the feeling of the poem beyond the poem's form, she creates a delay or interval for readers (Rilke would later call it a "heart-pause") in which they finish the poem and then hold onto the feeling it has voiced. In "Casabianca," for example, the reader might well experience the narrative events played out in tight, boxed-up rhythmic quatrains, but he or she is constantly reminded of the boy's feelings of anxiety, loss, mourning, and love so that he or she might understand rather than be consumed by them. As Liu argues, Hemans's poetry tends to be "constructed not so much out of feeling as 'for' feeling": the narrator refrains from indulging in hysteria or tragedy or sorrow so as to allow the boy's feelings to emerge as the poem's keynote. A poem written *for* feeling, as opposed to out of a now lost, emotive moment or subjective experience, releases us from the impasse of abstract emotions and channels us into the specificity of feeling. This specificity will change depending on individuals' interpretations of the poem (for instance, is the boy on the burning deck terrified, isolated, patriotic?), but it allows us to read for a precise rather than general experience of one of these feelings.

Liu's *Laws of Cool* might grant us further insight into the question of how feeling works in Hemans's poetry in its definition of literature as the cultural life of information or "knowledge work." What *is* the literary, Liu asks, when "literature" seems either subordinated to context (historicism) and entertainment (popular culture) or has simply passed away (the "death of literature")?[41] To think about this question is to address the ideology of art in the current moment: if in classical times the governing ideology was mimesis, and in the Romantic period it was a struggle between mimesis and subjective expression, our own moment is dominated by a "cool" aesthetic. This aesthetic dominates Western culture, and while Liu clearly seeks to move past it into a "warm" culture (where feeling is valued), he recognizes throughout his study that cool commands how and what we read. "Cool" texts are in; "warm" (sentimental) texts are out. Moreover, those who hold cultural power, in the contemporary Western world at least, are concerned only with what is cool or not cool.[42]

As an aesthetic, "cool" places center stage those edgy experiences of culture—"avant-garde art, music, film, fiction, poetry, dance, games, fashion, design, Web design, and so on"—that are best encountered by the reader or viewer whose mode of feeling is agitated and "manic," rather than sentimental and gentle.[43] The "cool" reader thus experiences the feeling a text evokes but cannot sustain such an experience and so rushes to freeze feeling into a thing to rationalize, rather than undergo. A reading of any text—a poem, for example—that fixes feeling in this way simply makes the emotion represented within it into a curatorial object to be found and put on display: a cool reading, like a new critical one, promises always to halt the thrill of the reading experience mid-emotion.

The problem with cool, then, is that while it offers knowing intellectuals a way of thinking about strong feeling in a rational age, it constantly threatens to block any kind of sustained emotional experience. It is, in Liu's words, a "viral" aesthetic that forces readers to go through an emotion as they might suffer the infection of a virus but weakens their capacity to feel anything at all, and demands that they destroy or freeze the virus/feeling. The implications of a viral aesthetic for an information technology culture offer us further insight here. A computer virus works as a "sequence of code" which, when activated, causes itself to be copied into other locations (the memory of a computer or network of computers) and manipulates the content stored there. A viral aesthetic also copies itself across a series of locations (cultural ones), causing readers to feel its presence and then forget their previous thoughts (just as the next cool thing displaces the last cool thing). Indeed, early, modernist cool, as opposed to contemporary cool, was entirely destructive, Liu suggests, resulting in nihilistic, existentialist art that served to repudiate both tradition and the commercialization of the visual. Liu compares this dark and determined destructiveness to Dorian Gray's portrait, eaten away by a moral rot that confirms the superficiality of cool consumption. Private or felt experience becomes unattainable, feigned, noxious, rendering life "damaged," as Adorno declared.[44]

New cool, however, represents a kind of "destructive creativity" (rather than a creative destructiveness), intent on restoring experience by providing a tonic to such alienated damage (even if it ultimately fails in its restorative aim). This alternative creativity is "less *fin-de-siècle* than Romantic," less Wilde than Wordsworth, the latter able to offer a vision addressing a constitution of the self grounded in a natural world that decays and then revives, offering the reader an organic continuity (a "motion and a spirit" that "rolls through all things").[45] Cool feeling, once raw and noir, is now "robust with feeling." Noting the contents of Netscape's "What's Cool?" Web site, Liu reveals that cool is constituted as that which provides the "gusto, rush, thrill" of information, luring the human browser with the uncomfortable promise of "fun" and couching such an invitation with "adjectival excess."[46] Yet how the human accesses such a rush is problematic for Liu, cool feeling remaining on a technological surface and vested not in the self but in material objects (the "retro" design of a Web site, the curve of a Marc Newson chair). As Liu argues, current modes of cool evoke "an emotional state so torn between incitements and proscriptions to passion" that they become "oxymoronic, even manic-depressive, in feeling."[47] By disturbing what came before, the viral element of cool creates something new, experimental, and expansive from its destruction, but at the same time threatens always to infect and paralyze. This is why Liu concludes his book by arguing that we "need an art and literature that are more than cool," and this "more than" is what Hemans gives us. The feeling she produces in her poetry is self-restorative, creating a reading experience in which feeling is felt always in the now. As Liu suggests in "Reading Hemans," the sentimental verse intellectuals have so long dismissed is precisely that which might lead to a reconnection with emotional and affective experience in our technologically led moment.

Read from Liu's post-cool perspective, Hemans's "The Image in Lava" (1827), for example, becomes a direct plea to the reader not to halt the emotional element of the reading experience. The poem concerns a mother and child caught in the eruption of Vesuvius that engulfed Pompeii in AD 79. When the site was discovered and excavated in the mid-eighteenth century, several impressions of bodies caught in the lava were discovered.[48] Hemans's poem asks us to turn from the ruined pomp of the imperial past to reflect on the constancy of familial love embodied in this private embrace:

Oh! I could pass all relics
  Left by the pomps of old,
To gaze on this rude monument,
  Cast in affection's mould.

Love, human love! what art thou?
  Thy print upon the dust
Outlives the cities of renown
  Wherein the mighty trust!
    (ll. 33–40)

The love portrayed here—intersubjective, social, human—induces a feminized poetic language which, for Isobel Armstrong, is exempt from commodification and, I would add, cool paralysis.[49] The poem insists that we look only at historical artifacts that have a human and therefore emotional aspect, and reject relics that pompously memorialize empire. We might have a "cool," detached interest in "relics / Left by the pomps of old," but the only response to the devastation of human life, Hemans suggests, is one of continued feeling. Like the boy in "Casabianca," the impressions of mother and child attest to a kind of presentist feeling that runs from the past into the future, embracing both.

As Elizabeth Bishop, embracing Hemans, puts it in her own poem, "Casabianca," "Love's the boy" as he is in any given moment—standing, reciting, holding his ground, burning, and loving.

Bishop's Burning Boy

Love's the boy stood on the burning deck
trying to recite "The boy stood on
the burning deck." Love's the son
  stood stammering elocution
  while the poor ship in flames went down.

Love's the obstinate boy, the ship,
even the swimming sailors, who
would like a schoolroom platform, too,
  or an excuse to stay
  on deck. And love's the burning boy.

Bishop, a self-proclaimed "minor female Wordsworth,"[50] published "Casabianca" in 1936. Her poem might be described as "cool," formally taut and encouraging the reader to experience the boy's anxiety, but pulling away from effusion (there are no exclamation marks, for example). Indeed, the poem allows the reader to experience emotion not through geography, time, or space, but in the processes Bishop's boy undergoes as he stands, recites a poem, stammers through it, attempts to be loved and to love. As Nancy Sullivan suggests, "The action of the poem emulates the action of love: it burns."[51] Some critics have read Bishop's poem as a restaging of Hemans's conservative nationalism and patriotism—a poem that replaces a cruel, if heroic, tale with a sensitivity to a young boy trapped in his own (burning) desire for soldierly recognition.[52] Aided by Liu's discussion of cool, however, we might see Bishop's engagement with Hemans differently—her poem a tool for rereading Hemans. If cool is a kind of paralyzing experience that drives the reader to flee from it into warm feeling, then Bishop seems to be deliberately draining Hemans's poem of its emotion in order to lay bare the loss such an action effects. In other words, by making the line "the boy stood on the burning deck" part of an elocution test for the boy in the poem, Bishop highlights the devaluation of Hemans's poetry in the twentieth century; the line was actually used in elocution classes, where enunciation, not meaning or feeling, was most important. Hemans's famous line, shorn of its sentimental charge, paradoxically reminds the reader of that lost emotion now squeezed out, encouraging the reader to move beyond the detachment of Bishop's poem into Hemansian emotion.

Bishop achieves this, I think, by presenting her burning boy as an aesthetic shadow of Hemans's martyr, who serves to illuminate the emotion at the heart of both personae: as a multiple of Hemans's boy, Bishop repeats what his predecessor feels but in a more damaged, perhaps cool way. Where Hemans's boy is bright and beautiful, "born to rule the storm," in Bishop's poem he becomes awkward and self-conscious, stumbling through a recital—Hemans's poem, one might hazard—he can hardly voice, "stammering" and "obstinate." Where Hemans's boy shouts loudly to his father through the noise of cannon fire, in Bishop's poem his voice fragments, the boy attempting to recite rather than actually reciting his poem, his expression burning up. Bishop's sailors are dynamic in that they swim away, but they long to be reinstated onboard with the burning boy. The implication here is that the sailors also long to return to their childhood experiences of emotion within the perceived security of the schoolroom, idealized from an adult perspective as consolatory and comforting.

However, the suggestion, at least, is that the actual experience was one of schoolboy awkwardness rather than security. Yet in both poems, the boy shines out from a scene beset with dead bodies and framed by fleeing soldiers: he is active—he is "moving," emotionally because of his plight and *actually* in that he wanders around deck while his father remains passive below.

We might conclude that Bishop's boy is the destructive creation Liu sees within contemporary feeling: his experience thrills us but the consequent grief halts that emotion—wartime murder is not cool (Liu: "In the vernacular of student discourse: why not kill someone? Well, it's not cool").[53] The kind of love that is a child on fire betrays the contradictions inherent in cool and demands that we, as readers, move beyond it and into the kind of unceasing love that elegizes and remembers what has been lost. Bishop's cool interpretation of Hemans's poem underlines the message of the latter's closing lines—that "the noblest thing which perished" onboard was a "young faithful heart" and that the emotion this provokes lives on in the reader. For Hemans's poem demands that it is the boy's capacity for feeling—his heart—that expires, where the feeling he endured does not, continuing as it does beyond his physical body in our readings of the text. Both poems, then, are focused on the expression of love and thus force the reader to turn to and evaluate his or her capacity to suffer emotion.[54] Bishop sustains this process inside the poem, allowing the reader to name the boy's experience even as it is stammered out, thus placing value on it at the same time as it threatens to burn away. Hemans, by contrast, liberates feeling into the reading space, repairing the experience her boy has gone through by privileging his own poignant reaction to war.

My closing remarks here are not designed to license "Romantic" reactions to feeling over modern ones, but rather to suggest that Hemansian feeling can be successfully recovered as restorative rather than cloying when understood from a post-cool perspective. Eliot implicitly encourages us to recoil from emotive poetry as well as from expressivist notions of identity and self. Liu, on the other hand, allows us to maneuver into a reading position that rejects embarrassment and embraces feeling, albeit a manic one that we must experience in an alienated, agitated, and sometimes depressive way.[55] What Bishop points to is what Liu demands at the end of *The Laws of Cool*—a mode of reading that forces us to experience the discomfort and pleasure of feeling through a poetry that provides responsive and careful terms for emotional expression. Her poem may be cool, but the reader response she hopes for is post-cool, even warm. This hermeneutic might in turn help recuperate Hemans's poetry for a readership that either despises her sentimentalism or distrusts her obsessive metrical order, and build up a critical language able to articulate questions about how emotion works and what it is. Reading for the "current of every newly-excited feeling," for "sudden lights and shadows," as Hemans urges us to do in her essay on Goethe, we might resist her twentieth-century detractors and embrace the lived emotional content of her poetry.[56] This content is one we might preserve by being "warm" rather than "cool" readers, as we encounter Hemans's poetry in a state of sustained heat—burning, without burning up, like her boy.

Notes

I would like to thank Isabel Davis for her comments on this paper. Thanks also to Richard Marggraf Turley and Damian Walford Davies, the editors of this volume, for their insightful advice.

1. T. E. Hulme, *Speculations: Essays on Humanism and the Philosophy of Art* (London: Routledge, 1924), 118.

2. Anne K. Mellor, *Mothers of the Nation: Women's Political Writing in England, 1780–1830* (Bloomington: Indiana University Press, 2000), 69ff.

3. Nanora Sweet, "'Under the subtle wreath': Louise Bogan, Felicia Hemans, and Petrarchan Poetics," *Romanticism on the Net*, 29–30 (2003), available at http://www.erudit.org/revue/ron/2003/v/n29/index.html (accessed 3 February 2005).

4. See Isaac Watts, *The Doctrines of the Passions Explained and Improved, Or, A Brief and Comprehensive Scheme of the Natural Affections of Mankind, Attempted in a Plain and Easy Method, With an Account of their Names, Nature, Appearances, Effects and different Uses in Human Life to which are subjoined Moral and Divine Rules for the Regulation or Government of them* (1729), 5th ed. (London: J. Buckland and T. Longman, 1770); Jonathan Edwards, *A Treatise Concerning Religious Affections in Three Parts* (1746) (Edinburgh: J. Ogle, 1812); Francis Hutcheson, *An Essay on the Nature and Conduct of the Passions and Affections with Illustrations on the Moral Sense* (1728), 3rd ed. (1742), a facsimile reproduction with an introduction by Paul McReynolds (Gainesville, FL: Scholars' Facsimiles and Reprints, 1969); and Adam Smith, *Theory of Moral Sentiments* (1759), ed. D. D. Raphael and A. L. MacFie (Oxford: Clarendon Press, 1976).

5. See Alan Liu's insightful contributions to "Reading Hemans, Aesthetics and the Canon: An Online Discussion," *Romantic Circles*, http://www.rc.umd.edu/peda-

gogies/usingRC/hemans.html (accessed 3 April 2005).

6. William Gladstone and Robert Peel, to name two founders of the Victorian liberal state, responded in this way to Hemans's poetry. See Gary Kelly, ed., *Felicia Hemans: Selected Poems, Prose and Letters* (Ontario: Broadview Press, 2002), 15–85.

7. Mackenzie Bell, "Felicia Dorothea Hemans, 1793–1835," in *The Poets and the Poetry of the Nineteenth Century: Joanna Baillie to Jean Ingelow,* ed. Alfred H. Miles (London: George Routledge and Sons, 1891), 53; Frederic Rowton, "Felicia Hemans," *The Female Poets of Great Britain, Chronologically Arranged with Copious Selections and Critical Remarks* (London: Longman, 1848), 407.

8. Eric S. Robertson, *English Poetesses: A Series of Critical Biographies with Illustrative Extracts* (London: Cassell, 1883), 185, 294; William Michael Rossetti, "Prefatory Notice," in *The Poetical Works of Mrs. Felicia Hemans,* ed. William Michael Rossetti (London: Moxon, 1873), xxv; Arthur Symons, *The Romantic Movement in English Poetry* (London: Constable, 1909), 294.

9. Symons, *The Romantic Movement,* 295.

10. Robertson commented: "The poetry of Mrs Hemans lacks any note of supreme passion," while Rowton insisted that "to *passion* she is well nigh a stranger." Robertson, *English Poetesses,* 183; Rowton, "Felicia Hemans," 409.

11. Janet E. Courtney, *The Adventurous Thirties: A Chapter in the Women's Movement* (London: Oxford University Press, 1933), 31; Charles William Sutton, "Felicia Dorothea Hemans 1793–1835" (1891), in *Dictionary of National Biography* (Oxford: Oxford University Press, 1995).

12. See T. S. Eliot, "The Metaphysical Poets," *Selected Essays* (London: Faber and Faber, 1999), 281–91.

13. See Marlon B. Ross, "Foreword: Now *Our* Hemans," in *Felicia Hemans: Reimagining Poetry in the Nineteenth Century,* ed. Nanora Sweet and Julie Melnyk (Basingstoke: Palgrave Macmillan, 2001), x–xxvi; Jason Rudy, "Forms of Passion: Victorian Poetry at the Boundaries of Sensibility" (Ph.D. diss., Rutgers University, 2003); and my chapter on Hemans in *Women Poets of the Nineteenth Century, Writers and Their Work* (Devon: Northcote House, 2006).

14. See *Felicia Hemans: Selected Poems, Letters, Reception Materials,* ed. Susan J. Wolfson (Princeton: Princeton University Press, 2000), 428.

15. Felicia Hemans, "Casabianca," *The Monthly Magazine or British Register* 2 (August 1826): 164.

16. Susan Wolfson, "Editing Felicia Hemans for the Twenty-First Century," *Romanticism on the Net* 19 (2000), http://users.ox.ac.uk/~scat0385/19hemans.html.

17. Myra Cottingham, "Felicia Hemans's Dead and Dying Bodies," *Women's Writing* 8, no. 2 (2001): 278; see Tricia Lootens, *Lost Saints: Silence, Gender, and Victorian Literary Canonization* (Charlottesville: University Press of Virginia, 1996).

18. Cottingham, "Hemans's Dead," 279.

19. See Gary Kelly, "Death and the Matron: Felicia Hemans, Romantic Death and the Founding of the Modern Liberal State," in *Felicia Hemans,* ed. Sweet and Melnyk, 199.

20. A. Mary F. Robinson, "Felicia Hemans," in *The English Poets: The Nineteenth Century,* ed. T. H. Ward (London: Macmillan, 1880), 334.

21. Ibid..

22. F. R. Leavis, *Revaluation: Tradition and Development in English Poetry* (1936; London: Penguin, 1978), 13.

23. Ibid., 10; I. A. Richards, *Principles of Literary Criticism* (1924; London: Kegan Paul, 1947), 98.

24. Richards, *Principles,* 287.

25. Ibid., 101.

26. Leavis, *Revaluation,* 15.

27. "The Metaphysical Poets" (1921), in Eliot, *Selected Essays,* 287.

28. Ibid.

29. Ibid., 288.

30. See my introduction to *Women Poets of the Nineteenth Century.*

31. See Suzanne Clark, *Sentimental Modernism: Women Writers and the Revolution of the Word* (Bloomington: Indiana University Press, 1991).

32. As ever, Nanora Sweet has been astonishingly generous in sharing her knowledge of Hemans's life and works; I am indebted to her for my discussion of Hemans and Eliot.

33. We might also note the influence of Hemans on R. W. Emerson, whose divinity school professor was Andrews Norton.

34. On Wordsworth's reception in America, see Leslie Eckel, "'Empire of the Muse': American Encounters with Wordsworth," *Literature Compass* 1 (2004), http://www.literature-compass.com.

35. "Tradition and the Individual Talent" (1919), in Eliot, *Selected Essays,* 21.

36. Harriet Monroe, "A Contrast," in *The Merrill Studies in The Waste Land,* ed. Bradley Gunter (Columbus, OH: Merrill, 1971), 20; see also Gail McDonald, "Through Schoolhouse Windows: Women, the Academy and T. S. Eliot," in *Gender, Desire, and Sexuality in T. S. Eliot,* ed. Cassandra Laity and Nancy K. Gish (Cambridge: Cambridge University Press, 2004), 180.

37. See McDonald, "Through Schoolhouse Windows," 185; and T. S. Eliot to Henry Ware Eliot, 31 October 1917, in *The Letters of T. S. Eliot, 1898–1922,* ed. Valerie Eliot (London: Faber and Faber, 1988), 1:203–4.

38. See Laity and Gish, *Gender, Desire, and Sexuality in T. S. Eliot.*

39. Alan Liu, contributions to "Reading Hemans, Aesthetics, and the Canon: An Online Discussion," *Romantic Circles,* http://www.rc.umd.edu/pedagogies/usingRC/hemans.html (accessed 3 July 2005).

40. Alan Liu, *The Laws of Cool: Knowledge Work and the Culture of Information* (Chicago: University of Chicago Press, 2004), 323.

41. See Alvin Kernan, *The Death of Literature* (New Haven: Yale University Press, 1990).

42. Liu, *The Laws of Cool,* 323, 3.

43. Ibid., 317–18.

44. See Theodor Adorno, *Minima Moralia: Reflections on Damaged Life,* trans. E. F. N. Jephcott (London: Verso, 1981).

45. Liu, *The Laws of Cool,* 340; Wordsworth, "Lines composed a few miles above Tintern Abbey, on revisiting the Banks of the Wye during a tour, July 13, 1798," ll. 101, 103.

46. Liu, *The Laws of Cool,* 231–33.

47. Ibid., 235.

48. Pompeii was discovered in 1748 and excavated from 1763 to 1820; see Wolfson, *Felicia Hemans: Selected Poems,* 424.

49. See Isobel Armstrong, "Natural and National Monuments—Felicia Hemans's 'The Image in Lava': A Note," in *Felicia Hemans,* ed. Sweet and Melnyk, 212–30.

50. Elizabeth Bishop to Robert Lowell, July 1951, in *One Art: Letters, Selected and Edited,* ed. Robert Giroux (New York: Farrar, 1994), 222.

51. Nancy Sullivan, "Perspective and the Poetic Process," *Wisconsin Studies in Contemporary Literature* 6, no. 1 (1965): 129–30.

52. See, e.g., John Palattella, "'That Sense of Constant Re-Adjustment': The Great Depression and the Provisional Politics of Elizabeth Bishop's 'North and South,'" *Contemporary Literature* 34, no. 1 (1993): 29.

53. Liu, *The Laws of Cool,* 237.

54. Charles Altieri, "Theorizing Emotions in Eliot's Poetry and Poetics," in *Gender, Desire, and Sexuality,* ed. Laity and Gish, 157.

55. For an excellent discussion of Eliot's views on emotion, see ibid.

56. See Felicia Hemans, "German Studies," *New Monthly Magazine* 40 (January 1834): 2.

Overcoming Kitsch:

Thoughts on Linguistic and Class Resource from Keats to Betjeman

John Bayley

In Keats's poetry something most unusual takes place. There had been nothing like it in English poetry before, but it will continue to flourish and increase in the late nineteenth and twentieth centuries. What I have in mind here is not easy to define, but it could perhaps best be suggested, or summed up, like so much else in English life, under the word *class*, and in the seemingly bizarre notion of class becoming, for poetry, an aspect of Romance.

Previously, the phenomenon of class had never really been visible in poetry, since poets had never been concerned with it as such. "Peasant" poets and artists might appear at any time between the seventeenth and nineteenth centuries, but their status and reputation as "peasants" was not strictly a class matter. John Clare, for example, is never in the least self-conscious about his subject matter or his background. But with the arrival of the "Cockney School" of poets, as hostile critics came to call it, class scornfulness and "superiority" was soon met by class resentment. Keats's antipathy to Byron, and to a lesser extent to Shelley, is not engendered by their poetry but by the way in which Keats detects, or feels he detects, an implicit sense of superiority that seems to confine him in an atmosphere of patronage: not patronage in the old sense in which art lovers were pleased to help indigent poets and artists, but a new style of class patronage that might praise with apparent generosity the artist or poet it singled out but at the same time regarded him or her as different—a species to be encouraged no doubt but one also to be regarded as odd, "outside," a little *comic* even, particularly when such poets attempted anything in the nature of the high style, the pathetic, or the old-fashioned sublime. The Cockney School was mocked particularly when it attempted the tender emotions of sex and love (Keats being a favorite target). "Namby-pamby" Keats was derided by Byron for his "p——ss a bed poetry,"[1] the reference being most obviously to *Isabella* and *The Eve of St. Agnes*. It was not that Byron, with his robust accounts of women and love in *Childe Harold* and *Don Juan,* objected to the treatment of such subjects per se, but rather that in his view and that of other socially "superior" poets and critics of the time, poets from Keats's class and background treated such matters in such a deplorably mawkish way.

Whether we think there is any truth in this charge or not, it remains significant that Byron and the critics should have leveled it—not only against Keats but also against his friends in the Hampstead world, most particularly Leigh Hunt. Leigh Hunt, loyal to Keats, did his best to refute the charge indirectly, and in a short piece—the best early essay that we have on Keats's poetry—warmly and intelligently praised the beauties of *Isabella* and *The Eve of St. Agnes.*[2] Tactfully and obligingly, Hunt also suggests that classically minded critics like Croker and Lockhart give Keats such grudging praise as they did because he latterly wrote his *Hyperion* poems in the classical spirit, hoping perhaps to mollify the men who had attacked *Endymion* and its successors. But however much *Hyperion* may have resembled a "classical revival" poem like Landor's *Gebir,* Keats was not, and could never have been, a Landor, as both he and Hunt knew very well.

In many ways, Keats was the least self-conscious of poets, but he was extremely conscious, nonetheless, of this essentially class-based criticism—a new phenomenon of the time—that his poetry had attracted. He belongs to the "new gentility," the class whose habits and pretensions would shortly be attracting the satirical attention of the novelist and humorist in Dickens, who was one of the same class himself. If we were not so familiar with the characteristic "Keatsness" of his great poems—if, in fact, we could read them as a prejudiced critic of his own time did—we would continually be finding evidence of the class-based nature of Keats's poetic speech and vocabulary. Keats's first reaction to what seemed to him the almost unbearably beautiful song of the nightingale is couched in a definite—though today almost invisible—Cockney idiom—"Now more than ever seems it rich to die."[3] Its familiarity for us, almost as much as its poise—it is a line that seems as rich as the rapt atmosphere of wonder in which Keats is composing—obscures the fact that he is using a phrase that would, in his social circle and that of his friends, be jolly, intimate, and above all *colloquial* (e.g., "wouldn't it be rich to get up a party next week with two dozen of claret?").

So Keats is actually using a piece of semi-genteel social slang in the sublime context of what he knew and intended to be the highest and noblest kind of poetry. So successfully does he do it that the modern reader is hardly aware of the fact, even though it may have been evident—sometimes painfully evident—to a conservative poetry reader of the time, one of those whom Wordsworth referred to as capable of "convers[ing] . . . about a taste for Poetry . . . as if it were a thing as indifferent as a taste for Rope-dancing, or Frontiniac or Sherry."[4]

The stateliness of Tennyson's language, like the deliberate eccentricity of Browning's, can be seen as ways of purposefully avoiding the kind of class-revealing bathos sneered at by critics and reviewers of "Cockney School" poetry. Even so, the young Tennyson did not escape from Croker's ill-natured amusement at the saccharine sentimentality of an early poem, "O Darling Room."[5] Tennyson smarted at Croker's gibe and resented it deeply. As we know from his letters, Gerard Manley Hopkins had something of the same consciousness of, and *wish to conceal,* not indeed his social but his unusual religious status. Who would have expected a Jesuit Father to write in such an odd and original way? And Hopkins's very early poetry is distinctly Keatsian.

The connection between what used to be known as the "obscurity" of modern and contemporary poetry and the poet's wish to remain anonymous, impersonal, and unidentifiable in terms of class or social being is one that does not seem to have been fully explored. Both W. B. Yeats and T. S. Eliot are in their own ways very different examples of it: Yeats through his doctrine of masks and the shedding of an all too identifiable many-colored coat of mythologies; Eliot through his doctrine of impersonality and hieratic self-concealment. (Both, we might note, are essentially extensions of former "Romantic" attitudes to the writing of poetry.) The doctrines of latter-day Romanticism—or at least this strain of it—held that the task of poets, their high calling, was, as Mallarmé had said (and he was one of Eliot's household gods), to purify the language of the tribe and render it more precise and more exacting. But purification and impersonality were ideals that the poets of the twentieth century were not always in a position to achieve, nor—in an important sense—did they always wish to do so. The language of a writer and a poet is his or her own thing—perhaps involuntarily so—and, as the example of Keats suggests, it is "rich" because of its individuality. W. H. Auden's view of the writer's and the poet's language is in sharp contrast to that of Mallarmé and Eliot. Time is indifferent, says Auden in his elegy "In Memory of W. B. Yeats," to all other considerations, taking no interest in ideals or morals, or the sacred, or the divine. Ignoring all such matters, it

> Worships language and forgives
> Everyone by whom it lives.[6]

Auden's view is perhaps the commoner one among English poets of recent times. A Welsh poet like Dylan Thomas writes of Wales, but his idiom is entirely his own and cannot be called either English or Welsh—it is purely Dylan Thomas, and by being his own achieves that degree of richness and singularity that is also true of Keats's idiom. A poet who is true, consciously or unconsciously, to his or her own language can never be vulgar or commonplace.

It is significant, though it seems to have gone unnoticed, that Auden subsequently excised the lines about time and language in "In Memory of W. B. Yeats." Why he did so can only be conjectured, but it seems likely that his later religious persona came to reject the notion that language—and specifically a poet's language—was *all* that mattered in poetry.

But, because it is his own, a poet's language is capable of the strangest possible permutations. As the example of Keats shows, it can embrace a range of registers, including that common Cockney idiom of the time, "it would be rich . . . ," and transform it for the poet's own purposes. Dylan Thomas invented his own language in the same way, producing a compound that owes something to the Anglo-Welsh idioms and rhythms of his childhood environment but more perhaps to the fashionable speech of London and Bloomsbury, the surroundings in which he came to feel most at home at the time he was becoming known as a poet in the mid-1930s. The compound is particularly seductive, and effective, in many of his later poems:

Before I knocked and flesh let enter,
With liquid hands tapped on the womb,
I who was shapeless as the water
That shaped the Jordan near my home
Was brother to Mnetha's daughter
And sister to the fathering worm.[7]

The complexity of the mixture is fascinating, and it did indeed fascinate other poets of the time like Edith Sitwell, who had a good ear for the new—which often means, where poetry is concerned, a combination of the naïve and the sophisticated, in a tone and with a conviction not heard before.

All modern idiom in poetry seeks to overcome the shadow of kitsch, the presence of something too comfortably done in words that no longer possess or invent their own kind of individual excitement. But for an artist, there can be many ways of startling and surprising what is banal and kitsch, and thus of shocking the whole concept out of itself. Dylan Thomas can do it by the sheer surprise and effortless elevation of his language, as in his superb "A Refusal to Mourn," referring to the death of a child by fire in the London Blitz:

Deep with the first dead lies London's daughter,
Robed in the long friends,
The grains beyond age, the dark veins of her mother,
Secret by the unmourning water
Of the riding Thames.
After the first death, there is no other.
(ll. 19–24)

So far from seeming secondhand or linguistically stale, the echo from Donne in the last line seems fresh, unearthly, and wholly surprising.

But it is even possible for a poet to give such a freshness and surprisingness to kitsch as the thing itself. Rather as Andy Warhol and other artists transformed the kitsch object by looking at it with a new and craftily reverent ebullience, so a poet like John Betjeman transforms the commonplace—the Romantic commonplace in particular—into his own sometimes comic and bizarre but always wonderfully new and lyrical enthusiasms. Things that to the bored and indifferent observer, and the unloving eye, seem merely ugly and vulgar are transformed by the poet into a landscape of new beauties.

Of course, the commonness of Romantic phrase and idiom ("rich to die"), which was quite unselfconscious in Keats, has in Betjeman and the modern Romantics become highly conscious and sophisticated. But the simple zest in words, and in living with and through them, is still there. If he could imagine the time change involved, Keats would probably recognize as in some sense his own sort of poetry the devout paean raised by Betjeman in salute to the Surrey landscape and its beauties, including the Southern Electric railway line:

Far, far below me roll the Coulsdon woodlands,
   White down the valley curves the living rail
Tall, tall, above me, olive spike the pinewoods,
   Olive against blue-black, moving in the gale.

. . . .

Fling wide the curtains!—that's a Surrey sunset
   Low down the line sings the Addiscombe train,
Leaded are the windows lozenging the crimson,
   Drained dark the pines in resin-scented rain.[8]

In a helpful tongue-in-cheek footnote, which might have enlightened a puzzled Keats as well as putting a more modern reader in the Surrey picture (date c. 1932), Betjeman glosses "the living rail" to Coulsdon: "*Southern Electric 25 mins.*" The point worth emphasizing is that Betjeman, by drawing our attention to these humdrum things in his own ecstatically aesthetic way, is doing for poetry what Warhol and others did for visual art. He is making kitsch into something rare and new, transforming the fatigue of the too-much-seen daily object into what is suddenly rich and strange.

Moreover, poetry is capable of further and more complex effects than the simple transformation of kitsch achieved by the new-style kitsch artist. For the first time, in these modern examples, we can see Romanticism—old style—discovering how to laugh at itself while still retaining its old and traditional characteristics of devout wonder and beauty. The Surrey landscape and its denizens, Pam and Miss Joan Hunter-Dunn, are transformed into a new kind of beauty, while at the same time, and without the slightest sign of patronage on their creator's part, these things become, and remain, simultaneously comical and touching. And yet Romantic strangeness and otherness is still very much a part of them: they have been as raptly seen, heard, and created by the poet as was Keats's Nightingale or Tennyson's Lady of Shalott. In these later modalities of the Romantic Vision, we see its powers of survival as well as our own perennial need for what its resources of new-old language can say to us.

Notes

1. Lord Byron to John Murray, 12 October 1820, *Byron's Letters and Journals,* ed. Leslie A. Marchand (London: John Murray, 1975–82), 7:200.

2. Leigh Hunt, review of *Lamia, Isabella, The Eve of St. Agnes, and Other Poems, Indicator,* 2 and 9 August 1820, 337–44, 345–52.

3. "Ode to a Nightingale" (l. 55), in *The Poems of John Keats,* ed. Stillinger.

4. *Lyrical Ballads,* ed. R. L. Brett and A. R. Jones (London: Methuen, 1965), 257.

5. J. R. Croker, review of *Poems* (1832), *Quarterly Review* 49 (April 1833): 81–96.

6. W. H. Auden, *Selected Poems,* ed. Edward Mendelson (London: Faber and Faber, 1979), ll. 50–51.

7. "Before I Knocked," in *Collected Poems,* ed. Davies and Maud, ll. 1–6.

8. *John Betjeman: Collected Poems* (London: Murray, 1979), ll. 5–8, 17–20.

Contributors

JOHN BAYLEY is Emeritus Fellow of St Catherine's College, Oxford. From 1973 to 1992, he was Thomas Warton Professor at Oxford University. His books include *Keats and Reality* (1962); *The Uses of Division: Unity and Disharmony in Literature* (1976); *The Romantic Survival: A Study in Poetic Evolution* (1979); *Shakespeare and Tragedy* (1981); *The Short Story: Henry James to Elizabeth Bowen* (1988); and *Housman's Poems* (1992), as well as a number of novels. He has written influentially on the Romantics and on writers such as Thomas Hardy, Dylan Thomas, Tolstoy, and Pushkin. His recent books include a trilogy on his relationship with his late wife, the novelist and philosopher, Iris Murdoch.

JOHN BEER is Emeritus Professor of English literature at Cambridge and Fellow of Peterhouse. His monographs include *Blake's Humanism* (1968); *Coleridge's Poetic Intelligence* (1977); *Wordsworth and the Human Heart* (1978); *Romantic Influences: Contemporary, Victorian, Modern* (1993); *Providence and Love: Studies in Wordsworth, Channing, Myers, George Eliot and Ruskin* (1998); *Romantic Consciousness: Blake to Mary Shelley* (2003); and *Post-Romantic Consciousness: Dickens to Plath* (2003). In addition to several collections of essays, he has edited Coleridge's *Poems* for Everyman's Library (new ed., 1993) and Coleridge's *Aids to Reflection* for the Bollingen *Collected Works* (1993). He is the general editor of the *Coleridge's Writings* series.

HUGH HAUGHTON is Senior Lecturer in the School of English at the University of York. He has published numerous essays on contemporary poetry and Irish literature, and a critical study of the poetry of Derek Mahon is forthcoming. Other volumes he has edited and introduced include Gustav Janouch, *Conversations with Kafka* (1985); Rudyard Kipling, *Wee Willie Winkie* (1988), *John Clare in Context* (1994), Lewis Carroll, *The Alice Books* (1998), Elizabeth Bowen,

To the North (1999), Sigmund Freud, *The Uncanny and Other Essays* (2003), and *Second World War Poems* (2004).

HARRIET DEVINE JUMP is Reader in English literature at Edge Hill College. She is the author of *Mary Wollstonecraft: Writer* (1994) and has published widely on Romantic and nineteenth-century women writers. She has edited *Diverse Voices: Essays on Twentieth-Century Women Writers in English* (1991); *Women's Writing of the Romantic Period, 1789–1836: An Anthology* (1997); *Women's Writing of the Victorian Period, 1837–1901: An Anthology* (1999); and, most recently, *Mary Wollstonecraft and the Critics, 1788–2001* (2003).

RICHARD MARGGRAF TURLEY is Senior Lecturer in Romantic and nineteenth-century literature, and codirector of the Centre for Romantic Studies in the Department of English Literature at the University of Wales, Aberystwyth. He is the author of *Writing Essays: A Guide for Students in English and the Humanities* (2000), *The Politics of Language in Romantic Literature* (2002), and *Keats's Boyish Imagination* (2004). He is currently completing a book on John Keats and Barry Cornwall and is coeditor of a volume of poetry, *Whiteout* (2007).

EMMA MASON is Lecturer in the Department of English and Comparative Literary Studies at the University of Warwick. She is author of *Women Poets of the Nineteenth Century* (2006) and, with Mark Knight, is writing *Nineteenth-Century Religion and Literature: An Introduction*. She is one of the editors of two forthcoming volumes on biblical hermeneutics: *The Oxford Handbook to the Reception History of the Bible;* and Blackwell's *Companion to the Bible in English*. Her current project is a book on feeling in Wordsworth's poetry.

LUCY NEWLYN is Professor of English language and literature at Oxford University and Fellow of St Edmund Hall. She is the author of *Coleridge, Wordsworth, and the Language of Allusion* (1986), *Paradise Lost and the Romantic Reader* (1993), and *Reading, Writing, and Romanticism: The Anxiety of Reception* (2000). She has edited *Coleridge's Imagination* (1986; with Richard Gravil and Nicholas Roe), *The Cambridge Companion to Coleridge* (2002), and Edward Thomas's *Oxford* (2005). She has also published a collection of poems, *Ginnel* (2005).

MICHAEL O'NEILL is Professor of English in the Department of English Studies at the University of Durham. His books include *The Human Mind's Imaginings: Conflict and Achievement in Shelley's Poetry* (1989); *Percy Bysshe Shelley: A Literary Life* (1989); *Auden, MacNiece, Spender: The Thirties Poetry* (1992; with Gareth Reeves); *Romanticism and the Self-Conscious Poem* (1997); and *A Routledge Literary Sourcebook on the Poetry of W. B. Yeats* (2004). He is the coeditor (with Zachary Leader) of *Shelley: The Major Works* (2003).

LISA M. STEINMAN is Kenan Professor of English and Humanities at Reed College in Portland, Oregon. Her books include *Made in America: Science, Technology, and American Modernist Poets* (1987) and *Masters of Repetition: Power, Culture, and Work in Thomson, Wordsworth, Shelley, and Emerson* (1998). She has published five collections of poetry, the latest of which is *Carslaw's Sequences* (2003).

DAMIAN WALFORD DAVIES is Senior Lecturer in Romantic and nineteenth-century literature, and codirector of the Centre for Romantic Studies in the Department of English Literature at the University of Wales, Aberystwyth. He is the author of *Presences That Disturb: Models of Romantic Identity in the Literature and Culture of the 1790s* (2002); editor of *Waldo Williams: Rhyddiaith* (Waldo Williams: Prose Works; 2001) and *Echoes to the Amen: Essays after R. S. Thomas* (2003); and coeditor, with Lynda Pratt, of *Wales and the Romantic Imagination* (2007). He is currently writing a book on the Romantic and Victorian shipwreck poem and is coauthor of a book of poems, *Whiteout* (2007).

JOHN WHALE is Professor of Romantic literature in the School of English at the University of Leeds. His most recent publications are *Imagination under Pressure: Aesthetics, Politics, and Utility, 1789–1832* (2000), *John Keats* (2005), and, as editor, *Edmund Burke's Reflections on the Revolution in France* (2000). He has also been involved in editing *The Complete Works of Thomas De Quincey* (2000–) under the general editorship of Grevel Lindop, and is currently working on Keats, Hazlitt, and pugilism in the Romantic period. He is also coeditor of *Stand* magazine.

Index

Credits

The essay "'In the Path of Blake': Dylan Thomas's 'Altarwise by Owl-Light'" is a revised and expanded version of a piece that appeared in *Romanticism* 3, no. 1; we are grateful to the editors for permission to print the essay in its new form here.

Plates 3, 8, and 9 of Copy D of William Blake's *For the Sexes: The Gates of Paradise* are reproduced by permission of the Pierpont Morgan Library; the images were kindly supplied by the Blake Archive (http://www.blakearchive.org). Blake's thirteenth illustration to Young's *Night Thoughts* is from William Blake's *Designs for Edward Young's Night Thoughts* (Oxford: Clarendon Press, 1980), and is reproduced by courtesy of Oxford University Press and the Trustees of the British Museum. *Christ in the Sepulchre, Guarded by Angels* is reproduced by courtesy of the Board of Trustees of the Victoria & Albert Museum.

Dylan Thomas's "Altarwise by Owl-Light," sonnet 1, and lines from "Before I Knocked" and "A Refusal to Mourn the Death, by Fire, of a Child in London": from *The Poems of Dylan Thomas,* copyright © 1939 by New Directions Publishing Corp., and *The Poems of Dylan Thomas,* copyright © 1945 by the Trustees for the Copyrights of Dylan Thomas; reprinted by permission of New Directions Publishing Corp. and David Higham Associates.

Excerpts from *The Diary of Virginia Woolf,* vol. 3: 1925–1930, copyright © 1980 by Quentin Bell and Angelica Garnett, reprinted by permission of Harcourt, Inc. Excerpts from *The Diary of Virginia Woolf,* vol. 4: 1931–1935, copyright © 1982 by Quentin Bell and Angelica Garnett, reprinted by permission of Harcourt, Inc. Excerpts from *The Diary of Virginia Woolf,* vol. 5: 1936–1941, copyright © 1984 by Quentin Bell and Angelica Garnett, reprinted by permission of Harcourt, Inc. Excerpts from *The Letters of Virginia Woolf,* vol. 4: 1929–1931, copyright © 1978 by Quentin Bell and Angelica Garnett, reprinted by permission of Harcourt, Inc. Excerpts from *The Common Reader,* copyright © 1925 by Harcourt, Inc. and renewed 1953 by Leonard Woolf, reprinted by permission of the publisher. Excerpts from *Three Guineas* by Virginia Woolf, copyright © 1938 by Harcourt, Inc. and renewed 1966 by Leonard Woolf, reprinted by permission of the publisher. The Virginia Woolf material is also reprinted by kind permission of Angelica Garnett and Anne Oliver Bell.

Credits

Excerpts from *Finders Keepers* by Seamus Heaney copyright © 2002 by Seamus Heaney; excerpts from *Government of the Tongue* by Seamus Heaney copyright © 1989 by Seamus Heaney; excerpts from *Opened Ground: Selected Poems, 1966–1996* by Seamus Heaney copyright © 1998 by Seamus Heaney, reprinted by permission of Faber and Faber Ltd and Farrar, Straus and Giroux, LLC.

Lines from Adrienne Rich's "Blood-Sister," from *The Fact of a Doorframe: Poems Selected and New, 1950–1984* copyright © 1984 by Adrienne Rich. Copyright © 1975, 1978 by W. W. Norton & Company, Inc. Copyright © 1981 by Adrienne Rich. Used by permission of the author and W. W. Norton & Company, Inc.

Lines from "The Idea of Order at Key West," from *The Collected Poems of Wallace Stevens* copyright © 1954 by Wallace Stevens and renewed 1982 by Holly Stevens. Used by permission of Alfred A. Knopf, a division of Random House, Inc., and Faber and Faber Ltd.

"Le Livre est sur la Table," from *Some Trees,* by John Ashbery copyright © 1956 by John Ashbery. Reprinted by permission of Georges Borchardt, Inc., on behalf of the author, and Carcanet Press Ltd.

Lines from "Snakecharmer," from Sylvia Plath's *Collected Poems,* are quoted by permission of Faber and Faber Ltd and Alfred A. Knopf/Random House, Inc. Lines from "That Morning," from Ted Hughes's *River: Poems,* are quoted by permission of Faber and Faber Ltd.

Lines from "The Nineteenth Century and After" and "Blood and the Moon" by W. B. Yeats reprinted by permission of A. P. Watt Ltd on behalf of Michael B. Yeats, and Scribner, an imprint of Simon & Schuster Adult Publishing Group, from *The Collected Works of W. B. Yeats,* vol. 1: *The Poems,* revised, ed. Richard J. Finneran, copyright © 1933 by the Macmillan Company; copyright renewed © 1961 by Bertha Georgie Yeats. Lines from "Meditations in Time of Civil War" reprinted by permission of A. P. Watt Ltd on behalf of Michael B. Yeats, and Scribner, an imprint of Simon & Schuster Adult Publishing Group, from *The Collected Works of W. B. Yeats,* vol. 1: *The Poems,* revised, ed. Richard J. Finneran, copyright © 1924 by the Macmillan Company; copyright renewed © 1952 by Bertha Georgie Yeats. Lines from "Leda and the Swan" reprinted by permission of A. P. Watt Ltd on behalf of Michael B. Yeats, and Scribner, an imprint of Simon & Schuster Adult Publishing Group, from *The Collected Works of W. B. Yeats,* vol. 1: *The Poems,* revised, ed. Richard J. Finneran, copyright © 1928 by the Macmillan Company; copyright © renewed 1956 by Georgie Yeats.

Lines from *The Collected Poems of Wallace Stevens* copyright © 1954 by Wallace Stevens and renewed 1982 by Holly Stevens. Used by permission of Alfred A. Knopf, a division of Random House, Inc., and Faber and Faber Ltd.

Credits

Lines from William Empson's "Doctrinal Point," from *Collected Poems of William Empson,* copyright © 1949 and renewed 1977 by William Empson, reprinted by permission of Harcourt, Inc.

Lines from Elizabeth Bishop, *The Complete Poems: 1927–1979,* copyright © 1979, 1983 by Alice Helen Methfessel, reprinted by permission of Farrar, Straus and Giroux, LLC.

Lines from Tony Harrison, *Selected Poems,* 2nd ed. (Penguin, 1987) reprinted by permission of Gordon Dickerson.

The lyrics of Bob Dylan: "Subterranean Homesick Blues," copyright © 1965 by Warner Bros. Inc. Copyright renewed 1993 by Special Rider Music. All rights reserved. International copyright secured. Reprinted by permission. "It's All Over Now, Baby Blue," copyright © 1965; renewed 1993 by Special Rider Music. International copyright secured. Reprinted by permission. "Love Minus Zero/No Limit," copyright © 1965 by Warner Bros. Inc. Copyright renewed 1993 by Special Rider Music. All rights reserved. International copyright secured. Reprinted by permission. "Open the Door, Homer," copyright © 1968 by Dwarf Music. All rights reserved. International copyright secured. Reprinted by permission. "Forever Young," copyright © 1973 Ram's Horn Music. All rights reserved. International copyright secured. Reprinted by permission. "Love Sick," copyright © 1997 Special Rider Music. All rights reserved. International copyright secured. Reprinted by permission. "Things Have Changed," copyright © 1999 by Special Rider Music. All rights reserved. International copyright secured. Reprinted by permission.

Elizabeth Bishop's poem "Casabianca" is quoted from *The Complete Poems: 1927–1979,* copyright © 1979, 1983 by Alice Helen Methfessel. Reprinted by permission of Farrar, Straus and Giroux, LLC.

www.ingramcontent.com/pod-product-compliance
Lightning Source LLC
LaVergne TN
LVHW010355080826
844660LV00016B/977/J

* 9 7 8 0 8 1 4 3 3 0 5 8 6 *